INDIAN SOCIAL SYSTEM

INDIAN SOCIAL SYSTEM

Shehzad Ahmad

ANMOL PUBLICATIONS PVT. LTD.
NEW DELHI - 110 002 (INDIA)

ANMOL PUBLICATIONS PVT. LTD.

H.O.: 4374/4B, Ansari Road, Darya Ganj,
New Delhi - 110 002 (India)
Ph.: 23278000, 23261597

B.O.: No. 1015, Ist Main Road, BSK IIIrd Stage,
IIIrd Phase, IIIrd Block,
Bangalore - 560 085 (India)
Visit us at: www.anmolpublications.com

Indian Social System

First Published, 2007

ISBN 978-81-261-3225-6

PRINTED IN INDIA

Printed at Mehra Offset Press, Delhi.

Contents

PREFACE

India is a home of several castes, tribes, ethnic groups and communities with varied social backgrounds. Each one of them has its own distinct identity in terms of traditions, festivals, habits and patterns of living. Yet, they all constitute a single and integrated nation. It is this paradoxical aspect, which Jawaharlal Nehru, the first Prime Minister of Independent India, called 'unity in diversity'. For such a wide variety of socio-cultural factors, India is said to have each day a celebration—now Eid, then Diwali, now this festival, then that, and so on. Hence, the country enjoys festivities for all 365 days of the year, which also give boost to overall economy of the nation.

Indian society is traditionally male-dominated. However, females are given due respect. Since they form an essential part of society, their rights to liberty, education, employment, etc. have been safeguarded by the Constitution of India. Though, intercaste marriage customarily is discouraged, it does not breach any law. Barring a few educational institutions, co-education is allowed at school and college levels.

Present book, *Indian Social System* is a comprehensive and exhaustive work, dealing with various aspects of Indian social system, at micro level.

Expectedly, this fine piece of work would come in handy in realising the true worth of Indian society.

Readers' comments and suggestions are anticipated.

— Editor

1

SOCIAL SYSTEM

No society can successfully work unless and until it is properly organised. In an unorganised society there are bound to be chaos which are sure to result in disorganisation. But at the same time if the organisational structures are too rigid then also there are chances of the whole structure breaking down and yielding and creating many other social problems.

One of the most important methods of maintaining social structure is through social groups.

Social Group Maintaining Structural System: Social groups are most effective methods of maintaining social structure. Maclver, in his *'Society'* has given schematic view of major types of groups in the social structure as follows:

Grouping/Organisation	*Basis of Grouping*
1. Major Category: Community Specific Types: Tribe; nation,' region; city; village; neighbourhood.	(a) Interest. (b) Occupation.
2. Interest Conscious unities: social class, caste elite, competitive class and corporate class.	(a) Like attitude of group members. (b) Indefinite social organisation.

Contd...

Grouping/Organisation	*Basis of Grouping*
3. Ethnic and racial groups; colour groups; Immigrant groups and nationality groups.	Distinction of status, prestige, opportunity, economic rank, length of residence.
4. Crowds: like interest crowds, common interest crowds.	Transitory Interest, Temporary Group.
5. Primary Group: family, play group, clique, club.	Limited size of membership, personal contacts between members, degree of , formal recognition, Type of interest pursued.
6. Large Association: State, Church, Economic Corporation, Labour Union etc.	Unlimited size of membership, Formal social organisation; Impersonal relation ship; Types of interests pursued.

Definition and Aspects of Structure: In every society there is a structural system, which the society wishes to preserve and is not interested in changing that unless there are sound reasons for the same. But what is a structure? There are many definitions which can be put forth but briefly speaking a good structure is one which can be put forth but briefly speaking a good structure is one in which there is a regularity and a kind of permanency. In the words of H.M.Johnson, "The structure of anything consists of the relatively stable inter-relationship among its parts; moreover, the term Tart' itself implies a certain degree of stability. Since a social system is composed of inter-related acts of the people, its structure must be sought in some degree of regularity of recurrence in these acts." In this system roles are always more stable than the role occupants themselves. The role occupants divide themselves into sub-groups and some such sub-groups live much longer than the individual members *e.g.* family will live much longer than any individual member.

There is always a close relationship between roles and subgroups, because each role occupant is required to perform certain duties towards the members of a subgroup in a social structure. These obligations which a role occupant is required to perform can be of two types *i.e.* those things which he is required to do and those which he must not do. Similarly his obligations can be of different types. He cannot discharge his obligations with some sincerity towards his business concern as towards his family.

The obligations which he discharges can be divided as obligatory norms and permissive norms,. Similarly there are different types of values and thus in a comprehensive social structure there are cultural patterns of knowledge and belief etc. Such a system also includes sub-groups of various types, regulative norms and cultural values.

Firstly the norms are not perfectly institutionalised and even if institutionalised, these cannot be allowed to operate on every occasion. In fact, in every big society there can be no uniform institutions and as such deviations in norms are bound to be there. Thus the whole structure is of relative nature.

It may however be pointed out that very rigid structure is also bound to make society static and create social disharmony and clashes.

Functions of Structure: Function may conveniently be defined as any contribution to the fulfillment of one or more of the social needs. When it hinders such a contribution it is called Dysfunction. Sometimes purpose and function are confused with each other. But sociologically both are different. Sociologically purpose is something subjective, whereas function and for that purpose even dysfunction is objective. Function is very relevant to action but action and function are not one and the same thing.

We have already said that a factor which hinders contribution to the fulfilment of one or more of the social needs is called dysfunction. Some of the dysfunctions may be discussed as under:

> When a person joins an office he is very active and has vigour but less responsibilities. As the time passes due to family liabilities, advancing age, sickness, etc. efficiency and vigour is reduced and

thus these factors hinder his contribution to social fulfilment. Similarly when an officer is posted with the responsibility of providing social security he is very active in the beginning, but gradually when he gets roots in the office, the whole security arrangement becomes a routine with him. In other words security of service has proved a dysfunction for him.

The functions can also be divided into manifest and latent functions. In the words of H.M.Johnson, "Manifest functions are those that are intended and recognised: latent functions are unorganised and unintended."

Distinction between manifest and latent functions is very narrow. Johnson has said that, "A function may be manifest for some participants in the social system and latent for others."

Functional Problems of Social Structure: In every social structure there are four important functional problems which every group must solve. These are:

(1) Pattern Maintenance,

(2) Adaptation,

(3) Goal Attainment,

(4) Integration.

From pattern maintenance point of view, we understand that the units of whole structure must learn the pattern and invest them with the appropriate attitude of respect. Sometimes pattern maintenance are subject to emotional disturbances and distraction. It is expected of a good social structure system, that these must be effectively managed.

In a good social structure groups and sub-groups try to adapt themselves to its social and non-social environments. Role of differentiation cannot, of course, be underestimated but at the same time it cannot be denied that no one person can perform simultaneously all the tasks that have to be performed by him in the society. Thus there is great need and necessity of adaptation in the society.

In every system, every society tries to attain certain goals through cooperative efforts. For attaining collective goals it is very essential that all resources must be mobilized in an effective manner, according to specific nature of tasks. But it must be remembered that there is relationship between adaptation and goal attainment because unless collective efforts are made, it will become impossible to attain goals.

In a society the people are required to work in close cooperation with each other. Without proper integration no social structure of system can smoothly work. It is desirable that in an integrated society all members must be loyal to the system as a whole.

Formal and Informal Social Structures: Social structure can be both formal as well as informal. Thus in a factory formal social structure is represented by the paper plan which outlines the divisions of function and responsibility, but informal social structure is indicated by informal groupings, the cliques. In the words of Maclver and Page, "The factors that give rise to primary groups in industrial organisation are present in all formalised social structures. Thus in governmental bureaux, military organisations, political parties, prisons, schools, labour unions and many others, the complete organisational picture includes the formal blueprint arrangements on the one hand and informal spontaneous grouping on the other."

Elements of Formal and Informal Structure: There are two important elements of structure which are maintained with the help of social groups. These can be both formal as well as informal. In the informal category fall voluntary associations. These associations go a long way in maintaining the structure. These are voluntary in the sense that it is not at all obligatory on the part of members to join any association. It is all left to him to join or not to join an association. Similarly it is also not obligatory or there is no binding an individual that once he has joined an association he must continue with that for all times to come. He can leave an association as and when he likes.

In an informal structure the members meet on informal occasions like the marriages etc. The position holders have some kind of relationship with each other. It may not be difficult to know the response of members on any important issue in anticipation of the actual occasion. In it secondary group plays a very insignificant role. Actual role and part is played by primary groups which take all the major decisions. In this structure few influential people through the members of the group, play their role and pull the strings from outside.

About a formal group Weber has said that in it every one holds some office and his position and authority is judged by the office which he holds. That also indicates his responsibilities as well. For each office there are certain minimum qualifications which the holder of the office must possess. Whole affair and system is quite impersonal and in it one can be replaced and is actually replaced by the other. Office does not belong to any person and every office holder is supposed to be impartial and view every problem without his likes and dislikes to interfere that. The rules which the holder of the office is supposed to follow must be precise, clear and without ambiguity.

If the holder of the office possesses any special qualifications that gives him more respect and regard. In fact with the passage of time every one gains some sort of specialisation. There is always a set hierarchy and chain of commands.

One of the important elements of formal structure is authority, which is needed for effective control as well as for achieving objectives. Its another characteristic is reward which means compensation in lieu of good work. It is essential for recruiting good persons, role differentiation and division of labour.

Not only this but in this types of structure there is always need for good communication system. Those who control communication are always respected. The authority is both rational and legal type and working is based on certain defined rules. It sets certain objectives before it to achieve.

Conventional Structure

Whereas in the society there are informal organisations which help in maintaining structure, there are also formal organisations without which structure in the society cannot be fully well maintained or made to function. At this stage we shall primarily discuss three such structures namely:

(a) Bureaucracy.

(b) Democracy.

(c) Authoritarian Forms(including dictatorship).

The Officials

It is a formal method of maintaining structure. It is a way in which the people are governed. A bureaucratic form of government is one in which governmental authority is not in the hands of duly elected representatives of the people but vested in a class of persons trained for the purpose. Such a class may be created either by nomination or examination by any other method. In fact, it is governed by officials who are whole-time workers in offices and continue to hold office during good behaviour. The people retire after a particular age and get some benefits of old age for serving the government faithfully, honestly and with integrity. A bureaucracy may be defined as "Government... which is composed of administrators especially trained for the public services who enter the employment of government, only after a course of regular study and examination and serve usually with good behaviour and retire on pension." In this system those who are at the helm of affairs are expected to maintain the structure which is given to them. They however, can interpret and twist it not in the way they like but considerably in a way which is convenient to them.

The greatest advantage of bureaucracy is that since the persons who are supposed to run the administration are whole-time workers, they have a lot of experience and background for working in the administrative setup. These workers are supposed to be above politics and political affiliations and as such it is expected of them to give the nation very clean administration and maintain whole structure with efficiency and impartiality. It is only in this way that the people can expect unbiased administration. In addition to this, it has also been said that in backward countries, where it is not possible for democracy to function successfully, this type of system can work smoothly and efficiently.

But the system also suffers from some defects. It may be an efficient system of maintaining structure but it does essentially mean a good form of running the administration as the bureaucrats do not come, in close contact with the masses and as such they cannot respect their sentiments. The laws accordingly may not be in accordance with public wishes and may ultimately not be respected by them.

In addition to this, in bureaucracy there is always red-tapism which not only means delay but expenditure in the administration which otherwise can be saved. There is also a danger that this form of working may ultimately become tyrannical by misusing its authority for selfish ends. The bureaucrats usually do not try to become an integral part of the social system. They try to become a class among themselves and thus put a great strain on the whole structure, which is not good for the society as a whole.

Bureaucracy and Political Parties: Michles in his *'Political Parties'* has discussed at some length about bureaucracy and political parties. He believes that political parties possesses many common traits with the state. According to him modern party like the modern state, endeavours to give to its own organisation the widest base. Thus arises the need for a strong bureaucracy and these tendencies are reinforced by the increase in the tasks imposed by modern organisation.

Bureaucratic Leader: In bureaucracy leader plays an important role and he is delegated some functions. There is bifurcation of functions. The leader has delegated functions because here is pressure of work, problems are complex and wide ranging and time and ability to solve these very limited. The problems and interests which implement to organisation are of a quite different kind than those which arise in a running organisation. There is hierarchy of values attached to the kind of work. Positive valuation of office raises new problems for the bureaucrats.

The delegation of functions introduces a relation of dependence. A leader bureaucrat must seek a personal base within a group itself. Actions of such leader are taken as policies and adopted with an eye more to the effect of action or policy on power relations inside the organisation rather to the achievement of its professed goals. Struggles within the group tend to become exclusively struggles between leaders. The bureaucrats construct an ideology peculiar to their own social positions.

Leadership identifies particular administration with the group as a whole. An incumbent tends to adopt the ideology of centralization. It tries to create the ideology of centralization. It tries to create the ideology of collective submission and tends to become the centres of conservatism.

Bureaucracy in India: Bureaucratic system is quite well known to India. It was quite well developed under the Hindus, under Chandra Gupta Maurya and under the Muslims during Mughal rule. Under the Britishers, Indian Civil Service was one of the best organised and efficient bureaucracy. It produced some very well known and efficient bureaucrats who enjoyed international reputation for their work and understanding. It is this steel of framework which was responsible for running administration in India after independence and making our parliamentary system of government and democracy a success.

Bureaucrats in India were educated, enlightened and recruited through well established and competitive examination system. They are supposed to be and were actually impartial in the discharge of their duties. They enjoy security of service and its role day by day is increasing. But at the same time bureaucrats are charged of their being a class among themselves. In addition, it is also now being alleged that it is becoming less efficient and more corrupt. It is having no effective contacts with the masses. It is trying to grab more powers, thereby posing a serious threat to our democratic and parliamentary system.

People's Rule

Democracy is another way of maintaining formal structure. In this system the people are allowed to have a share in deciding the type of structure and system of governance they will like to have and the extent to which they need changes in the existing social structure. It shall be absolutely wrong to say that origin of democracy lies in any of the modern institutions. It is in fact one of the oldest institutions in the world. We find that city states, in the time of Aristotle and Plato, practised this.

It was also in practice in some parts of India in the ancient times. Roman empire at the time of its glory also knew and followed it. It, however, got eclipsed in the Middle Ages but emerged with more energy, vigour and force in the writings of Rousseau. Since then it is very rapidly progressing. There is perhaps now no institution in the world which is not actually running or professes to be running on democratic lines.

The word 'Democracy' is derived from Greek words

'Demos' and 'Cratio' which respectively mean 'people' and 'power'. In other words to the Greek it meant a form of government in which power was vested in the people. In the Middle Ages it was a reaction against consolidation of power by the feudal, despots and the church. With the progress of industrialisation, this institution was used as a check against industrial magnates in particular and capitalists in general. In 19th century it became symbol of struggle against all types of aristocracies in all walks of life. Today democracy is the only hope of depressed classes who find in it signs of their welfare. It gives them hope and right of self-expression and thought to be the only suitable form for imparting political education to the millions.

Various definitions of democracy have been put forth by various thinkers to depict its characteristics and salient features. Seeley has said that "it is a form of government in which everyone has a share." Bryce has said that it is a form of government "in which will of the majority of qualified persons rules." According to Dicey, in this form of government, "the Governing body is comparatively large fraction of nation." According to Gettell, "Democracy is that form of government in which the mass of population possesses the right to share in the exercise of sovereign power." But the most suited and acceptable definition of democracy is that of Abraham Lincoln, who defined it as "Government of the people, for the people and by the people."

Thus according to this definition it is assumed that in a democracy: (a) Sovereignty resides in masses, (b) Structure is based on the consent of people, (c) All adult citizens have the right to vote and to stand for election as a candidate and have share in deciding the type of structure, (d) Government is responsible for looking after the welfare of the community as a whole and give to the people the type of structure they wan, (e) By certain means which are devised by the government, the people remain in constant touch with the authorities which frame policies. And lastly (f) The people are given certain fundamental rights which are justiciable in courts of law.

Democratic State, Government and Society: Democracy is not only a form of government but also a type of state as well as society. A democratic state is one in which ultimate sovereignty is vested in the people who have a right to change the government and have active participation in the final formation of policies.

A democratic government is one in which the majority party governs and continues to govern as long as the people express confidence in it. In this form of government every citizen has a share in the formation of government.

A democratic society is understood to be one in which there is a sense of equality and in which economic, social and political disparities do not retard the progress of the members. In this society, the people are not judged by the wealth but by the qualities which they have. In such a society there is no distinction of caste, colour and creed. In it there is faith in the personality of man. In fact it is the democratic society which is responsible for healthy democratic government and state.

Forms of Democracy: Democracy is of two types namely (a) Pure or direct democracy: (b) Representative or indirect democracy. A pure or direct democracy is one in which the people directly participate in their own affairs, *i.e.*, in the formation of policies. They speak for themselves and do not require the assistance of representatives to speak on their behalf. Such a type of democracy is possible only in small states where the people can assemble at one place to express their will. It was being practised in Greek city states and today is being practised in Switzerland where devices of Referendum, Recall and Initiative have been introduced for ascertaining the wishes of the people.

Indirect or representative democracy is one in which representatives of the people duly elected by them speak on their behalf. The people, as such, have no right to participate in the running of administration. They are required to get in touch with their representatives, and let them know their viewpoint and ideas. The elected representatives shall only have the right to speak for the constituency to which they represent. These days this type of democracy is the most well known and is prevailing in almost all democratic countries.

Merits or strength of Democracy: It is a system in which ultimate sovereignty vests with the people. They are ultimately to decide the nature of laws which they are to obey. They are the masters and thus enjoy maximum liberty. They have to decide the structure which they wish to follow. It is the system in which there is no possibility of violence. The people have always right to change the system by peaceful means. It believes in the ballots rather than the bullets. Democracy has faith in the capacity of people to decide their own affairs. Accordingly people develop a sense of self-confidence, social dignity and self respect. They also get intellectual development and rise from narrow outlook of egoism and try to promote national character and patriotism. It is again this system which looks after the welfare of all classes of people because those at the helm of affairs are ultimately responsible to the people as a whole and not to any particular community or class of people.

Democracy is a system in which people are called upon to give their opinion. Thus every party arranges meetings and educates the masses about living political and social issues. Thus people get educated and remain in touch with day-to-day political and social problems. Since the people themselves make laws, they feel that they are their own law makers and as such there is no justification in their breaking those laws. There is thus very little possibility of breaking the laws and chances of committing crimes are minimised. In this way there are few chances of social stratification and pressure on the existing structure is very much reduced. The structure does not come under many strains.

Since everything is done in the name of people, the masses feel that they are everything in the country and the society. They also feel that this is their own land which promotes patriotism even in a common man. They try to maintain social harmony and a peaceful atmosphere. They develop love, affection and sense of duty towards society and get ready every time to sacrifice their lives and property for the motherland and the society to which they belong.

It is a system which is self-corrective. Once an error is committed, a lesson is learnt and effort is made to rectify the mistake. It is, in other words, a method of trial and error in which corrections are not made by any outside authority but from inside by the masses. Had this basic principle been followed perhaps many of our social problems would have not existed today.

In this system there is the possibility of fixing responsibility on some one. The society gives responsibility to people to maintain or modify existing structure. In case they fail to do so, they are exclusively held responsible for that.

Weaknesses or Demerits of Democracy: In a democracy there is no secrecy. Everything becomes public in it and as such it is not possible to act and execute plans before their becoming public. In many of the cases it is not in the national interest and in the interest of society to discuss a problem in the public with the result that democratic governments have no national secrecy. It is a system in which there is no place for quality. The heads are counted, not weighed. The views of one man who is socially conscious are equal to those who has no interests in the society.

Democracy has been called the cult of incompetence because in this system it is not possible to take quick decisions. Much of the time is wasted in criticism and thus structure comes under heavy pressure before it is rectified.

This is a costly system. After regular intervals elections are to be conducted and each election means expenses which a poor nation like India can ill-afford. In addition to this, the people who are already overburdened with taxes do not react favourably to this type of expenditure. Here every one is treated as 'equal', *i.e.*, having equal qualities and capabilities but in actual practice it is not so. It is a system in which the psychologists take objection. They feel that here the individual and his reasonings and arguments submerge in an appeal from the platform, as a matter of respect to the personalities and also to symbols and slogans. Individual members kill their conscience in order to obey social discipline. Thus, psychologically it is not a welcome. It is a system in which structure is supported and maintained by the 'amateurs'. The people who are returned in elections either due to their social influence or the influence of castes, etc., are quite fresh. They have no experience and do not know the technicalities of administration. They have no experience of maintaining structure.

It is alleged that it is a system which is supposed to be maintained by mediocres. Able persons with qualities of administration and those who are well off do not like to throw themselves in the mud and dust of elections. It is accordingly controlled by demagogues and opportunists. Only those who have the art of speaking can captivate the feelings of masses and command their faith. The people listen to speakers with more attention than to a sincere worker having unquestionable loyalty towards the nation but not having the art of delivering a speech. An integral part of democracy is party system, without which it cannot function. Accordingly it inherits all the defects of the present party system particularly those relating to maintenance and disturbing social structure.

Conditions for Successful Working of Democracy: Democracy is one of the most popular and living institutions of the world which, it is hoped can bring about structural changes without violence. No doubt it suffers from some serious defects yet at the same time, it is the only way of hope for introducing peaceful changes. It is believed with some reasonableness that if the world is to save itself from the horrors of another war, the people must be given an opportunity to discuss calmly their own affairs across the table. But at the same time if democracy is to succeed there must be fertile ground for it.

People should be educated enough to understand national and social structural problems. They should also understand the value of opinion and should use that consciously. Not only this but at the same time they should have a spirit of toleration. They should not feel irritated over trifles but should be broad-minded enough to tolerate criticism of others. At the same time, both the majority and minority viewpoint should be harmoniously blended. The people must have civic sense and possess virtues of good citizenship. They should be active participants in the social process. In addition to this, it is expected that the people should not bow before illegal actions and unconstitutional decisions either because of social pressure or gratification. The people in offices, on the other hand, must have a high standard of moral character. They should realise their duties and responsibilities and perform these with no selfish ends but in the collective interests.

If democracy is to work successfully it is essential that there should be no gross economic inequality as that will make democracy futile. Those economically strong are bound to misuse their authority and power for their selfish ends and shall try to change the structure to suit their convenience. It cannot be denied that those who have power must wield that according to their own interests. Economic inequality makes society 'class divided' in which 'haves' always have an upper hand over the 'have-nots'.

The people should be vigilant enough to safeguard their own interests. They should also see to it that none encroaches upon their legitimate rights granted to them either by the constitution or law of the land. It has been said that, "Constant vigilance is the price for liberty". The more the people are vigilant the more rights and liberty they shall be enjoying.

Press is the mouthpiece and spokesman of public opinion. It is thus a link between the people and the authorities. In fact, it is an integral part of democracy and most essential in its successful working. It is, therefore, imperative that it should be considerably free and allowed to express unbiased viewpoint of society on all matters.

As regards speech, it is also essential that the people should be free to express their opinions. In a democracy if there is no freedom of speech, it cannot work at all. Democracy functions on the basic assumption that people should have the fullest opportunity to express their views so that there should be no revolutions. In a democracy people who are returned to the legislature by the electorates have generally no experience of administration. It is, therefore, essential that they must be given proper training. It is healthy if all those intending to become members of legislature are asked to serve in the first instance in local institutions before they are returned either to a legislative assembly or parliament. It should be a prerequisite for joining any legislature. It is essential that there should be social equality and each community should have complete confidence that it shall be treated at par with the other communities. There should be spirit of brotherhood among all the communities and no factionalism, provincialism or casteism as it was in India in the past or maltreatment which is being meted out to Negroes in the U.S.A. These are slurs on the fair name of democracy. Powers should not be concentrated in the hands of any one individual or institution. There should be clear demarcation of powers so that one agency does not encroach upon the rights of individuals or any other agency. As far as possible, those in office should be made to feel that they are servants of the people and not their masters and are to maintain structure in such a way that there is no disharmony.

Effort should be made to find out such leaders who are of high character and possess valuable qualities and have virtues of head and heart. Such leaders should have broader outlook of life and should also be above factionalism. They should view public questions not with a narrow outlook but with an open mind.

Judiciary is always expected to play a very vital and important role in maintaining political and social structure. It is most essential that it must be free and above the influence of either the executive or the legislature, as the people always have high hopes in it.

Democracy inter alia implies existence of political parties, elections, voting pattern and legislatures. These are formal institutions and very essential for maintaining social change.

Political parties are a useful and effective link between the government and the people and the brokers as well as propagators of viewpoints suited to their ideologies. These help in developing as well as killing social organisations and institutions. These wish to bring both social and political changes and if successful occupy chairs and position of power and authority. These try to justify their actions and secure legitimacy to what they plead, propagate or stand for. There is no democratic society, system or institution which can work successfully without political party system. These are the mechanisms through which political institutions in democracies successfully steer.

Elections are unavoidable in a democracy in which every voter is expected to participate. In every election burning problems are focussed and debated. Such problems and issues can be both national as well as international. How much the people are interested, very much depends on their participation and involvement. These are held periodically and in each election the electorates get the fullest opportunity to express their grievances on the one hand and expectations from the representatives on the other. Those who are elected, sit in the legislatures and are eligible to speak on behalf of the voters. In all democracies the governments are made and seated out of power as a result of election.

Next then come the legislatures, which are constituted on the basis of some predetermined formula and the basis. Such a basis can be adult franchise, manhood franchise, limited franchise etc. Similarly a legislature can be either unicameral or bicameral. It is the majority party in the Lower House of the legislature which forms the government.

Autocratic Type

Monarcy: Monarchy is one of the oldest institutions of not only a particular part of the world but of the world as a whole. It was known to the most primitive people when they joined state. In the past it was considered as a holy institution.

There are various forms of monarchy. It can be elected monarchy, in which monarch is elected by the people or by their representatives. Similarly monarchy can be hereditary. Under it the monarch automatically comes on the throne according to a well established and recognised law of succession. Generally the eldest son of a ruling monarch succeeds him after his death. Such a type of monarchy is now prevailing in England. Monarchy can also be absolute as well as limited. Absolute monarchy, according to Garner, is one "in which monarch is not merely the titular head of state but is actually the sovereign, that is, his will is the law in respect to all matters, upon which it is proclaimed. In short, he is bound by no will except his own".

Such a type of monarchy was prevalent in the whole of Europe as well as in India in the Middle Ages. In those days it was considered that the king was the fountain head of justice and his decisions could in no case be challenged in any other manner. Limited monarchy is one in which real power is not vested in the monarch but has been taken away from him either by one method or the other. All the powers are exercised in his name though in actual practice he has shed many.

Monarchy has its own strength. It is believed that it is the best form of government because it combines efficiency and secrecy. An enlightened monarch can do a lot in making rapid progress of his country. There is possibility of maintaining absolute secrecy in this form of government. In monarchy neither national time nor energy is wasted in party factions or useless debates. Since king rules the nation with impartiality and justice, it can inspire its faith and can keep up national morale. Whole nation looks towards him with faith and confidence. There is continuity in policies and as such it is possible to follow a consistent policy for quite some time it is also said that in actual practice real progress has always been made in a monarchy.

But it has its weaknesses too. Monarchy is a government of chance in the sense that there is no guarantee that every monarch shall always be enlightened and keen about public welfare. Our experience has shown that most of the monarchs were either mediocres or had no capacity to rule at all. In absolute monarchy, there is concentration of power in the hands of ruling monarch and thus the possibility of power and authority being misused. In this form of government, people have no chance and opportunity to take initiatives and even reforms come from above. It is not a self corrective form of government. Thus even if there is, some enlightened monarch who introduces reforms, he does not get active cooperation of the people.

In this form of government people do not enjoy any liberty. Thus in a monarchy life and liberty of the people is at the whim and discretion of monarch. The people are reduced to the level of living and eating cattle.

Dictatorship: Dictatorship is not a new but an age-old institution. It was known to the Romans where the whole governmental authority was vested in the hands of Presidents, called Consuls, who were virtually replaced by dictators as emergency warranted. In the past however, dictatorship was more or less legal and a dictator always derived his authority and power from some statutory provision. But modern dictatorship is quite different from what it was in the past. In the past dictator used to be an individual who come to power as a result of coup d'etat. He comes to power by force and retains authority by force, alone, but as we shall subsequently see modern dictatorship has its own features.

Causes for the Rise of Dictatorship: The destructive 1st and 2nd great world wars have given great momentum to dictatorship. As the 1st World war came to a close, in Italy, Fascist Party came to power in 1023, and the same year Primo de Rivera got power. In Germany, Weimar Constitution gave birth to Hitler. In 1929 there was upheaval in Poland and in 1931 King Casol of Rumania dismissed his Parliament. Then came the great revolution in Russia where the Czarist regime was overthrown and dictatorship of the Proletariat or of the working class was established which was intended to overthrow the authority of the capitalists. Not only this but these great wars made England and the U.S.A. think in terms of concentration of powers and the cabinets were virtually dictators for handling all war affairs. In England Ramsay Macdonald got a 'blank cheque' for handling the war situation whereas in the U.S.A. Roosevelt got many more powers than what Presidency usually enjoyed.

Many new states which were born as a result of war, had no capacity to work on democratic lines. They, therefore, wanted concentration of authority in one person who could take quick decisions and carry the nation on the path of progress and prosperity. It was considered for quite some time that democracy was an ideal form of government but gradually its defect came to light. In addition, the democracy failed to keep pace with the changing times and more so in emergencies where it completely broke down. It failed to afford any solution to economic and social problems which faced nations at every stage. Economic self-sufficiency was the catch word of every nation. Self-sufficiency being an attractive slogan gave rise to dictatorship which, it is felt, could achieve this laudable object more quickly as against democracy. 1929 saw economic depression primarily because of the U.S. economic policy.

The world was very much sure that its solution was not in democracy but in dictatorship. A dictator alone could solve firmly and face boldly these economic problems. As the League of Nations failed and various attempts at disarmament also went to cold storage the world began to get ready for another world war. It required a very strong national leader with all powers in his hands to face and ward off any outside attack. This was supplemented by the activities of Hitler and Mussolini and gave rise to dictatorship.

Features of Dictatorship: Here the leader is glorified. He is elevated to great heights and is considered to be the most competent person. He represents national unity and is the symbol of national honour. There is no opposition to challenge his authority. In other words there is 'one leader, one party and one programme' under dictatorship. Under dictatorship there is great respect for the state. The dictator will always glorify the nation and place it above every other nation in all respects. The authority of the state is considered unquestionable. A dictator will try to honour that because it is believed that it is an indication of health of a state. He will always try to create war atmosphere so that economic aspect is ignored. The nation shall always be made to feel and work under a shadow of war.

In dictatorship individual has neither any liberty nor personal freedom. The people have no right to criticise the conduct and actions of a dictator. One cannot raise slogans like liberty, equality and fraternity but is obliged to talk of duty, discipline and obedience. Dictator will try to glorify his race and represent it as one having the noblest heritage. Their race is considered to be supreme and honourable as compared to others. A dictator will always like to give a totalitarian outlook in which each and every attempt is made to control each aspect of society including religious and cultural. In fact, there is no aspect of human life in which punch of state intervention is not felt. In dictatorship, dictator will never be satisfied with what he had got. He will always try to expand his area of operation. In it, it is only the executive government which has powers. Legislature and judiciary have no say in the affairs of state administration.

Dictatorship and Monarchy: In both these cases there is rule of one autocratic ruler and his will is supreme in the state. Again in both the cases the head of the state has actual and effective powers.

But in spite of this the difference between the two exists. In dictatorship, a dictator comes to power because of his personal qualities and virtues which the nation has appreciated. He has a programme to execute and nation is there to help him in its execution. But in monarchy, monarch comes to the throne by a system already decided by law. Nation neither knows his qualities nor his programme. Another point of difference is that a monarch does not belong to any political party. He is an institution in himself. On the other hand, a dictator belongs to a particular political party and is required to carry out the programme of that party.

Modern dictatorship is different in the sense that the dictator tries to pose that he is there to protect the interests of the subjects. He has no other hunches and selfish interests. Super powers try to impose their dictatorship by making poor nations economically and militarily dependent on them.

Merits and Demerits of Dictatorship: It is a type of

organisation in which there is quickness to action and promptness in arriving at decisions. There is no wastage of time and energy over useless talks and discussions. Both Hitler and Mussolini opposed making programmes. For them action was only programme. Dictatorship is a form of government in which there is efficient administration which checks delays and corruption and employing underhand means for getting the work done. Here there are more chances of quick reforms. A dictator always feels that his state is more or less his personal estate. He believes in giving quick reforms and a neat administrative set up to his people.

Dictatorship encourages decency which is most urgent. In fact, it is health of state. Fear of severe punishment makes all people work quickly and efficiently. But it has its demerits as well. Dictatorship means regimentation which crushes human liberties. Even if the people want expression of their thoughts and feelings these are denied here. It is the form of government in which individual initiative is denied and gradually killed. This lack of initiative denies healthy development of culture and traditions which are life and soul of a state. Since dictator comes to power with force and glorifies it there is always a danger of misuse of force. Use of force is a never-ending circle since one action leads to another. In fact dictatorship glorifies force which is never appreciated and can never be praised. A dictator always keeps the nation in fear of war. He creates war atmosphere and as such more and more money is invested on upkeep of army and making arms and ammunitions rather than using public money for raising living standard of the people. A dictator is more interested in maintaining his position than anything else. He is interested in his security rather than that of the state.

Dictatorship may be an ideal form of government in emergencies and in abnormal circumstances, but it is beyond all doubts that this form of government is not suited to normal times and circumstances. It also does not believe in internationalism, without which no state can live in the world of today. On the other hand it believes in self-sufficiency which is more ideal than real and practicable.

Distinction Between Democracy and Dictatorship

	Democracy	*Dictatorship*
1.	In it violence is condemned. encourages healthy criticism and discussions round the table for resolving differences and solving problems.	It is based on violence and no criticism is tolerated under it. There is no question of sitting round the table for discussing problems and disputes.
2.	In democracy the people have a significant share in the running of their own administration. The government remains in power as long as the electorates desire it to remain in office.	The people have no share in the running of administration nor are the masses consulted in any way. The people cannot overthrow a dictator.
3.	Under democracy everyone is considered an end in itself. All state activities are directed for development and growth of human personality.	Every one is considered only means to an end which is glorification of state and indirectly that of the dictator.
4.	Democracy stands for mutual understanding and coexistence at international level.	Dictatorship does not stand for establishing international relations.
5.	In democracy tight of self determination is asserted and the people are expected to struggle for getting their rights and also for performing their duties.	Here there is no question of rights but only right is honest performance of duties.
6.	It is government by publicity and propaganda.	Here there is no question of creating public opinion. The public is supposed to work on the lines chalked out by the dictator.
7.	Democracy is considered a symbol of struggle against the tyranny and unhealthy actions of the tyrant in whatsoever form that might be.	Dictatorship is a form of government which is based on tyranny and as such it is not supposed to be against any other tyranny or high-handedness of one against the other.
8.	Since democracy is a process and is based on evolution, there is no possibility of violent changes in the structure of society.	Dictator comes to power suddenly and is overthrown all of a sudden. In preserving himself he does not hesitate to bring about violent changes in the society.
9.	In a democracy there is public support for the representatives who have been returned to power by the electorates.	There is no question of public support and cooperation in dictatorship. It must be extended no matter even unwillingly.

System of Power and Authority

Patterns of Power and Authority: The most fundamental structural feature of industrial organisation is a graded or hierarchically ordered system of power and authority. 'Power' refers to the ability of one person or group to get things done, even against the will of others or their natural inclinations. Power includes ability to persuade, to educate, to provide definitions of the situation, to determine the problems which will come up for discussion, to control the possible alternatives of action, to coerce use of physical force or sanctions. Therefore, power must rest on some sort of legitimate claim to the right to rule and to demand obedience.

Max Weber has made an important contribution to the understanding of Power and Authority in society in his construction of Three types of Imperative Authority. He constructed his types of authority on the basis of his definition of the corporate group. Corporate group was defined as a set of social relationships within which order was enforced by a leader and an administrative staff employing a set of rule which included limitation of membership.

The three types of Imperative Authority are

1. Traditional Authority
2. Legal-Rational Authority
3. Charismatic Authority.

Traditional Authority:This system of order and type of authority were regarded by members who lived in it as having always existed and having always been binding on them and their ancestors. This system had 2 elements (1) Its body of rules was a body of concrete rules, the legitimacy of which rested simply on the part that they always had been so. This was the authority of 'immemorial use' or 'immemorial custom'. No questions arose about their consistency, nor was only rational justification thought of. (2) The leader and administrative staff formed a hierarchical system of statuses of persons who were legitimately empowered to exercise authority.

In this large scale centralization of authority people were subjects of the leader. There was certain distance between the subjects and leader and the leader granted his followers "bundles of rights" on a personal basis and grant 'Fiefs' as the basis for reciprocal obligation. The structure of authority entailed a clear class structure (*e.g.* a feudal structure).

Legal-Rational Authority: This type of authority rests on a number of features which were all interdependent but focussed on the Rule of Law itself. Characteristic of this was the existence of a body of abstract or generalized rules which had been intentionally established and therefore possessed rational justification. These new legal rules could be established by the agreed procedures of the governing group and therefore they could claim the obedience of the members of the Corporate group. The allegiance of members of the Corporate group was not to persons who were incumbents of statuses, but to the impersonal order of the law and of the accepted legal-rational procedures itself. The entire order of the administrative staff was essentially that of a bureaucratic nature. The hierarchical definition of levels was such that each official was subordinate to the one above and responsible for the one below. This supervisory power included a degree of power in hiring, firing, promoting and demoting the personnel in lower offices.

Charismatic Authority: This resided in the direct appeal to others due to the qualities possessed by particular persons. Charisma refers to, 'Gift of Grace'. Here the obligation of obedience is a matter of personal loyalty within the area of accused obligations.

In modern bureaucratic organisation authority is legal-rational. The means employed by the organisation to obtain obedience of its members is by the creation of universally recognised and legitimate seats of authority and chains of command. Legitimate authority exists when those who are subject to this authority feel an obligation or duty to comply with its demands.

The authority of each office in an organisation is defined by rules which carefully determine the extent of the authority. Rules specify those individuals and offices which are subject to the authority of a particular office. Rules specify the means of compulsion which each office may use. If commands are to be recognised as legitimate, they must emanate from certain universally recognised and respected sources and come through definite channels of communication which are recognised as legitimate. Every individual in the organisation must know what the lines of communication are. Therefore lines of communication must be short and competent persons must be present at each stage of the line of communication.

For the senior official to be able to issue workable orders there must be accurate and up-to-date information about condition on the levels where orders, are being carried out. Such information will pass up the lines of communication.

Functions of Informal Organisations: An informal organization consists of a number of factors. It is composed of the animosities and friendships among the people who work together. It contains the primary groups, clique and congeniality that develop in a shop or office. It further consists of the folkways, mores, norms and values which guide the behaviour of workers.

The informal relationships which we mentioned above may exist between groups where departmental members meet informally at social or during tea or coffee breaks. Secondly, there are large informal groups which may arise as a result of some particular issue in the organization. Thirdly, there are the very important primary groups often small and of a face-to-face character which constitute the actual groups. Fourthly, there can be groups of friends sometimes only two or three meeting regularly, sometimes sharing hobbies or leisure time are outside the organization.

The informal organization performs a number of latent functions for often the formal organizations is insufficient as a means to achieve the manifest ends for which it was set up. People who plan the ends or goals of the organization and the means to attain them realize this and sometime enlist the help of the informal groups.

Psychologists are aware that many individual satisfactions arise from face-to-face interactions. Thus, Brown emphasises that the primary group is a social instrument conditioning the individual's attitudes, opinions, goals and ideals. He also points out that it is one of the fundamental sources of discipline and control. Often it is the interaction within primary groups that makes the work more enjoyable for the people.

Of course, often the interests of the management and small groups can differ; it has been noted that small groups develop their own norms regarding the maximum turn out for a worker. When he tries to improve on that he is called a rate buster. Loyalty to the group may mean that output and speed are related to the level of skill of the weaker members of the group rather than the best endowed.

The informal group is marked by the spontaneous interaction of a number of people (the number usually being small) over a relatively long period of time. The members of an informal group play certain roles tending toward the accomplishment of certain ends, but this action arises and continues without conscious purpose or direction. It is not, for instance, a number of people getting on the bus to go to work, or pouring through a factory gate, or rushing toward a cafeteria. Such groups may be called crowds.

The members of a crowd may act in certain definite ways toward each other; *e.g.*, men may be courteous to women and considerate of children. However, there is nothing permanent in this relationship. The people in a crowd do not act toward each other as members of a stable group. The regularity of this behaviour is cultural rather than social; that is, the culture demands certain types of behavior toward certain social objects—*e.g.*, women or children—no matter in what group they may be found. The informal group, on the other hand, is made up like the formal group, of a relatively stable set of roles, values aid personalities.

Unconventional Segments

The informal group was, in a sense, "discovered" during the course of the well-known experiments at the Hawthorne, Illinois, plant of the Western Electric Company which took place in the late 1920s. The purpose of the experiments was to rest for correlations between various factors and the output of individual workers. Previous experiments with the effect of variation in the amount of light at work had failed to reveal significant connections between output and physical factors. Consequently, it was decided to isolate several workers in a test room where the amount of production could be measured accurately while several conditions were varied. Ingenious arrangements were made to record the rates of production of the individual workers and the variations of the test factors. In addition, a record was kept of daily events, including conversation between the workers and other forms of interaction. A special observer was installed in the test room to take note of what was going on and to keep records.

The results of the experiment were surprising to the experimenters. It was found that apparently none of the factors being tested had much relation to productivity. This conclusion was reached because, no matter which factors were held constant and which varied, production continued to rise until it reached a high plateau, from which it apparently could not be shaken. This held true when improved methods of payment were tried, when rest pauses of various lengths were introduced, and when the length of the working day was shortened. Even after some of these favorable test factors—*e.g.*, rest pauses and shorter hours—were removed and the test conditions were returned to the general conditions of the plant, production continued far above the average rate. The investigators were forced to conclude that some other factor was working to maintain high productivity.

The factor in this case, then, was high morale; an intangible feeling of confidence in, and satisfaction with, the work, the test, the supervision, and prospects for the future. High productivity was then considered a natural outcome of this high morale, although the exact nature of the connection remained a matter of debate.

A new "social situation" was created by the experiment. There can be little question of the nature of this new social situation; it was undoubtedly an informal group. This group arose in an industrial situation marked by a minimum of formal social relationships between workers and between workers and management.

Leadership in the group of girls working in the Western Electric Company developed gradually. One of the girls established herself in this capacity through superior ability and enterprise. A system of status also emerged, and by the end of the experiment it had become quite hardened. This system of status assigned positions to each of the girls and determined the roles that would be played within them (that is, roles within the informal group).

Thus, besides the leader's role, there appeared the roles of scapegoat, of jester, of lieutenants to the leader. Even the experimenters, who were very prominent throughout the whole test period, were assigned roles within the group. A system of differential prestige attached to these roles soon appeared. Thus, in time the girls formed a series of social relationships at work which had little to do with bureaucratic relations or with the technology of the job. The informal group performed two important functions for its members. On the one hand, it offered the workers opportunities for achieving certain personal satisfactions which could not be attained within the regular social structure of the factory.

The group, for instance, provided certain sort of human relations that the formal structure of the plant could not. Within the group, the girls could communicate with relative freedom; they could exchange experiences, joke, quarrel. Furthermore, the group assigned definite statuses and roles, positions of power, prestige, and leadership which gave definite satisfactions to those playing the roles. Thus, the girl who became the leader of the group was an able person who would have had small chance of showing her ability within the formal social structure of the plant. On the other hand, the group functioned to attain certain group goals which were, apparently, strongly believed in by the girls.

The girls felt that they held a favoured position in the plant. This position, they believed, could be maintained only by continuing a high level of production. The function of this group, therefore, came to be maintenance of the productive level at all costs. To that purpose girls were chided if they fell behind their quotas, and discipline at work was strictly maintained. In the eyes of the girls, the function of the informal group as a whole was to maintain economic security.

Role of Unconventional Segments: Many different interpretations of the causes of informal groups and of their significance are possible. Some branches of management have looked at the informal group as the result of the worker's natural laziness, or rebelliousness, or unwillingness to cooperate in the sometimes exacting tasks of industry.

Others have seen in the informal group just the opposite—the natural expression of man's friendliness and his needs for cooperation. Organized labour has looked upon the informal group as the natural protective device of a group of unorganized working men, against the overweening power of management; that is, the informal group has been considered as a sort of reunion. Finally, some have seen the informal group as the answer to the worker's need for an outlet to his sentiments and emotions. The informal group must be understood in relation to the role and personality situation of the worker. It should prove possible to incorporate the insights of other schools of thought within a role and personality framework.

There would seem to be a plausible explanation for the formation and nature of informal groups in industry. Their overall function is to provide alternative outlets for the aspirations of working men, that is, they operate to mitigate the effects of strains arising from discrepancies between the worker's role and his capacities. The informal group is an outgrowth of, and a reaction to industrial technology and industrial bureaucracy. It is, therefore, the function of the informal group to afford the worker: (1) relief from monotony, boredom, and fatigue; (2) opportunities of status; (3) an increased flow of emotional responses, (4) opportunities for independence and (5) increased security.

It provided the girls with alternative outlets for socialization, which undoubtedly relieved the monotony of work. Furthermore, on this experiment the workers were provided with a group goal, which made a real demand on their talents and creativity. Under that circumstances, the gap between worker and role was closed.

Spontaneous Groups

Associations, by and large, are voluntary and it is left to every person to join an association or not. The need and necessity of such associations is usually not felt in rural settings and small communities where the people know each other personally and have face to face contact with each other. Need of such associations is felt in urban settings where the people do not know each other, Not only this, but their common interests are even not protected if they do not collectively struggle for the same. Need of the associations is therefore, felt by the consumers of goods of day-to-day use, users of buses and other means of daily transport, workers in the industries and even by those who sit on the pavements and work in the houses as domestic servants. In fact more is the number of members, better organised work base and leadership it has, more forceful voice it has. Every effort is made by the leadership on the one hand and those effected by activity on the other, to have associations.

Some Salient Features of Formal and Informal Structure: Where in a structure the emphasis is on office, the legality of authority, and the hierarchy, it constitutes the formal structure. These elements of formal structure have been described by sociologists as authority, reward and communication.

Authority: Every organization, as indicated above, has an aim to achieve, and it is not possible to achieve it in absence of it having legitimate authority for the purpose. It is essential for exercising the effective control. In absence of power, which in effect is authority, no organization can be operational. Authority involves the element of sanctions; without the sanction, the authority, would be ineffective.

Rewards: For participation and performance of roles in the organization, reward system is considered essential for the members. The reward system, it has been emphasised assures the recruitment of personnel, and the maintenance of the acceptable level of efficiency.

As the rewards are controlled by higher officials it would bring about the integration of authority with the execution of the organization work; and the manipulation of rewards would bring about role differentiation, and division of labour which is expedient due to the technological developments.

Communication: Communication is the soul of organization. Sociologists have laid full emphasis on the full communication among the members of organization. The communication should be short and direct in accordance with the communicative channel. In an organization one who controls the communication channels has the obvious advantage on all others.

An analysis of formal structure is also provided by Max Weber. He calls it the ideal type. In a complex society, according to Weber, there is a rational-legal type authority, where people act according to the defined rules. He regarded bureaucracy as a model and called it as an ideal-type. He did not use ideal in a moral sense, but in the sense that it was unaffected by only external influence. He used ideal purely in the abstract sense. To him a formal organization is thus based on efficient coordination and has a set objective to achieve.

The essential features of formal structure, on the basis of Weberian analysis are:

(i) *The Office:* The position that an individual holds in a bureaucratic organization, is according to Weber an office. The duties of the office, that is of one, who holds it, are defined. The office is distinct from its holder. It does not belong to any person, except the one who has the required qualifications for it. The occupant holds it for the time being. The holder of the office is not indispensable, but is replaceable.

(ii) *Office has Impersonal Character:* The office is held in an impersonal capacity. Since office does not belong to a person, therefore, the relations of the holder to the office is impersonal. The interaction in the office is not allowed to be impeded by one's likes and dislikes. It is only by an impersonal attitude to the office that an efficient and rational service can be rendered. According to Weber: "The dominance of a spirit of formalistic impersonality, *'Sine tra et Studio'* without hatred or passion, and hence without affection or enthusiasm".

(iii) *Rules and Regulations:* As indicated above, all social organizations are normative, but under the formal structure these must be *clear-cut and defined.* These are laid down in writing—and constitute the rules and regulations, which the organization and the holder of the office have to follow in an impersonal manner.

(iv) *Specialization of Function and Technical Competence:* Complete system of division of labour makes specialization of functions and technical competence on essential attribute of formal structure. Impersonal character of bureaucracy, makes it specialized functioning, and division of labour makes it technically competent. Qualification is, therefore, the basic criterion for holding the office.

(v) *Centralization of Hierarchy of Offices:* In the bureaucratic system, authority is centralized; alongside a definitive authority is assigned to an office. There exists in it, therefore, a chain of command from top to lower levels. This makes, every holder of office responsible to his superior in the hierarchy; and, someone else responsible to him.

Restructuring the Society

The formal structures thus are bureaucratic. They include large organizations—administrative, political, economic etc. These however, need be contrasted from the informal structures, which are not in the regular order. These have not the scientific structural form. These lack the objective ness. The salient features of informal structure are:

1. *It is a Position System:* Among the position holders there are informal relations. The members may meet informally at social functions. It is pervasive throughout.

2. *It is the System of Anticipated Responses:* As a result of some particular issue, affecting a large number in the organization, a large informal group may arise, and mobilize the public opinion against or in favour of it within the organization. To anticipate the response, it may have, may not be difficult.
3. *There is the Dominance of the Primary Group in an Informal Organization:* In an informal organization, the actual authority, rests in a primary group.
4. *Individual Influence cannot be Ruled Out*: There may also be few individuals in or outside the organization who may be in a position to exercise influence from time to time on the matters of organization.

Society is normally held together in symbiotic relationships as its interdependent parts work together in balance. Some conditions and situations, however, may disturb this balance and result in social disorganisation. Such situations, together with possible causes, are discussed in this chapter. It is important to understand the concepts of social organisation, social disorganisation and social reogranisation as changes that take place in rural society, since rural areas all over the world are in the process of change, for a variety of reasons and at a varying rate or pace of change. Whatever may be the factors that bring about unbalance and "disorganisation" of society it is important to understand both the cause and process involved.

The concept of social reorganisation for instance, has replaced the traditional concept of disorganisation. Specific illustrations of alleged "disorganisation" of certain social institutions of Indian rural society have been cited to clarify the concepts described in this chapter and their relevance to the behaviour of rural people in society. It is important to recognise in these illustrations that the changes that have taken place are best viewed as reorganization of various aspects of the institutions in society.

Society has been described as an organised body of individuals and groups, having structure and function, with a complex of form or systems of social relationships involving social roles, values and norms The components are so organised that they are normally held together in various relationships that enable them to operate effectively toward the achievement of social goals and objectives. In society, the individual and groups that compose society are held together in social cohesion, much like the human body is held together by the interdependence of its components. The human body has different organs such as arms, legs, stomach, heart and lungs which relate to one another to form various systems such as the respiratory system, the digestive system, the nervous system, the reproductive system, etc. Each system performs specific functions which, working together, enable the body to operate with normal effectiveness.

Society in its social organisation functions similarly. Life in an Indian rural market centre may serve as an illustration of such organisation. In the early hours of morning, farm produce begins to arrive from other villages. Farmers set up their stalls, and restaurants and teashops begin serving the farmers, local selling agents and other early customers. As the regular bus (and perhaps rail) system commences, wholesale buyers arrive. All shops for supplies and services now open and the general public come to the market for business and pleasure. Schools and public offices open, after lunch the tempo of activity seems to accelerate as more village people come to participate, not only in trade, but also in the social aspects of market day.

Throughout, each individual normally knows what to do and what is expected of him or her within the complex of social organisation at that time and place. Market taxes are paid, goods are located in prescribed places, livestock are handled and housed in the manner expected, selling agents are contacted, and transactions carried out according to prescribed procedures. As many as 10,000 people may participate in social relationships of various types and forms, each filling various roles and acting normally in accordance with prescribed norms of conduct, behaviour and operation.

The illustration implies a vast complex of interdependent relationships that compose society and that hold it together. Such interdependence in social organisation has both symbiotic and non-symbiotic phases. The symbiotic interdependence refers to the various interdependent roles and functions and the division of labour and functions that make up life. Considering the number of persons and the intricate relationships and function involved in the clothes worn, food eaten or mail services and telegraph facilities that are often taken for granted by an individual, and tracing each item back to its origin will produce and appreciation of the network of symbiotic interdependence that exists in society.

Non-symbiotic basis of interdependence also serve society as forces for social cohesion. Cultural factors, such as common religious beliefs, loyalties, and shared ideological convictions are nonmaterial factors that hold people together in society. Thus, the Hindu, Christian, and Muslim religion unite those who subscribe to beliefs contained in each. National loyalties likewise serve to unite what may sometimes be diverse groups of people.

Both symbiotic and cultural ties are fundamental and important in holding society together and in maintaining social integration. Through the process of socialisation, an individual's needs and behaviour are patterned according to the symbiotic and cultural aspects of society. Society creates certain social needs and wants and, at the same time, teaches socially acceptable ways of meeting these needs which involve links of mutual interdependence with other people in society and values that must underline behaviour in relationships with others for satisfaction of needs and wants.

Thus, while symbiotic and values ties which hold society together are distinct from one another they are themselves interdependent on one another and together effect human behaviour and relationship in society.

Social Disorganisation: Often, changes in the normal routine of life create a disturbance in the balance in the functioning of the existing parts, and the customary and socially approved ways of life no longer/prevail. Social disorganisation refers to such a situation or state of affairs in society. Some events, natural calamity such as flood and earthquake, war, rebellion, strike, lockout or otherwise—creates disorder and confusion rather than order in society.

Means of social control break down, and normal functioning of society ceases to exist. In social disorganisation, for example, patterns of authority break down with the "subordinate" no longer abiding by the orders of his superior officer; laws protecting person and property break down and give way to arson, looting, burglary, rape and murder; rules laying down conduct and behaviour of students in respect of teachers and administration are defied and educational institutions may be closed.

Considered in its broadest sense, social disorganisation is due to change in human environment, including social environment, cultural environment and in some instances, such as an earthquake or flood, natural environment. Change as a matter of degree varies from society to society, being minimal in primate and so-called static societies and varying in rapidity as one moves toward more complex, dynamic societies. Disorganisation implies such change as has produced problems for people in society about which they are conscious.

For the most part social disorganisation in its worst form does not occur through the deliberate intent of an individual or group, but is by-product of the action of various social forces that operate impersonally and an aftermath of changes that were not actually aimed at changing the social order. Social disorganisation represents a temporary period of confusion and disorder which persists until society establishes normality and order once again.

Landis has emphasised the regulative system of social control in society as being vital to the concepts of social organisation and disorganisation. He refers to the latter as a counter process of social control which "consists essentially of a breakdown of social control so that disorder and confusion rather than orderliness prevail", and represents social organisation on a continuum: (Diagram).

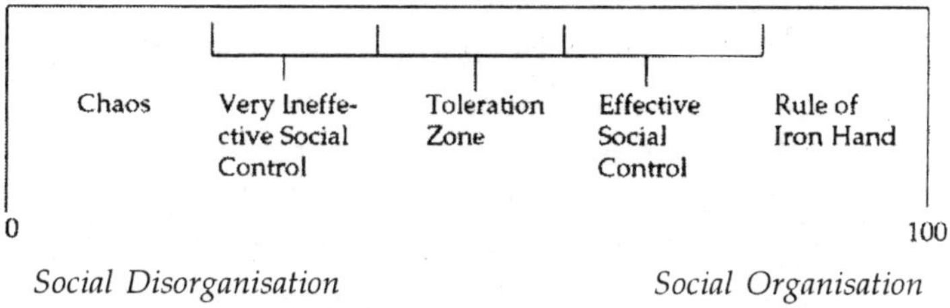

Diagram: Social Organisation is a Continuum Social organisation extends from the chaos of revolutionary disorder on the one hand to extreme and intolerable social regimentation on the other. The problem of every society is to maintain effective social control without suppressing the individual to the point where he will revolt. Over the long span of history a society may move from one position on the continuum to another. This movement may be gradual or violent, depending upon the nature of the social control in use in a particular instance and on the nature of the individuals in the society [Landis, 1958, p. 518].

Disruption of the functions of a social unit of society such as a group, community, institution or organisation or of society as a whole, depending of course on the degree, extent and area of disruption, can result from several causes. The more important basic causes of social disorganisation have been identified as follows:

A. Maladjustment or conflict between human beings and their natural environment, especially under circumstances of radical change such as epidemic, flood, famine, war. Such conditions significantly disrupt the normal functioning, not only of certain units of society, but of the entire society. It may take years for society to make modifications and adjustments in its organisation in relation to the natural environment that bring about the desired balance or stability in life; an earthquake within a few minutes may produce conditions that completely disrupt this stability and cause social disorganisation.

B. *Conflict of Norms:* The norms within society may conflict with changes in patterns of economic or other aspects of life and may lead to disorganisation. Oilseeds produced by farmers in an Indian village have traditionally been taken to the village oil-presser. With electrification and the development of small industry in towns power oil mills have been established and have assumed the function of the oil presser to a large extent, causing economic and social repercussions for the oil pressers, who form a part of the rural social structure. With the introduction of power oil presses a conflict in norms of behaviour between the traditional and the new has caused disorganisation of a unit of society and, through linked effect, on other units. In other rural societies conflict of norms has been more evident and clearly exhibited, not as the introduction of new norms of behaviour because of changed conditions, but in cases where ethnic and religious groups with differing norms have come in contact with each other. Usually, disruption of functions and social disorganisation has resulted.

C. *Unequal Rates of Cultural Change:* The concept of cultural lag has been discussed. When different aspects of culture exhibit unequal rates of change, social disorganisation may result, for various parts of culture are interlinked and if one part changes rapidly while a correlated part lags behind, strain is likely to be created between the two unequally moving parts. Introduction of electricity in a village for the first time may, for instance, disrupt the work pattern in a village where nightfall with darkness usually heralded bedtime and dawn meant early rising for work. Further, electric power has brought to many rural areas the power flour mill, and consequently has disrupted the work pattern of the housewife who used the early hours of the morning to grind flour in her own domestic flour mill. The disruption of some of the allied social functions have also been involved.

Social disorganisation thus results from conflict between basic factors of human experiences, from influence of man's natural environment and his culture, of heredity and culture and of other parts of culture. The geographic cause of natural environment is more pronounced in primitive and simple rural cultures, and unequal rates of cultural change is very pronounced and evident in dynamic modern societies.

Society seems to pass through various stages of a cycle during periods of time as it is subjected to various forces of change. From a state of organisation with relative equilibrium or stability, it may become disorganised with disruption of its functions in part or wholly. The period of disruption of normal functions, or disorganisation, may be considered temporary, as society strives to regain balance and "normality" through reorganisation, emerging with organised functions of various parts of society and society as a whole. Changing societies are in a constant process of disorganisation and reorganisation [Plans and programmes of directed change attempt to expedite and simplify the process of change at minimum cost and avoidance of waste].

Social and personal disorganisation have been referred to as the "costs" of social change and resultant from it. Disorganisation has allegedly occurred and continues to occur in certain areas of society in which rapid changes are taking place. The following may serve as illustrations of alleged "disorganisation" of certain aspects of society in India:

1. *"Disorganisation" of the Family:* In rural India the traditional joint family system has been and continues to be subjected to the influence of various factors that have disrupted the functioning of this system. Briefly the system involves the joint residence under one household, of parents, their married sons and their families and their unmarried daughters under the headship of the father. Sons remain subject to the direction and will of their father even after marriage and have farm work (if farmers) and other duties assigned. While the father is head of the household, the mother has charge of the home with unmarried daughters and daughters-in-law responsible to her. The domestic affairs of the home are managed under her direction. When a daughter gets married she becomes a part of the joint family of her husband. Roles and conduct of behaviour and decision making are clearly defined in the joint family. Limited farm holdings causing economic necessity of securing additional income from non-farm sources, job opportunities in urban area, increased contact and communication with urban areas, impact of education and ideologies that emphasise diversification of occupation, community development programmes, migration to urban areas and several other factors have served to disrupt this system. A general upsurge of individualistic feelings among youth and adults, together with an awakening to rights and privileges, have also served as functional factors in the situation. Homes have been established as nuclear

families independent in varying degrees from the parental home and the traditional joint family system has been disorganised to a large extent in the face of rapid change, although it still persists to some extent in rural areas. Another, aspect of change that has made for the disorganisation of the joint family system has been the changing role of women, although less evident in rural than in urban areas. With such basic changes implemented after national independence as equal voting and other rights of women, supporting legislation, together with special programmes of welfare for women for their development and leadership, there has been a disruption of their traditional functions and roles that has affected family and community life in various ways. In some areas women have been elected to the village Panchayat sometimes in leadership positions. In urban areas there have been radical changes in the traditional role of woman as homemakers and child bearers. Together these and other changes have contributed to the "disorganisation" of the rural family and specifically of the joint family system in north India.

2. *"Disorganisation" of Some Economic and Religious Institutions:* The Hindu Caste System in India is an organisational structure of Hindu society with religious foundation and sanction and economic implications. For years certain of its basic aspects have been the target of reform and change by eminent leaders. This major force, together with increased communication, breakdown of isolation of villages, industrialisation, promoted programmes of development, legislation for equal rights of all citizens and other such factors have diversified the restrictive occupational nature of the Caste System and done much to minimise its discriminatory nature. The traditional caste system has

by and large "disorganised" in urban area and in rural areas the pace of its "disorganisation" is moving with rapidity. Many active forces, both within and outside of the system, are making for its "disorganisation". For instance, alternative economic pursuits and locations will be sought by many in the light of industrialisation. This "disorganisation" of the system will also have a bearing on the religious institution, but because of its all inclusive nature, Hinduism will probably be in a position to cope effectively with such "disorganisation".

3. *"Disorganisation" in Education:* Educational institutions in India have been in general considered to be in a state of "disorganisation". Repeated protests, strikes, demonstrations, and acts of violence resulting in repeated closure of colleges and universities all over the country over the past several years certainly point to a state of confusion and instability. Scholars and educators have stated that the pursuit of scientific knowledge is simply not possible in such a state of confusion, and unless remedied expeditiously, the long term effects on society as a whole may be disastrous. Several causes have been attributed to the situation. One is interference of political parties in the affairs of educational institutions as a means to gain their political ends by using students and teachers as tools for this purpose. Another that prevails, though to a much lesser degree than before as a result of implementation of educational reforms, is the continued lack of relevance of the content of education to the needs of society and as a whole, to the needs of the independent nation. Another is the heavy demand for education and the inability of educational institutions to meet the demand within their limited resources and at the same time, maintain desirable academic standards. Several other

> causes have been identified, such as lack of perspective and planning, faulty sense of priorities, and general confusion of thought in respect of the purpose and role of educational institutions by individuals and groups concerned. Whatever the causes, the disruption of traditional functions and a large degree of confusion in educational institutions and in the general sphere of education in the country can be referred to as "disorganisation".

While the examples illustrate social conditions in various aspects of life that have been described under the traditional concept of "disorganisation", there is, however, a growing reluctance on the part of sociologists and rural sociologists to accept this traditional concept and to use the term "disorganisation". Social change is a fact and a constant Ceaseless phenomenon in society. Whether or not programmes that attempt to direct and promote change exist, changes in various aspects of society, and society as a whole do occur.

The traditional concept of disorganisation employs as its criteria for assessment such conditions as disruption of normal functions, imbalance in functioning of various parts, failure in operation of social controls on human behaviour in society, confusion in behaviour among individuals and groups, and change in roles. But all of this occurs during the process of social change constantly happening in society in some form and aspect or other.

Old roles are modified, or are replaced by new roles, institutions are modified and change in form, structure and function give way to new forms and functions as society through them adjusts to meet changing needs.

> "The crux of the problem lies in the inability to distinguish between so-called breakdown of a traditional role and the appearance of a new role" [Cuber, 1968, p. 535].

What has been traditionally considered "disorganisation" can be considered as merely emergence of new organisation of society or reorganisation. Social conditions involved in change appear to be disorganisation because we are acquainted and "familiar with the roles which have come out of the past, but we are unfamiliar with the roles which are shaping up for the society of tomorrow" [Caber, 1968, p. 535].

Thus the alleged "disorganisation" of the rural family and "breakdown" of the Hindu caste system in India with its impact and bearing on aspects of some economic and religious institutions in society, constitute a reorganisation and reformulation of these parts for the society of tomorrow.

"Disorganisation" is thus objectively indistinguishable from normal social change. Use of this term has resulted in much erroneous thinking because "disorganisation" has connotations of abnormality, of disapproval, of a situation that is undesirable. Social change is a normal phenomenon and is quite as likely to result in an improvement of social conditions as in conditions that are worse.

The traditional concept of social disorganisation has hence become less useful as an objective concept for rural sociologists and sociologists, although it does have utility in describing such situations as earthquake, flood, war and riots. Such conditions exist for a relatively short period of time and there is strong probability that at the end of this period of confusion and disruption, order will be restored more or less on the same pattern as before.

2

Social Backdrop

Integrity of the Nation

India is a vast peninsula with a total land area of about 33 million sq kms and population exceeding 800 millions. Its length from north to south is about 3,200 kilometres and breath from east to west is nearly 3,000 kilometres. Because of its huge size both in area and population India is generally referred to as a subcontinent.

India owes its name to the mighty river Sindhu (the Indus, which is now in Pakistan.) The huge river which carries an annual inflow twice that of the Nile and thrice the combined inflow of Tigris and Euphrates was the most imposing feature of north-western part of the Indian subcontinent. The early Aryan settlers in India were amazed at the sight of the huge river and called it Sindhu meaning a huge sheet of water. Sometimes it is used as a synonym for ocean.

In 518 B.C. the Persian Emperor Darius conquered the area around the river Sindhu and made it a *satrapy* of his empire. The Persians pronounced 'S' as 'H'. Hence, Sindhu became

Hindu. Later the Greek invaders changed 'Hindu' into India. Since then the foreigners have referred to the entire country from the Himalayas to Kanyakumari as India.

The early people, however, called their country 'Bharata Varsha', that is, the country of Bharata and his progeny, a famous king mentioned in the early *puranas*. Bharata Varsha is supposed to be a part of an island continent known as Jambu dvipa. The Muslim invaders called the country Hindustan. The British rulers called the country India and the same name was retained when the country was partitioned and became free on 15 August, 1947.

Unity in Diversity: The diversity of India is unique. Being a huge country with a large population, India presents endless varieties of physical features and cultural patterns. It is only in India one can find people professing all the major religions of the world. In short India is "the epitome of the world".

Population Density

The impressive fact about India is its size and population. It is as large as Europe minus Soviet Russia. Many states of India like Andhra Pradesh and Madhya Pradesh are larger than many countries of Europe like, United Kingdom, France and West Germany. In fact the area of the state of Andhra Pradesh is larger than the countries of United Kingdom, France and West Germany separately. India is the second most populated country after China. Every fifth individual on the earth is an Indian.

Physical Features: Diversity: The second unique feature about India is the extreme diversity of the physical features. Only in India can one find the world's largest mountains covered with snow throughout the year. The Himalayas or the abode of snow is the source of the mighty rivers like Indus, Ganga and Yamuna. These perennial rivers irrigate extensive areas in the north to sustain the huge population of the country.

At the same time northern India contains arid zones and Thar desert of Rajasthan where nothing grows except a few shrubs.

Again it is only in India that one can encounter different types of climates like the polar (Arctic), the temperate and the tropical. The climate of Kashmir which is cold even in summer contrasts with that of Kerala's climate which is hot and humid even in mid-winter. Likewise, there is nothing common climate-wise between the states of the North-East region and Rajasthan. The states of North-East India are noted for their heavy rainfall and Cherapunji in Meghalaya held the world's highest record of rainfall. Its rainfall of about 500 inches a year contrasts with less than 3 inches of rain per year in some areas of Rajasthan like Jaisalmer and Banner.

Diversity of Race: India is an ethnological museum. Majority of the people of India are descendants of immigrants from across the Himalayas. Dr. B.S. Guha identifies the population of India into six main ethnic groups, namely:

(1) The Negrito,

(2) Proto-Australoids,

(3) Mongoloids,

(4) Mediterranean or Dravidian,

(5) Western Brachycephals, and

(6) Nordic Aryans.

People belonging to these different racial stocks have little in common either in physical appearance or food habits. The racial diversity is very perplexing. As Jawaharlal Nehru stated:

> In the North-West frontier province there is already the breath of Central Asia, and many a custom there, as in Kashmir, reminds one of the countries on the other side of the Himalayas. Pathan's popular dances are singularly like Cossack dancing. Yet with all these differences there is no mistaking the impress of India on the Pathans.

Diversity of Language: The census of 1961 listed as many as 1,652 languages and dialects. Since most of these languages are spoken by very few people, the subsequent census regarded them as spurious. But the 8th Schedule of the Constitution recognises 18 major languages. They are: (1) Assamese, (2) Bengali, (3) Gujarati, (4) Hindi, (5) Kannada, (6) Kashmiri, (7) Konkani (8) Malayalam, (9) Manipuri, (10) Marathi, (11) Nepali, (12) Qriya, (13) Punjabi, (14) Sanskrit, (15) Tamil, (16) Telugu, (17) Urdu, and (18) Sindhi. But four of these languages namely Sanskrit, Kashmiri, Nepali and Sindhi are not official languages in any state of the Indian Union. But all these languages are rich in literature. Hindi in Devanagiri script is recognised as the official language of the Indian Union by the Constitution. The second largest language, Telugu, is spoken by about 60 million people, mostly in Andhra Pradesh. Most of the languages spoken in north India belong to the Indo-Aryan family, while the languages of the south namely, Telugu, Tamil, Malayalam and Kannada belong to the Dravidian family.

Diversity of Religion: The major religions of India are Hinduism, Islam and Christianity. Besides, there are the followers of Buddhism, Jainism, Sikhism and Zoroastrianism (Parsis). India is not religiously a homogeneous state even though nearly 83 per cent of the population profess Hinduism.

Novel Integrity

Despite the above mentioned diversities; India has never lost the ideal of unity. It is wrong to suppose that the unity of India is the gift of the British rule. From times immemorial it found noblest expression in the thoughts of our sages and poets. The entire country was referred to by the common name Bharata Varsha and the people are referred to as 'Bharata Santatih' to emphasize the oneness of the country and its people. The fundamental unity was reiterated in the *Vishnu Purana* thus:

Uttaram Yatsamudrasya

Himadreshchaiva dakshinam

Varsam tad Bharatam nama

Bharati yatra Santatih

(The country bounded by the seas on the south and the Himalayas on the north is called Bharatam. There live the progeny of Bharata.)

Heritage in Common: Ramayana and Mahabharata are the epics of India and are read with much devotion even in the distant nooks and corners of the country. That the great epics have helped in fostering the unity of the country since early times to the present day need no emphasis. They are rightly regarded as the common heritage of all the Indians.

Apart from the epics, the Sanskrit language fostered the unity of the country. Even though it was not the language of the masses, yet it remained a common medium of communication between the elite in different and distant parts of the country. Further, Sanskrit is regarded as the mother of the modern Indian languages. Even in the languages of the South, especially Malayalam, Telugu and Kannada, the number of words of Sanskrit origin used is as high as 60 to 75 per cent.

Sanatana Dharma (Hinduism) is still the religion of the overwhelming majority of the people. The main sects of Hinduism, namely Vaishnavism and Shaivism have their important places of worship all over the country.

The places of Hindu pilgrimage such as Kasi and Haridwar in the north, Tirupati and Rameswaram in the south, Dwaraka in the west and Jagannath Puri in the east are visited by people from all over the country fostering national integration since the ancient times.

Sir Herbert Risley admitted that: "Beneath the manifold diversity of physical and social type, language, custom and religion, which strikes the observer in India, there can still be discerned a certain underlying uniformity of life from the Himalayas to the Cape Comorin. There is in fact, an Indian character, a general Indian personality, which we cannot resolve into its component elements."

Indian Nationals

A number of anthropologists have given a variety of classifications of the Indian people. Dr. B.S. Guha, Dr. J.H. Hutton and Sir Herbert Risley have given a broad seven ethnic group classification:

1. The Mongoloids
2. Indo-Aryans
3. Dravidians
4. Mongolo-Dravidians
5. Aryo-Dravidians
6. Seytbo-Dravidians
7. Turko-Iranians

Another Analysis Presented by J.H. Hutton in 1933, Classified the Population into Eight Groups:

1. The Negritos
2. Proto Austroloids
3. Early Mediterraneans
4. Advanced Mediterraneans
5. Armenois
6. Alpines
7. Vedic Aryans
8. The Mongoloids

However, a detailed and clear analysis of the Indian population is given by Dr. B.S. Guha. According to him there are six main racial groups and from these a few sub-groups got formed which formulate the Indian population.

The Negritos: There sub-group survivals are found among the Kadars and Palagans of Cochin and Travancore Hills; Nagas of Nagaland; Rajmahal tribes of Eastern Bihar and among the Andamans.

The Proto-Australoids: They have left no trace as such in India.

The Mongoloids: This racial group is largely visible in Sikkim, Bhutan and North-Eastern region.

The Mediterranean: These are of three types: Palaco-Mediterranean who are of medium height, dark-skinned and slight build. They are largely to be found in Kannad, Tamil and Malayalam areas; the Mediterranean are fair complexioned and are found in the Punjab, in other words the Aryanized people; Oriental Mediterranean are people with long noses and fair skin, found largely in the Punjab, Rajasthan and Uttar Pradesh'.

The Alpinoid: The Alpinoid are also of three types: The traces of the first are found in Gujarat; the second type are found in W-Bengal, Orissa, Kathiwar, Tamil and Coorg tracts and the third type are close to the Parsis.

The Nordic: The Nordic or the Aryans.

Traditional Hindu Social Organisations

System of Varna: The Hindu *sastra-karas (i.e.* those who have written the *Sastras,* the scientific treatises) have taken man into account as a social being with reference to four broad factors that influence his life and its conduct: He is considered in relation to: (i) *desa,* (place, region) which may be said to be the regional approach to the study of society; (ii) *kala* (time) which, we may say, constitutes the historical approach to the study of society, (iii) *srama* (effort) which takes into account man with reference to his nurture and development in the contemporary environment; and (iv) *guna* (natural traits), which refers to the natural inherent psycho-biological equipment of man.

An attempt is made here to study the Hindu thought under the last two headings, *i.e.* man as a social being in connection with his natural development *(srama)*, and in connection with his natural endowments *(guna)*. Here we may note that in substance, all the Hindu sages agree that any plan or scheme of social organization which aims at the best functioning of every human being as a social unit, must, in the first instance, take him into account from these two aspects: First, it must consider man as a social being with reference to his training and development in the natural and social environment in order to enable him to fulfil the final aim of his existence; and secondly, this has to be coordinated with another scheme which studies" man with reference to his natural endowments, dispositions and attitudes. The first of these is the problem undertaken in the scheme of the *ashramas;* the second is thought out in the scheme of the *Varnas.*

Ashrama and Varna System: The two organizations of the *Ashrama* and the *Varna (vamasrama-vyavastha)*, which, to put it briefly, refer to the problems of the nurture and the nature of man, rightly serve as the cornerstones of the Hindu theory of social organization. And, we may also note here that the scheme of the asramas as thought out and devised by the Hindus is a unique contribution in the whole history of the social thought of the world, without even a parallel in any other thought-system, excepting, perhaps, to some extent, in Plato's *The Republic.* The same may be said to be true to a great extent of the varna-organization also.

Both the schemes of the *ashrama* as well as the *varna* presuppose, and are fundamentally based upon, a certain point of view in regard to the problem of life and its conduct, upon a certain basic outlook, a certain philosophy of life.

The whole of the life of an individual was, for the Hindu, a kind of schooling and self-discipline. Now, during the course of this schooling, he had to pass through four stages, four grades of training, as it were called the *Ashramas.* And, in regard to the *ashramas,* too, every item and stage and phase had to be defined in terms of the already defined relations between man and God. Here, therefore, practically we start with supernatural basis; upon this, we erect the superstructure of man's earthly career.

The earthly existence has thus to be defined primarily in terms of *dharma;* and *dharma* has to be interpreted in the concrete in term of *karma.* The *asrama* scheme, therefore, defines our *dharma* in and through a life of worldliness, of *Samsara,* before it, and beyond its pale; and, in practice, it seeks to delineate the implications of *dharma* in terms of *karma.*

In order to understand the psycho-moral basis of the *asramas* proper, it is advisable to look into the theory of the *purusharthas* which concern themselves with the understanding,-justification, management and conduct of affairs of the individual's life in relation to the group, in and through the *asramas.* The *purusharthas* are four, *viz., dharma, artha, karna* and *moksha.* We speak of these *purusharthas* as the 'psycho-moral' bases of the *asrama* theory, because, on the one hand, the individual receives a psychological training through the *asramas* in terms of lessons in the use and management of the *purusharthas;* while, on the other hand, in actual practice, he has to deal with the society in accordance with these lessons. It is in the light of the understanding of the meaning and place of the *purusharthas* in the *asrama* scheme that the right method, way and outlook for the management of each of the *asramas* can be comprehended.

It is usual to translate these terms *dharma, artha, karna and moksha* in English by such words as morality, wealth, desires or passion, and salvation respectively. But the Sanskrit terms are potent with deeper meanings than these English words singly convey. Thus, the word *dharma* is derived from the Sanskrit root *'dhri'* meaning to hold together, to preserve.

The social implications and meaning of *dharma* as a principle for maintaining the stability of society is brought out by Sri Krishna in three verses in the *Mahabharata:* In advising Arjuna as to what is dharma he explains that "*Dharma* is created for the well-being of all creation", and further that "all that is free from doing harm to any created being is certainly *dharma;* for, indeed, *dharma* is created to keep all creation free from any harm." Shri Krishna proceeds, next, to give a still more comprehensive view of *dharma:* "*Dharma* is so called because it protects *(dharanat)* all that is created. *Dharma,* then, is surely that principle which is capable of preserving the universe." *Artha,* on the other hand, is to be understood as referring to all, the means necessary for acquiring worldly prosperity, such as wealth or power.

And *Kama* refers to all the desires in man for enjoyment and satisfaction of the life of the senses, including the sex drive to which the word *karna* more prominently refers. The term refers to the native impulses, instincts and desires of man, his natural mental tendencies, and finds its equivalent, we may say, in the use of the English terms "desires", "needs", "basic or primary motives", "urges", or "drives" and the collective use of the term "karna" would refer to the totality of the innate desires and drives of man. The term is also often used in a broader sense to include socially acquired motivation too. *Dharma, artha* and *karna,* therefore, refer respectively to the moral, material and mental resources, accessories and energies available to man.

Of these three, *artha* and *karna* refer to two of man's earthly belongings, while *dharma* stands on higher level. At its lowest level of manifestation, *karna* is understood in the sense of pure sex drive, and is said to be one of the six 'enemies' of human being.

But it is equally true that a human being cannot conduct his life without *artha* which constitutes the material means of living, and *karna* which helps the propagation of the species. Therefore, it is needed that the correct quality and quantity, the place, and the time of *karna,* have to be determined and laid down by the wise sages. This is done in terms of *dharma,* which defines, for man, the proper quantum, place, season, for the right functioning of *artha* and *karna.* By attending to his *dharma,* therefore a person is able to live a proper life even though it may be lived in terms of *artha* and *karna.* As Vidura says: "It is by the help of *dharma* that the sages have been able to cross the world. The stability of the universe depends upon *dharma; artha* and *karna* too, depend for their proper management upon *dharma. Dharma* is the foremost of all; *artha* is said to be middling: and *karna,* at is said by the wise, is the lowest of the three. Therefore, we should conduct our lives with self-control paying major attention to *dharma"*

In the opinion of Manu, the good of humanity lies in a harmonious management or coordination of the three *(trivarga), viz., dharma, artha* and *karna.* Says he: "Some declare that the good of man consists of *dharma,* and *artha;* some say that *dharma* alone will give it; while the rest assert that *artha* alone is the chief good of man here below (on earth). But the correct position is that the good of man consists in the harmonious coordination of the three".

This advice, is meant for those who weigh the issue from the viewpoint of the immediate and worldly objectives of life. But, from the point of view of the final purpose and meaning of life, *moksha* alone would prove to be the best guide. With reference to the supreme end of *moksha,* therefore, the other three immediate objectives of life become but the means for the attainment of that end.

Bhakti: the Root of Religion: *Bhakti* is the root of our *dharma.* It is the method of pleasing the gods and goddesses. It is through *bhakti* that a religious person tries to control his mind and soul. It is the channel for approaching Him. *Bhakti* and *dharma* are so much identified with each other that it is believed that a *bhakt* must be a religious man and a religious man cannot be so unless he is *bhakt.* It is however, repeatedly made clear in our religious books that *bhakti* should be used as a method for self-purification but not for achieving personal ends or gains. According to P.H. Prabhu,

> "Thus Bhakti as a means of attaining the end, is conceived as based on an intellectual foundation and not on mere emotional or sentimental one. Nor is it to be taken resort for redress against personal afflictions, griefs or shortages in wordly comforts...And the Bhakti Sutras of Narada says that it is the form of the highest devotion or affection towards same one. In Hindu society there is however, no restriction on the way in which people worship their gods and also whether worship is in the open or in the temple. There is in fact perfect freedom in so far as Bhakti is concerned".

Moksha: The whole Hindu social system and organisation aims at Moksha. It is the desire and will of every Hindu that he or she should attain Moksha, *i.e.,* salvation, when the soul rises above all lines of wordly life. It then rests in eternal peace and does not suffer the tortures of life and death. This is considered to be the supreme and ultimate end of the life. To quote P.H. Prabhu again, *"Mere meritorious action will not lead to the attainment of the supreme bliss (which is moksha); it will lead, at best, to happiness during the next birth. The state of supreme bliss from whence there is no return of this mundane existence can be obtained only by attaining knowledge of the self.* In fact, all our actions, charities, alms giving, worship, etc., are directed around one activity namely, *moksha.* Our saints and sages spend whole of their life in jungles for the attainment of *moksha* only.

Marriage: the Base of Family: Marriage and family are other important institutions of our social system and organisation. Undoubtedly marriage and family are very old institutions and are also found in all societies. There are however certain rules and regulations which govern family life and so the conditions of the married life and with whom marriage should or should not be performed. Marriages among such near relatives as the father and daughter or sister and brother are forbidden in almost every society. But marriage occupies a very significant role in so far as Hindu social system is concerned. Whereas in other societies, particularly in western society, marriage is considered more a friendship rather that a bond with a religious sanction, *vice-versa* is the case in Hindu society.

In our system marriage is considered not only an institution necessary for procreating the children but it is essential for a household. Without children one cannot even die religiously. P.H. Prabhu says in this connection that,

> "For the Hindu, then, marriage is Samskara, and as such, the relations between the marrying parties are of sacramental character and not a contractual nature. For, apart from the necessity of begetting a son in order to assist the householder in the discharge of his obligations (rinas) it has been ordained by the Dharma Sastra that wife is a necessary complement as the Grihpatni (i.e., the lady of the house) for the proper and full execution of his Dharmas as the Grihpati (i.e., the lord of the House)".

Indian Women

Then we come to another important aspect of Hindu social organisation, namely, the attitude of Hindus towards the women. It is clear from all accounts that during the Vedic period women were respected in the society. However, gradually women lost respect in society, and came to be considered as inferior and unequal. Due to the frequent education and other facilities were denied to the women and she had to adopt the *Purdah* system.

Trivarga: In Hindu society there are 4 *Purusharthas* namely

Kama, Artha, Dharma and *Moksha*. But three *Purusharthas* namely, *Kama, Artha* and *Dharma* combined together are called *Trivarga*. The *Trivargas* discuss the three main aspects of human life namely material, moral and biological. The *Kama* discuss biological, *Artha* material, and *Dharma* moral aspect of the life of a Hindu. In Hindu society *Trivarga Dharma* plays a more vital and important part than the other two components; namely *Kama and Artha*. It is moral aspect, *i.e., Dharma* of life which regulates two other aspects namely, *Anha* and *Kama* or what can be said as material and moral aspects of life.

Rinas: Hindu social system believes that after coming into the world each and every individual undertakes certain obligations which must honestly and sincerely be discharged. These begin with parents who bring up the children from their childhood after facing all the difficulties. Then the obligation is towards the teachers and saints, etc., who guide the course of life of a child for the future. Thereafter come the gods and goddesses, who are supposed to have given birth to the child and who will receive him after his death. These obligations are technically called *rinas*. These rinas in Hindu philosophy are known as *Patri Rina* (parental obligations), *Rishi Rina* (duty towards the teachers and saints) and *Deva Rina* (duty towards the gods and goddesses). It is enjoined upon all the Hindus that throughout their life they should try to discharge these obligations and while doing any action they must not forget these duties. The obligations can best be discharged by studying the *Vedas*, by begetting children in accordance with the provisions of *dharma* and also by performing duties as a *grihasthi, i.e.,* by remaining in the *grihastha ashrama*.

Patri Rina can be discharged by way of having children, because they alone will continue the race. The children are equally expected not to forget that the parents suffer for them when they are not capable of holding themselves. Similarly, each and every individual is required to remember that his teachers and saints are always makers and unmakers of his life and can mould future course of his action in the way they like. It is, therefore, very essential that all respect should be shown to *Rishis* and teachers. Similarly respect should be shown to sages, gods and goddesses who will receive them at the end of his life.

Ashram Vyavastha: *Ashrama Vyavastha* is one of the fundamentals of our social organisation. According to this system life is to be divided into four Ashramas namely: (1) *Brahmacharya Ashrama,* (2) *Grihastha Ashrama,* (3) *Vanaprastha Ashrama,* and (4) *Sony as Ashrama.* Each *Ashrama* is considered very important for the development of a person and his faculties. It is also believed that each one will live in each *Ashrama* for a period of at least 25 years.

Evolution of Ashrama Vyavastha: The word Ashrama is derived from Sanskrit word 's-rama' meaning thereby to exert itself. Ashrama therefore stands to mean a place where exertions are performed or the action of performing such exertions is initiated. In the words of P.H. Prabhu, *"The word therefore, signifies a half a stoppage, on a stage in the journey of life just for the sake of rest in a sense, in order to prepare oneself for further journey"*. He further says, *"The Ashramas then are to be regarded as resting place during one's journey on the way to final liberation which is the final aim of life. The four stages of life, says Vyasa in the Mahabharata, form a ladder or flight of four steps. The flight attaches to Brahmins"*. German scholar Paul Deussen also says that *Ashrama* means a place where people make efforts and the people labour. The *Ashramas* are considered steps towards *Moksha,* which is ultimate end of human life. According to Hindu philosophy *Ashramas are* considered essential for schooling and self-discipline.

It is argued by some of our social thinkers that originally there were only three *Ashramas* and not four. They opine that there was no *Vanaprastha Ashrama.* According to them Chhandogya Upanishad mentions about 3 *Ashramas* only. They believe that Manusmriti also refers to only three stages of life.

One however, finds that Jabala Upanishad mentions about four stages. It is however, usually believed that there were four *Ashramas* in Hindu social system through which an individual was required to pass before he could reach *Brahaman*. At least four *Ashramas* have come to stay since times very long past.

Entry Age: There is no unanimity of opinion about the age of entry to *an Ashrama*. Usually however, it is believed that each *Ashrama* was of 25 years span and an individual was normally required to live up to 100 years. Prof. M.N. Srinivas however, makes us believe that *Brahmacharya Ashrama* was only up to the age of 16. According to him, *"The first stage of studentship (Brahmacharya) under a teacher came to an end at about sixteen when the boy married and entered the second stage of Grihastha or householder"*.

P.H. Prabhu says, *"There are differences of opinion among different authorities concerned as regards the particular age at which one is expected to enter each of the Ashramas, and the period of life he is expected to spend in it"*.

System of Ashramas

As already pointed out some thinkers make us believe that there were only three *Ashramas* whereas there is a usual belief that Hindu life was divided into four *Ashramas*. These were: (a) *Brahmacharya Ashrama,* (b) *Grihastha Ashrama,* (c) *Vanprastha Ashrama* and (d) *Sanyas Ashrama.*

The Brahmacharya Ashrama: A boy at the age of 7 was required to join this *Ashrama* and his parents were required to arrange a *guru* for him, who was his spiritual guru as well as teacher. It was expected of the student to exclusively devote himself to the service of the *guru* and serve him without reservations. He resided in the campus under the overall supervision and control of the teacher. He was not to care for worldly life and was also forbidden to live a life of comfort and luxury. *Guru* gave him all that was best with him. He also helped him in the realisation of the ultimate truth. It was expected of the pupil that he should not go near the opposite sex, as long as he was Brahmachari and thus maintain absolute purity of character.

Initiation of a person into this *Ashrama* makes him *Dwija* or twice born. This is also called *Upanayana initiation.* It is more or less unanimously agreed that this period was important in the life of a pupil. It was during this period that he became a man of letters and also that he appreciated need and necessity of devotion to duty towards the teachers on the one hand and society on the other.

The Grihastha Ashrama: Next stage in the life of a person was considered to be the one when he left his studies and joined the worldly life. According to P.H. Prabhu,

> "After the course of study is over in accordance with the Dharmas laid down for the Brahmachari, he takes a bath, symboled of his completion of that Ashrama course; so he now becomes a Sanataka. He now becomes fit to enter the next Ashrama, viz., the Grihastha Ashrama".

This ceremony is technically called *Samavartana.* This is considered to be the most important period of the life of an individual. It is believed that the future course of his life depended on this Ashrama. It was the test of his ability, wisdom, social morality and social adaptability. What he had learnt in theory was put into practice in this Ashrama. It was his duty to maintain his family in a dignified manner. He was required to earn wealth in accordance with *Dharma, i.e.,* by righteous means. He was to have the children during this period. According to P.H. Prabhu,

> "The individual has to fulfil his obligations (rinas) to the members of his family, to his deceased ancestors, to strangers and gods in order to become fit to enter the next Ashrama of Vanaprastha".

Importance of Grihastha Ashrama: In the Hindu social organisation, *Grihastha Ashrama* has been considered as a turning point in the life of an individual. One finds that Shanti Purva of Mahabharata discusses the significance of this *Ashrama,* when Yudhishtra decided to become a *Sanyasi* in disgust against the worldly life. It is believed that it is in this *Ashrama* that *Dharma, Artha* and *Kama* exist together and these can be used for *Moksha.* Similar praises about *Grihastha Ashrama* are found in Smriti literature as well. It is this *Ashrama* which lends support to other three *Ashramas.*

Now a question that naturally arises is as to why so much significance has been attached to this *Ashrama,* when it is usually believed that all the four *Ashramas* are of equal significance. Was it due to importance of sex over knowledge or renunciation? No, certainly not. Prabhu makes us rather reasonably believe that it was primarily because, it was thought that each and every individual might not live for hundred years and thus might not pass through all the four Ashramas of life.

Since Grihastha *Ashrama* combined *Dharma, Artha* and *Kama,* therefore, it could be used as a stage for Moksha, even if there was no opportunity for passing through other stages. He says, *"Thus it is said that in the Grihastha Ashrama alone can the three Purusharthas be practised together, and the three rinas could all be discharged satisfactorily".* He further says that, *"We may say that such a view of Grihastha Ashrama was due to the fact that the Hindu Sanskaras perhaps found that it was, in practice, not always possible or was exceedingly difficult, for the average individual to follow the course of all the four Ashramas one after the other, considering the actual average life-span of man, which could be in most cases much less than only 100 years and that therefore, they wisely suggested that one can hope for salvation even if he continued in the Grihastha Ashrama till the end of his life, provided that he discharged in that Ashrama the three rinas and practised the three purusharthas in the manner prescribed?"* This Ashrama was also important because a person could learn to live in adjustment with the others. He was also to learn to sacrifice, selflessness, live life of pity and also that of sympathy.

Then another cause of importance is that the *Brahmachari*, the *Vanaprastha* and the *Sanyasi* all knock at the door of *Grihasthi* for alms and charity and for promoting all religious and social activities.

The Vanaprastha Ashrama: It is the third Ashrama of life. It was hoped that an individual will join this Ashrama at the age of fifty. By this time, it was expected that the person concerned will begin to renunciate his worldly life slowly and gradually. He will, now in a way, begin to say good-bye to his married life. It was however, fully well understood that at this stage of life he might, not have fully discharged his obligations in the worldly life. He might, therefore, continue to live in the family, along with his children. But what he should do is that gradually he should start withdrawing so that after some time he was in a position to lead a free life without any wordly obligations and start controlling his mind and soul. He should now start searching for *Moksha*. At intervals he might even go to jungles for meditation.

Now he should start living on vegetables and fruit. He should also not eat sweet things and meat. It was expected of him to use deer-skin or the bark of a tree as his clothes. He should also sleep on the floor and reside under a tree without any attachments to outside world. He should continue to perform sacrifices and utilise his time for getting knowledge and take steps for purging his body. He should also lead a life of self-control, friendliness and charity and also develop compassionate attitude towards all creatures. In the words of P.H. Prabhu, "*Now, in the Vanaprastha Ashrama, as the name itself suggests, the individual has to leave the shelter not only of the family (Kula) and of the home (Griha), but of the village (Grama) too; he must go to the forests (Vana) and live there all the while striving to bring under his control senses of enjoyment...*" It is expected of him that he should start giving responsibilities to his children so that they start picking up the work and try to become self-supporting in worldly and economic life.

The Sanyas Ashrama: It is the last *Ashrama* of a Hindu life. In this *Ashrama,* usually a person is supposed to enter at the age of 75 years. It is at this stage of life that he is required to give up worldly life and lead a life of renunciation. He should not care for *Artha* or *Kama.* He should be above all worldly attractions and also should not care what was happening around him in the world. He should have neither desires nor anxieties. He should struggle to control soul and try to get *moksha* or spiritual freedom. It is said that in this *Ashrama* the person is not supposed to depend on the support or help of anybody. He owned the whole world and yet disowned everything which he had, including his children and family.

Under the Hindu social organisation aim of life is *moksha,* which can be attained through passing the *Ashramas.* Each *Ashrama* enjoins certain duties on the individual and it is proper fulfillment of these duties and obligations that one successfully passes from one *Ashrama* to the other. These *Ashramas* have been called as schools of human life. It is in these *Ashramas* that one is in a position to discharge his *rinas* (obligations) which are towards the teachers and sages, towards the parents and towards gods and elders. It is in the proper discharge of these *rinas* that one can think of *moksha.* Hence the greatest significance of *Ashrama* system lies in the fact that it helps in getting salvation.

Ashramas Vyavastha and Modern Society: Modern society is very complex and complicated one. Every individual has economic worries and is passing through difficult economic times. There are financial strains which are causing many worries for him. Most of the poor and middle class people are not in a position to go on getting education up to the age of 25. Everyone wants to get settled in life at the earliest so that he and the parents are relieved of economic worries. Similarly, it is difficult for most of the people to have completely discharged their obligations by the age of 50 and to start leaving the world. One finds that those who seek employment in public and private sector are permitted to continue in active service up to the age of 60. Most of them till the age of their retirement are not in a position to discharge their Worldly obligations. *Ashrama* system has also become outdated because in many cases people do not live up to the age of 100 and death both natural and accidental, comes earlier than that age. This is happening in spite of the fact that longevity in age has very much increased. Not only this, but one also finds that settlement in life, in different stages is not due to one's own will and determination because throughout the world employment opportunities are limited.

Hindu society thinkers have fully appreciated the place of *karna* in human life. According to them *karna* is the urge of human life and it must be satisfied. They believe that it is essential both for the production of children and for continuity and perpetuity of the race. It is great source of joy and pleasure and it will be difficult to check this natural urge of man which he inherits from his birth. But what the society did not permit was unbridled *karna,* which could bring more harm than good to the society.

It is the ultimate aim of every human being to get salvation. Perfection and spiritual attainments are not only desirable but the end of human life. Some of the thinkers believe that it is the most important *purshartha* and the remaining three are only means while this *purshartha* is end of all these means. Leaving that apart, all our sages and saints have always aimed at attaining *moksha.* A study of *purshartha* makes it amply clear that there is a healthy blending of material and spiritual principles and aims of life in *purusharthas.* Whereas *Artha* and *karna* deal with material aspects, whereas *moksha* and *dharma* deal with moral aspects of human life. Unless both are blended together perhaps perfection cannot come.

Cultural Changes: Religion in India has always played a very big role. But in those days it was not taken in narrow sense of the term, but in a very wide sense. The aim of the religion was to promote *dharma.* It meant the promotion of righteousness and justice. It also meant growth of virtue. Then another feature of the *dharma* was that it was not a very complex system. Both during Indus valley and early Rigvedic period we find that it was a simple affair. There were no temples. The people worshipped in the open. There was worship of nature. There were no rituals and also no need of a *Purohita.*

Everyone worshipped in the way one liked. Not only this, but religion was not at all costly. There was no priestly class as such. It was subsequently under the later Vedic age that the system changed. Now from nature the worship of nature gods started in which the people started building temples in which the images of gods began to be kept. The whole worship system began to grow complex and complicated. Need of the priest was also felt for the performance of religious ceremonies with the result that a priestly class developed with the sole aim of performing religious ceremonies. Many rituals developed around religion. Costly religious ceremonies came to stay which the people could hardly perform. Costly temples and images of gods began to be built.

As the time passed with that religion began to become a burden, but still none dared to speak against religion. The respect and regard for *rishis* and *sages* very much increased. Even the kings had to leave their thrones when a sage from the jungles came to visit a darbar. The regard for religious books like the *Vedas* and the *Sastras* on the one hand and Ramayana and Mahabharata as well as Bhagwat Gita on the other was still very high.

The Hinduism: Hinduism is the ancient most religion of the people of India. It forms the basis of Hindu society. Our whole social system is based on it. We derive our sources for our social and religious life from our *Vedas, Sastras* and such other religious books as Bhagwat Gita, Ramayana and Mahabharata. Our society, to begin with was evil free. It was a society in which there was no caste system. The people believed in simple living and purity of character. Their food habits were very simple and social customs and ceremonies not complex and complicated. With the passage of time many evils crept up in our society. For centuries together, these evils continued to hollow our sound social system but a stage came when it became intolerable for our social and religious reformers. Shocked by the evils of our social system like caste, dowry, *sati* and child marriage, our social and religious reformers decided to reform the society without caring for the opposition from the orthodox sections of the society.

Literary Strong: The *Upanishads* occupy a very important place in it. It is in the *Upanishads* that such complex and complicated questions have been discussed as what is *maya*, soul, the philosophy of rebirths, *karna* and *mukti* (or salvation). The *Upanishads* do not encourage unnecessary religious practices and ceremonies. Throughout there is keen desire for probing the problem and finding a solution for the same. The spirit of enquiry is all pervading in these *Upanishads*. Truth, knowledge and immortality are the basis round which everything revolves in the *Upanishads*. These help solving very complex and complicated problems of life.

The other two religious books of Hinduism are the Ramayana and the Mahabharata. Both these throw a lot of light on the life and society of those days. It tells us how social conditions of those days had changed. In Ramayana age there was no love for power. For the sake of his father Rama will leave his throne and go to the jungles. There was immense love among the brothers. Lakshmana will accompany his brother and Bharat will not sit on the throne as according to him it was the trust of his brother. Not only this but there was the highest regard for the women. In order to keep the morale of his people high, Rama will not mind leaving his wife Sita and sending her to jungles. But conditions had drastically changed under Mahabharata. Now there was quarrel among the brothers for getting the throne. The respect for women had come down. She should now be put on dice.

The *Vedas* and the *Sastras* however, shine unabated in our religious literature. No other religious piece of work can occupy better religious position than these. Among the Hindus they are great source of inspiration.

Bhagwat Gita tells us about the philosophy of life and death. It contains the sermons which Lord Krishna gave to Arjuna on the battlefield. These are eternal for every Hindu.

Effect of Buddhism: Buddhism made first bold attempt to solve our social problems. It boldly challenged caste system and inequality which the system created. It pointed out evils which had crept into our society, and raised a voice against the costly customs and practices which Hinduism had introduced and which had made it impossible for the poor to perform religious ceremonies. It also boldly opposed system of untouchability. It suggested that the people should not accept everything and every religious dogma blindly. On the other hand it suggested that our religious principles should first be tested and it should be made sure that these sounded to reason, love, pity, benevolence and the spirit of forgiveness which was disappearing from the society, an attempt was made to bring all back. Similarly Buddhism preached non-violence as against violence which had created social problems. It even opposed deriving of too much authority from our religious books. It created a sense of respect for the women and did not contribute to the idea of child marriage or ban on widow re-marriage. In this way Buddhism made a bold attempt to challenge the evils of our society.

Buddhism had deep impact on Hinduism. It was a missionary religion and preachers of Buddhism exposed the weaknesses of Hinduism and the latter tried to reform itself.

It was now realised that unless religion was reformed it will die down. The hold of caste system which was very rigid so far was very much weakened. Many costly rituals had to be given up. Sacrifices at religious and other occasions had to be reviewed. There was intellectual freedom for all in religion because Buddhism believed that in religion blind faith should have no place. It was now propagated that all that appealed to reason should be accepted. In a sense it prompted revolt against Vedic religion.

It boldly propagated the philosophy of equality of man which was opposed to caste system of Hinduism which had got deep roots in India and thus attracted many who so far stood condemned. Every one was now allowed to be admitted to Buddhist monasteries. His great eight-fold path very significantly developed ethics and simplicity in society. It laid stress on truth, pity, non-violence, benevolence and forgiveness, which again were appealing to the people and attractive for them. Buddhism made the people realise that one is the architect of one's own faith and self reliance. It gave religions philosophical simplicity. It very significantly helped in the contribution of literature and in Buddhism Prakrit language was given more importance than Sanskrit and for some time the latter received a setback.

For the spread of Buddhism, monasteries, rock pillars, rock caves and images of Lord Buddha were made. These became beautiful art pieces. In this way Buddhism very much helped in the promotion of art. Buddhist missionaries also went abroad for the spread of their religion and thus India's prestige in foreign countries was enhanced enormously.

The Jainism: Like Buddhism, Jainism also attemped to put an end to sacrifices, rituals and customs which were a burden on our society. It also opposed child marriage and dowry system. It wanted to end disparity between men and women on the one hand and man and man on the other. It pointed out that purification of soul could be through self-sacrifice rather than anything else. Thus Jainism made an attempt to solve social problems of our society. It bitterly opposed violence and was equally opposed to discrimination of man against man.

Impact on Hinduism: It openly condemned all sacrifices and costly rituals. This appealed to the people. It wanted that one way of attaining salvation was to renounce this world and live in the jungles. It also laid stress on fasts and meditation on the one hand and on charity on the other. It believed that none with a soul should be killed. Its teachings were very simple with the result that Jainism spread quite quickly.

Brahmo Samaj: Neither the Muslims nor the Britishers made any serious attempt to touch our social system. In fact they followed policy of non-interference in our social life. The most agonising aspect of our social life which touched Raja Ram Mohan Roy and his Brahmo Samaj was against *Sati* system. He awakened public opinion both in India and England against this system. In the long run he was successful in getting *Sati* system legally banned. It was a curse on the fair name of Hindu society and under Brahaminism it was considered very essential. It was obligatory for a widow to burn herself on the pyre of the husband. Banning of the system very much weakened priestly classes and thus this single step alone had deep effect and great impact on the Hindu society.

Prarthana Samaj: Then another organisation which boldly pointed out our social evils was Prarthana Samaj. It was opposed to orthodoxy and superstitions which had not only crept into Hindu society but were deep-rooted in it. The members of this Samaj were opposed to blind faith and wanted that the women should be given equal rights with men.

Arya Samaj: But a bold jolt to the Hindu society from within came from Swami Dayanand Saraswati and his Arya Samaj. Arya Samaj brought to the front all that was good in the Hindu literature and thus created among the Hindus, sense of pride and self respect. Its founder Swami Dayanand Saraswati very boldly pointed out the evils of Hindu society. He condemned idol worship and asked the people to worship one supreme God. He was also opposed to caste system and advocated inter-caste marriages. He wanted that the women should be given high education and in all walks of life should be treated equal to men.

Similarly he stood for the purity of character, simplicity in worship and also piety and benevolence. According to him most of our social problems could be solved if the foreigners withdrew from our soil. In this philosophy materialism and spiritualism went hand in hand. He inculcated spirit of *swaraj*. According to him 'our' worst ruler was much better than the best foreign ruler. He also condemned the system of offering sacrifices at the time of *yajna*. He also wished that religious education should not be denied to the so called *Sudras*.

Arya Samaj has deep impact on the Hindu society. It was forced to look into its drawbacks and tried to remove the evils. It also laid stress on bringing the so called *Sudras* back in its fold and thus provided a breathing hope for all those who had lost hope of better life.

Rama Krishna Mission: This mission also came with a heavy hand on our social evils. Swami Vivekananda in the USA very beautifully and to the amazement of the whole world, expounded ancient Indian Hindu philosophy and religion. He pointed out to the world that due to foreign rule Hinduism could not occupy its rightful place in the world. In India the Mission wanted to uplift women and wanted to end casteism and untouchability. It also wanted to end many evil superstitions and costly customs. According to the Mission proper consciousness about India's past on the one hand and spread of education and, literacy on the other could solve many of our social problems. It revived glory of ancient India and tried to make every Indian realise that India's past was so glorious that every Indian could feel proud of it. The Mission also stressed that Mother India was the spiritual *guru* of the whole world and still she has to perform the role of spiritual world leadership. The world is to learn much from India even today.

Impact of Islam

Before proceeding further it will be proper to study the impact of Islam on Hindu culture. The Muslims came to India as invaders but decided to settle down here. They followed a different type of culture than the they followed by the Hindus. They did not believe in caste but had faith in the concept of equality of man. They believed in the concept of brotherhood and were quite prepared to accept in its fold the people belonging to all religions. They did not believe in idol worship at all. In fact they were idol breakers. They had no faith in non-violence. In addition, they also did not believe in costly religious rituals and ceremonies. Instead of monogamy they believed in polygamy. The idea of dowry was not known to them.

Due to prevailing circumstances under the Muslims the system of child marriage started. The *sati* system also became quite common.

In the field of architecture new styles started of which Red Fort, Jama Masjid, Qutab Minar, Taj Mahal, Fatehpur Sikri etc. are the living examples. The Mughal rulers, except Aurangzeb all loved architecture and fine arts. Under them paintings too received great encouragement. Under Jahangir painting received considerable fillip and emperor himself was the great lover of paintings. No less attention was paid to music. Tansen lived during 'the reign of Akbar.

Persian, Arabic and Hindi literature was produced generously. The works were produced both in poetry and prose. Humayun Nama, Ain-i-Akbari, etc. were brought out during this age. In fact there was no aspect of national life, including dress, food and drinking habits, life style, trade and commerce, language both written and spoken which was not influenced by the Muslim way of life. Urdu language is the product of this age. The long association of the Hindus and the Muslims has left a deep impact on Hindu life style, which is felt even today.

Modern West and its Impact: But Hindu social system and organisation were also influenced by modern West. As the Western influence over India increased every social institution came under strain. West did not believe in giving inferior position to the women and developed that thinking in India. The West believed in human equality and not in caste system. Thus hold of caste began to weaken somewhat. The women were not given high education in India but under the influence of the west, schools and colleges for women began to be opened.

In addition, the system of child marriage and also that of dowry in India was quite prevalent. Under the influence of the West both these systems also received jolts. Then another field in which social system received set back was religion. In India in the name of religion there was exploitation and everything unhealthy was done in its name. The rituals were costly and, in many cases, unscientific. But under the influence of West religion began to be tested on scientific lines and many of the superstitions which were believed in the Hindu society were shaken from the roots.

The institutions of marriage and family also came under the influence of the West. Some began to consider that marriage is a friendship and not a religious bond. In fact there was no social institution which did not come under the influence and impact of the West.

The system of child marriage began to decline. *Sati* system was banned by law. Due to western education awakening came both among the men and women and the latter tried to become economically self-sufficient. Since marriage began to be considered as friendship, therefore, women thought of institution of divorce as well. Food habits and dress drastically changed, The people of India began to dress themselves in western style. Vegetarian foods began to be replaced by non-vegetarian food. There was trend towards urbanisation and industrialisation with the result that cottage industries received a setback. The people became poor. Village autonomy system too received a great set back and trend towards migration to the cities began.

A lot of new literature which touched every walk of our national life was produced. It inspired many Indians for freedom struggle. New ideas emerged. Efforts were made to portray the ancient Indian culture in bad light. In addition, there was considerable development in architecture and new massive buildings in new style were built.

Caste system which had strongholds in India was very much weakened. The system of civil marriages and inter-caste marriages also started and gradually became more and more popular. Both the boys and the girls were now given freedom to choose their life partners and thus instead of arranged marriages, the system of love marriages got introduced in the society. A voice was raised that the marriages should be only at mature age. Divorce was considered as a way out for solving many family problems. Due to industrialisation and urbanisation people started leaving their home villages and in this way joint family system began to disintegrate and in its stead single family system became more popular. Small family size began to be preferred over the big one. The educated women refused to completely merge themselves with the personality of man. English language became very popular and began to dominate over all other Indian languages. On cultural occasions English dances also became popular.

Cultural Monuments

Religion in some form or other has been with man since times unknown. It is one of those few characteristics and activities of man which are independent of his animal nature. It has developed in response to his felt needs, external and internal. To trace its origin is impossible, and to define it is no less. It is evolutionary in character. Most of the definitions of religion oscillate round the concept of the super human; belief and practice; rituals and rites. According to Robertson, it is not however, "a vague fear of unknown powers, not the child of terror, but rather a relation of all the members of a community at heart, and to protect its laws and moral order".

'According to Ogburn "it is attitude towards super human powers". The super human, the unseen, the supernatural and the beyond, have always attracted the minds of men, the primitive and the modern alike. To propitiate the unknown the primitive, evolved beliefs and practices, to draw strength and support. The religious rites and rituals, sacrifices and ceremonies and the forms of worship rudimentary or non-rudimentary too were evolved in response to the--cultural requirements.

The emergence of gods and their fading away to provide room for the new, and the resentment against rituals etc., and the substitution of new in their place speaks of the changing conditions and of the new social expectation. In fact the movement from the nature gods such as the *Prithvi* and the *Indra,* conceptional gods such as the *Yama* and the *Vishnu,* from impersonal to personal gods and to the great realization of the *Ekam Satya* to the belief in the communion of the self, with the universal self is the expanding experience from the material to the spiritual and from the self to the supreme. While ritualism and orthodoxy provoked challenge from time to time, the intellectuality and spirituality provided the relief, hope and the eternal inspiration down the ages.

Customary Rituals

We have no idea of the religious beliefs and practices of the Indus Valley (3250-2750 B.C.) people, except what is deduced from the finds. The worship of Mother Goddess or the *Sakti;* of male deity, the *Pasupatinath,* accepted as the earliest predecessor of the *Shiva;* of trees in their natural state and of their indwelling spirit; of animals and of numerous other objectives appear to have been common.

The religion of the Vedic (2750-1500) people was elaborate. It consisted of worship to gods, sacrifice and rituals. They had the nature gods such as the *Indra,* domestic deities, the *Agni;* abstract gods, the *Sraddha* (faith) or *Manyu* (wrath) the water system, the *Apsara;* and the aerial spirits, the *Gandharas.* The sacrifice consisted in the offerings of the milk, ghee, grain, animal flesh and the *Soma* to gods to secure the boons. For the performance of the sacrifices, they had seven different classes of priests.

The worship of indwelling spirit of Nature remained popular. The Vedic Rudra, is the successor of the Indus Valley three faced male deity commonly called *Pashupathinath. Brahma and Vishnu* are described as the direct successor of the four armed figure among the signs of the Indus script. Animal sacrifice, very important among the Indus valley people made a deep impact on the vedic people. The *Homa,* which is now a fire sacrifice, was in the beginning slaughter of animals and was known as *Pasu Kamta.* Animal sacrifice, in fact continued and remained part of the religious practice of the vedic people. Some of the "vigorous enough" religious practices had to be adopted in the interest of popular appeal. The use of sandal-paste and of vermilion for religious ritual; turmeric and vermilion in wedding ritual became common and are now a part of our heritage. On the occasion of the *Homa* sacrifice rice-barely mix were important offerings and it continues to be so offered even today.

This religion of rites and rituals was seriously challenged, time and again it was put to severe tests, but its resurgence, testifies its vitality and appeal. It could not be eliminated; though occasionally it got eclipsed.

The animals like elephant, bull, buffalo and lion, so well known to the Indus Valley people, were adopted as the vehicles of the gods and goddesses. The galaxy of gods and goddesses, ancient vedic and non-vedic gave a new dimension to the religious sense of the people all over the country, came to be the belief and hope of the newly assimilated millions. There developed immense religious catholicity among the royalty and the communality. Reigning kings believing in one cult, extended full patronage to the believers of other cults within their kingdom. Kings and commons did not find it necessary to worship the same god and follow the same cult of their predecessors.

During the medieval period, when proselytizing zeal of the Turk hordes caused devastation all over the North, the orthodox resistance saved the heritage from getting lost. Every village and hamlet, temple and pathshala worked to sustain the ethics of the heritage, although it appeared as though the rites and rituals were losing their hold.

This system, the oldest form of Hinduism, is generally called Brahmanism. It is the handiwork of time and circumstances. Nobody is its creator and none its progenitor. It has grown concomitant to out social order. The pivot around which it turns is the Brahman *purohit*. He accepted the path of service and sacrifice and for himself, claimed nothing. For his high intellectuality, reflecting spirituality and total humanity, he remained distinguished and earned the gratitude of all, his wisdom to balance the political authority on the high-ethical standard in the interest of individual and society remains exceptional in all the history of mankind. His persuasion in initiating the settlers to the Indian way of life remains remarkable. His contribution to social organization, political system and to social ethics; mathematics and astronomy remains distinguished. Down the ages his spirituality has come handy to the country. He has been the progenitor (or supporter) of all the religio-social and political movements.

Intellectuality vs. Spirituality: The spirit of curiosity, the freedom of thought and expression and the immense social experience, generated in the closing period of the Vedic Age, disgust against all pervading religious dogmatism, in the efficacy of the cumbersome rituals and rites, in the expected boon securing offerings and sacrifices and in the multiplicity of gods.

The system had become too much to reconcile with. Dazzling streaks of intellectuality and spirituality soon found broader expression and greater acceptance. It touched the high climax in the *Upanishads.* The issue raised and answers provided in the *Upanishads* have been elaborated further in the *Ramayana,* the *Mahabharata,* the six schools of philosophy and in *Bhagavadgita.*

The Upanishads: *Upanishad* means sitting before the teacher, who imparts the doctrine and to receive the same. There are one hundred and eight *Upanishads.* The most known and distinguished are twelve. These are: the *Aitareya, Kausitaki, Chhandogya, Kena, Taittiria, Katha, Svetsvatara, Brihadaranyaka, Isha, Prasna, Manduka* and *Mandukya.* The *Chhandogya* and *Brihadaranyaka* are considered the oldest. They are pre-Buddhist and are dated 800 B.C. The *Upanishads* expound and explain the concepts of the *Maya* meaning that the material world is an illusion, the *Punarjanma,* the rebirth, the *Karma,* action, and *Mukti,* the final deliverance. The emphasis, in the *Upanishads* is on the *Jnana Kanda,* the true knowledge.

The *Upanishads* open before us a new world of thought and action: of knowledge of self and the Absolute Self; of objective inquiry and of spirit of adventure all in the pursuit of truth with earnest sincerity, demanding total disregard to dogmatism and misbelief.

There is nothing negative or pessimistic in the *Upanishads.* Asceticism is not the way to salvation. The saving knowledge one can gain without renouncing the world. Where mind is full of cares and desires, salvation is a remote possibility. Discipline of mind and harmony with the external world, which is only an aspect of inner reality is implied. The emphasis is on action and discipline; on social action and individual salvation; on the fulfillment of the obligations in a spirit of detachment. There is, in the *Upanishads* the buoyant confidence to do, to achieve, and to rise above the rest.

Great Epics

The two great epics, the *Ramayana* and the *Mahabharata*, provide immense sociological material to understand and appreciate the manner in which socio-cultural dynamics worked to bring about political unification of the country and invested it with a socio-cultural system as well to sustain and strengthen it. These continue to guide and inspire old and young alike. Whatever, the time of their compilation, the historical periods they cover, fall much beyond it and have links with the Vedic past.

The age of the *Ramayana*, historically, preceded that of the *Mahabharata*. The *Ramayana* is the earliest poetic literature. It is composed by the sage Valmiki. It is appreciated for the characterisation of an ideal father, son, brother, wife, husband, friend or devotee. This reference-model has influenced and stimulated the father-son, brother-brother, husband-wife relations, in a unique way, in all their dimensions. For its sociological and ethical content, the *Ramayana* remains everybody's book of common prayer. Millions in this country, have sustained themselves, and drawn strength from the charm of the *Ramayana*, in their daily course of life and activity. Its influence remains a force, even today.

The *Mahabharata* is second of the two epics. It was composed by sage Vyas. With time, the original text has been changed and altered several times to accommodate within its bounds, the beliefs and practices of the tribes and people who got rolled in the contemporary social system. In this sense, the Mahabharata presents real, legitimate and historical picture of the phenomena the society had gone through over a long historical period.

The one lakh verses it consists of are highly revealing to the end. "It is eight times the length of the *Illiad* and the Odyssey put together. Its appeal is universal, all over the country. The *shantiparva* (1,400 verses) and the *Anusaanparyva* (3000 verses) are the richest part from ethical point of view. The emphasis on the supremacy of *Dharma* and on its role in all fields of social activity. Here are mysticism, theism and *bhakti*". For their comprehensiveness and depth of meaning, for their social import and ethical content, epics are venerated and respected read and studied, racked and listened to, sung in the audience halls and public assemblies, performed in the theatres for the select and in the open for the lay and the learned alike.

They provide solace and comfort, inspiration and guidance to high and low, educated and illiterate in towns and villages all over the country. No epic anywhere in the world has commanded so much respect so long and has influenced so many people, generations after generations, in all conditions of life as have the *Ramayana* and the *Mahabharata*, Bhagavatism and the Bhagavadgita *Bhagvatism* is the doctrine taught by Sri Krishna. He is known in the Bhagvata religion as Shri Bhagvan; his teachings are contained in the Bhagavadgita. He was born of the ancient Virshni or Satvata branch of the family of Yadu, whose home was in the region of Mathura. His mother was Devaki. He learned his doctrine from the sage Ghora Angirasa. The Chandogya Upanishad refers to Krishna, as the son of Devaki. In the Mahabharata, he is presented as the friend of Arjuna.

The Bhagavadgita is a part of the Mahabharata; yet it stands apart and distinct. It is a poem of eighteen chapters of seven hundred verses. It is not sectarian, its appeal is universal.

The Bhagavadgita opposed the sacrificial and ritualistic religion of Vedas; It regards life as the field of active struggle between good and the evil. There is the falling back on the ancient concept of the Supreme. There emerges the concept of personal god, with individualized and universal characteristics. The concept of *Avtara,* the divinity, in the human form, constitutes the significant aspect of the Indian religious thinking. The *Avtara,* for the protection *of Dharma,* the righteous living and for the eradication of *Adharma,* the unrighteousness, is born again and again.

In the Bhagvadism, Vasudeva Krishna is accepted as the *Avtara* and is *Paramatman,* emphasising the transcendence; he is *Jivabhuta,* the essential life of all. According to the *Bhagavadgita,* there is no escapism, no shutting of oneself in the closet of monastery or cave and no running away from action. The constant effort should be, it emphasises, to sustain good. "He who knows himself in everything and everything in himself will not injure himself by himself. Every person around me is myself at a different point of space and time and at a different grade of being. When one realises that all beings are but the self *(atmaivabhuti),* One acts not selfishly but for all beings.

The psychological setting in which the Bhagavadgita is revealed is everyday experience. Individuals and societies at times are confronted with intellectual, moral, social and political crisis and violent convulsions. When there is the loss of norm and anomie prevails, as Durkheim would call it, when "the conflict between the self affirming law of good and the forms that impede it, force is sometimes necessary to give the law a good chance of becoming a psychological fact and a historic process. We have to act in the world as it is, while doing our best to improve it" (S. Radhakrishnan).

The Mahabharata and the Bhagavadgita, thus filled the sociological abyss that had come to be caused by the heterodox approach. Their emphasis on action, on performance of one's duty and on over all positivism is refreshingly assuring. In the order and conflict relationship, the role of change, and of the supremacy of righteousness is fully emphasised. While upholding the cause of social order based on *Dharma*, and use of power for social good, individual is advised to gain worldly perfection. Life being an endless continuity, every preceding improvement brings forth, still more improvement.

Philosophical Schools

The spirit of restlessness and the intellectual curiosity led our ancestors into the deep regions of mind to understand the nature of the Soul, of the Universal Soul and of the beyond. The subject remains, elusive and yet attractive to human mind. This probing gave rise to the well-known six schools of philosophy: the *Nyaya,* the *Vaishesika,* the *Sankhya,* the *Yoga,* the *Mimansa* and the *Vedanta.* These schools of thought were evolved long before the rise of Buddhism. The Brahmanical, Jain and the Buddhist thinkers, from time to time interpreted them in the light of their beliefs and experience.

Nyaya: It means logic or analysis. It is reasoning in a systematic manner. An object of knowledge is examined step by step and critically. The idea being to emphasise that in all fields of activity, clear thinking and logical arguments is essential. It was, therefore, made an essential part of educational curriculum. The Nyaya system of philosophy expounds the belief in the rhythm and unity in life and nature. It assumes belief in personal god and in individual soul. It is accepted to be the work of Aksapada Gautama.

Vaishesika: It means individual characteristics. It accepts that the four elements, time, space, soul and matter have individual characteristics. Atom is ' described eternal. It is held to be the basis of nature. It accepts the *Dharma*, the moral law as the regulatory force in universe. It is the axis around which the universe rotates. Its rationalistic approach goes against the hypotheses of God. It is the work of Uluka Kanada.

Samkhya

It means the Count: It is also known as the *Dviata* or the dualistic philosophy. In this system, the *Purusha,* the constant spirit; the Soul; and the *Prakrati,* the changing nature the matter are accepted as the fundamental elements. It holds universe to be the result of the interaction between spirit and matter. It accepts, the existence of effect in the nature of cause. It does not accept the existence of God. This school of thought has been referred to in the *Upanishads* and also in the Bhagavadgita. The founder of this school was Sage Kapila.

Yoga

It means Discipline: It is the method of disciplining the body and mind. The psychological assumption is that by proper disciplining of body and mind, one achieves higher levels of consciousness. It is essentially rationalistic and experimental in approach. The belief in personal God, is not essential in the Yoga system. Yogic practice is said to awaken the *Kunddalini* in a yogi. And, once the yogi has it, he is said to gain superpowers.

Mimamsa

It means Enquiry: This school was developed to explain the Vedas; and to defend their authority. It held the Vedas to be the first, original, supreme and unchallengeable. It lays out a scheme of right living in accordance with the *Dharma.* It is ritualistic and has largely influenced the popular forms of Hinduism.

Vedanta

Upanishads: It supports the monistic philosophy of the universe. It holds that the ultimate reality is the *Atman,* the Absolute Soul, which is indivisible and all pervading. The *Purusha* and the *Prakrati* are thus the two aspects, of the single reality. These are not independent of one another, but interdependent.

Social Continuity and Change: In spite of the fact that several reform movements tried to reform our society and many of our social and religious leaders tried to see that social evils were eradicated from our society, yet on the whole the change has been slow. A question arises as to what are the factors which are opposed to changes and wish to have continuity in our social system. Some of these being:

1. Indians are not in favour of violent changes. By and large they are orthodox and wish to cling to the old institutions.
2. Most of the institutions in India are linked with God. These are given religious tinges and it is felt that any violation of any social institution will be displeasing to God and violation of either one religious practice or the other.
3. Each institution has some social roots and is the outcome of either one social system or the other. It is felt that any change in one is sure to adversely effect the other, for which society is not prepared.
4. In the society the forces of change are always weak whereas those interested in maintaining *status quo* are always strong and latter can swing the balance in their own favour.
5. Undoubtedly each social institution has its own advantages, which in no way can be underestimated.
6. A vast majority of population in India is illiterate and as such it becomes difficult to convince them of the need of eradication of evil social institutions.
7. A vast majority of the people in India live from hand to mouth and they are always more interested in earning livelihood rather than in attending to social problems.
8. India is a vast country and people live in far flung areas where access is difficult. It becomes difficult for our social and religious leaders to reach the people,

particularly when means of transportation and communication are difficult.

9. Our foreign rulers did not make any effort to make the people conscious of social problems, leave alone removing the evils.

Our leadership in independent India and even prior to that during freedom struggle did not favour complete break with the past. Gandhiji favoured the idea of continuance of small scale industries rather than installation of heavy industries, which he felt was not at all suited to India. Indian leadership has always believed that radical and drastic changes in any field are bound to do more harm than good to the society.

Due to these reasons India has maintained continuity with the past. Though the society has adopted some essential changes India has for example, accepted the system of co-education, higher education for women, secularism, abandoning of caste system and untouchability, yet it has basically maintained its social structure. Traditionally most of the Indians are God-fearing. They have faith in religion and in the supreme power of Almighty. They do not wish to tell a lie or commit sins. They are hospitable and according to them marriage is not a friendship but an eternal tie. They have the highest regard for their parents and teachers as well as elders. In India thus there is both change and continuity.

There is, however, continued increasing tendency towards change. Process of industrialisation and urbanisation has become quick. It is now realised that unless there is rapid industrialisation, the country will be economically backward. In the religious field blind faith in religion has come to an end. Though vast majority in India still resides in villages, yet migration to cities has started. Many religious reforms have been introduced. In the political field monarchy of the past has been replaced by democracy. Not only this, but if there is centralisation of powers at the centre, the system of democratic decentralisation at the villages has been encouraged. The philosophy of equality before law is accepted all over and the concept of liberty is very popular. Democracy has made the people believe that all are equal. Rapid progress without traditional resistance, is being made in the field of science and technology and philosophy of humanism has emerged.

Thus India is accepting changes which have been introduced in the west but is not prepared to completely shun the past. Thus the process of continuity and change is going on unabated and at times it becomes fast whereas at other times it is slow.

3

SOCIAL SETUP

Prior to the introduction of cooperation, the rural India was characterised by social isolation and physical segregation and was cut off from the wider world.

The rural populace, owing to these conditions, was known for its illiteracy, ignorance, unawareness, poverty, unemployment, domination and exploitation of the haves over the have-nots, casteism, untouchability, religiosity and other social evils.

In view of the prevalence of these socio-economic problems and geo-physical characteristics, the rural people had limited options for their development. Consequently, the rural area remained backward and the mass living in these backward pockets was affected socially and psychologically.

This has resulted in the shaping of their behaviour in tune with the prevailing social structure, so that the rural people were known for socio-economic inequality, submissiveness, dependency, inferiority, egoism, lack of initiative, motivation, mutual assistance due to all sorts of segregation in their social life leading to various restrictions in social relationships. This has in turn ultimately affected the inter-personal, inter-group, caste-class-leadership and behaviour of the people.

Collaboration in Practice

The concept of 'cooperation' gained currency and took its shape for the first time in India in 1904 with the cherished objective of providing credit to the needy and of combating rural indebtedness and thereby alleviating the sufferings of the weaker and exploitation of the privileged upon those under-privileged. With the introduction of cooperative credit societies, the cooperative movement in India got a start and achieved notable progress in the fields of agricultural credit, equated with the values of democratic functioning.

Being a developing country, India is devoted to integrated development-through the democratic participation of people in such development endeavour. The cooperative organisation however, supports and supplements such endeavour of promoting the socio-economic uplift of the downtrodden to achieve all-around development and economic progress. In short, the objective of economic growth with social justice is better achieved through the cooperative and collective social action of the affected segments.

Traits of Collaboration: The cooperative movement has the following characteristics ensuring all the aspects of democratic functioning in the promotion of the socio-economic development of the affected segments.

- The cooperative body is a voluntary organisation and anyone can enroll, if he is agreeable to its objectives, philosophy and principles.
- The cooperative organisation is primarily based upon democratic principles and without any place for exploitation, monopolistic functioning, domination, superordination, and so on.

- This movement has the philosophy of all for each and each for all.
- The cooperative organisation is free from the defect of egoism, which is an element of capitalism.
- It is based on self-help and the promotion of mutual aid of the people, who enroll in this organisation for the purposes of fulfilment of their needs.
- Cooperative action indicates the working together of large number of people in a manner suitable for the promotion of their socio-economic development.

Group Action by Society

Cooperative organisation, as already pointed out, facilitates the enrolment of the affected segments and ensures their democratic participation in the affairs of the organisation. Since the people who got together have the common purpose of promoting their well-being, their cooperation invariably ensures collective action. In the process of their collective action for their uplift, there emerges a type of behavioural pattern in tune with the cooperative spirit, characteristics, philosophy and principles of cooperation. The concept of cooperation and the establishment of cooperative enterprise in a society of our kind not only leads to the empirical operation of the principles of democracy but also effect changes in the behaviour of the participating members in cooperative action.

The organisation behaviour in cooperative institutions involves the following principles:

- Open and voluntary membership
- Democratic control
- Limited interest on share capital
- Fair distribution of share capital
- Promotion of cooperative education
- Cooperation among cooperative bodies.

The practice of these principles of cooperation by members leads to changes in their behaviour and social interaction and relationship hitherto identified between and amongst the various segments in rural social life.

Collaborative Nature

Cooperation, being an organisation of affected segments meant for the promotion of socio-economic well being of the participating members, facilitates the operation of democracy at the micro-level. As human society is characterised by a web of social relationships, the organisation of a cooperative society strengthens their social bond and effects change in their behaviour in tune with the principles, philosophy and objectives of cooperation. The cooperative organisation could affect human behaviour in the following aspects.

1. Cooperative organisation involves systematic social contact on the part of the promoter (who for all practical purposes come from the upper strata) with those members, in whom all motivation lead to information dissemination and generation of the awareness on benefits available from emergence of cooperative movement. The task of the promoter has crucial importance in the initial organisation of cooperatives. The nomination of a promoter paves the way for the establishment of vertical contact, leading to horizontal identity in the name of cooperative society. In the process of rapport establishment in villages there emerge peoples get-together irrespective of their socio-economic, political, religious and educational background. This in turn results in greater social interaction and gradually eliminates all the socio-economic hurdles, which once acted as stumbling blocks in their social interaction.
2. The getting together and greater social interaction in the midst of members, irrespective of their social

identity on a common platform leads to the imbibing of certain social values such as equality, freedom of expression, democratic participation and control, exercise of rights in a free and fair atmosphere, etc., and accords social honour to all members. The principle of equality enshrined in the constitution of cooperation further accelerates the transmission of this value amongst interacting members.

3. A cooperative is not only a social organisation of the weaker segments, but a cooperative business venture devoted for the economic upliftment of these weaker sections. By utilising the benefits available from cooperatives, the weaker sections strive to develop themselves through their collective social action. Since economic development is the basis for all other development, social change occurs in their midst in view of their participation in the cooperative endeavour.

4. Cooperative business involves the pooling of resources of the participating members as well as the tapping of external assistance for the benefit of one and all. In the process of sharing their resources for mutual benefits, there seem to develop social considerations such as other mindedness, concern for others, priority to the deserving etc., All these social considerations pave the way for social cohesion, solidarity, unity, peaceful coexistence, cooperative spirit and a feeling of brotherhood, etc.

5. Besides being a socio-economic organisation, the cooperative organisation is a moral movement, which develops in the village. It develops various social values and moral qualities in the Indian farmers. Through the cooperative movement, village people have developed fellow-feeling and so they may be relieved from the effect of the evils of extravagance, litigation, drinking, gambling etc. The morality injected through cooperative

movement has been summed up as follows: "Litigation and extravagance, alcoholism and gambling are at a discount in a good cooperative society and in their place will be found industry, self-renunciation, straight dealing, education, thrift, self-help and mutual benefit."

6. As a result of cooperation, many of the social evils are at a discount people now. Instead of taking an interest in the social evils they take more interest in the working of the cooperative business. Due to mutual cooperation, they are able to seek the advantage of the experience of others. They are also motivated to undertake various community jobs. This movement has brought about social consciousness and people have become wiser and more clear about the advantages and disadvantages thereof. As a social movement, cooperation has added various social qualities to the minds of participating members.
7. Being a voluntary organisation cooperation instills in the minds of the members a feeling of working together. It also develops in them such social qualities as sympathy and cooperation, and owing to these sentiments, they develop a fellow-feeling towards other people and train them also in the art of working together.
8. Through the cooperative movement people, could take interest in social work. As the cooperative societies are meant for the welfare of the people the spirit of social service and selflessness develop in the minds of the members of these societies. These qualities are responsible for the development of moral faculties. Once people come to know one another, they do not indulge in litigation and other evil habits. All the members treat others as their own kith and kin. As a result of this feeling, the entire atmosphere is changed into one full of moral qualities.

9. As a result of cooperative organisation, the village level societies experience social transformation from the traditional social order to a modern one. The inevitable outcome of this transformation is social change in their midst. The traditional barriers are liquidated due to the large social interaction of various social segments hitherto divided on socio-economic considerations. Consequently, the beneficiaries are the lower echelons of the social hierarchy.
10. Social evils such as casteism, untouchability, social and physical segregation and other social disabilities experienced by these weaker segments are liquidated to a great extent owing to vertical unity and horizontal solidarity of the deprived in the form of cooperation. Consequently, the economic hardships experienced by them once are no longer a reality now.
11. In view of the opportunity for integrated development routed through cooperation, the rural communities experienced socio-economic development, generated consciousness, promoted equality which together ensured their well-being. The one time socio-economic disabilities such as inequality, untouchability, submissiveness, dependency, inferiority, egoism, lack of initiative, motivation, social and physical segregation, etc., all decrease in view of the emerging cooperative social order in the village society.
12. The principles of cooperation relating to open and voluntary membership, democratic control, fair distribution of share capital etc. ensures equality, irrespective of personal background, in the minds of members and generate an interest in the affairs of cooperation which ultimately generates a feeling of oneness in their midst.
13. As women are affected due to the prevalence of socio-cultural obstacles, the cooperatives offer a fair chance

to their socio-economic uplift through their enrollment and establishment of producer and industrial cooperative societies. Here the cooperative enterprises act as the catalyst, enabler, and facilitator of women development. The stigma attached to women hitherto is erased through their collective action and endeavours, women seek better social treatment, income generation in the family, community and society at large.

To sum up, the cooperative movement has facilitated for the enrolment and collective action of the weaker segments for the purposes of the promotion of their socio-economic development. As a voluntary organisation of the weaker segments the cooperative societies opened up vistas for the practice of democracy at the micro-level. The cooperative organisation brought the people together in the rural areas—once known for various kinds of social discrimination.

In fact, the cooperation built up among them stimulated to eliminate all social barriers and promoted unity and social solidarity. The socio-economic problems such as untouchability, social segregation, physical distance, submissiveness, inferiority, exploitation, domination, poverty, indebtedness, etc., are minimised to a great extent, if not totally eliminated. In view of these developments, the rural societies experience a transformation in their social structure—leading to change in behavioural patterns. All these developments ultimately resulted in the institutionalisation of the cooperative social order in village society.

Moral for Repayment

Prior to the introduction of cooperative credit, the only source of credit available to the cultivators were the moneylenders. This was purely a non-institutional source of credit which people approached. For, they could get money at the time they needed without any formal application or legal proceedings. It was peaceful in one way, but the moneylenders' terms were always extortionate as they charged a higher rate of interest. It became worse, when the borrower failed to repay the amount in time. It was a question of status in the village community. It led to pauperisation and proletarianisation. The moneylenders were certainly not an institution meant for evolving thrift, self-help and savings among the poor farmers.

The government of India noticed that, being in the clutches of the moneylenders (non-institutional) the "Indian farmers are born in debt, live in debt and die in debt." The government felt that the farmers should be helped through some type of institutional effort.

Towards the close of the last century, the success of the schemes of cooperative finance which had originated in European countries came to the notice of several local governments. In 1982, Sir Frederic Nicholson was deputed by the Madras Government to review the theory and practice of agriculture and other land banks in Europe and devise ways and means by which a similar movement might be popularised in the country. He came up with the formula "Find Reiffeisen" to solve the problem of rural poverty aggravated by chronic indebtedness and usurious practice at its worst.

Accordingly, a committee under Sir Edward Law was appointed by the Government of India, whose recommendations formed the core of the Cooperative Credit Societies Act of 1904. By virtue of this Act, the cooperative movement in India got a breakthrough.

The establishment of cooperative credit societies paved the way for the provision of financial assistance through institutional arrangements. For procuring agricultural and rural credit. Cooperative credit societies started taking root with the idea of relieving the Indian farmers from the parasitic clutches of non-institutional sources and the process of helping farmers to help themselves was effectively set in motion.

Paradoxically, what realised now was only the organised resistance of the farmers towards the repayment of cooperative credit. This phenomenon is mainly due to the interference of political parties and government in the affairs of the cooperatives, coupled with lethargic management and indisciplined members, which ultimately wrecked the movement. The overdue was accumulated for years, creating an atmosphere, where the cooperative credit movement is unable to succeed in its endeavours.

Financing and recovery represent two sides of the same coin. Financing without recovery bears no fruit; recovery without financing too has no needs. These two aspects are however interlinked, interdependent and inseparable.

While there was phenomenal increase in the flow of credit to the agricultural sector through institutional sources, parallel growth was seen in the overdues of such loans. Effective financing could be judged not merely from the quantum of credit extended, but from the quality of loans expanded. The latter was reflected through the recovery of loans. The recovery performance was an index for judging the operational efficiency and organisational competence of a financing institution.

From time immemorial, the private agencies like moneylenders were providing credit to agriculture. Of the total rural credit, their share ranges from 50 to 60 per cent. They too function under the same socio-economic-political climate in which the banks operate; but seldom they face recovery problems, because they fulfil a few criteria of a sound system of lending, viz, adequate quantity of timely credit to the right people.

The (Cooperative) philosophy of need-based, purpose oriented, productive credit was seen in the letter rather in spirit, because it could not reach the right people at the right time, leading to poor recovery. This must be overcome and the movement must be given a fresh life. To do this, it is high time that repayment ethics in rural cooperative credit transactions are introduced. An ethic of particular kind is an idea or moral belief or principle that influences the behaviour, attitude and philosophy of life a group of people about performing something right and wrong. Repayment ethics of cooperative credit implies the moral considerations towards the repayment of cooperative loans in the minds of the members.

In order to increase repayment ethics or morality in repayment of cooperative credit, some sort of attitudinal change has to be effected in the minds of the borrower member of cooperatives.

When we deeply probe into the matter to understand the reasons for non-repayment, we realised that many societies often were found to be managed by vested interests, with the result that the small farmers, marginal farmers and other members belonging to the weaker sections of the society were not properly served, and a few locally influential big farmers enjoy the benefits. Inferences from many studies conducted in this regard reveal that big farmers often don't have the habit of repayment. They make wilful defaults.

The reasons understood for the default among the small and marginal farmers are; these farmers have to borrow from the societies on account of their possession of a limited amount of landholdings and a limited degree of financial solidity. The persistence of inadequacy in the volume of loan assistance rendered by the societies, which is too little and too late, exerts a push effect on them to take recourse to the professional moneylenders for pecuniary assistance at exorbitant and uneconomic rates of interest.

In view of the two-fold responsibility to pay back the loans, the common psychology which shapes their behaviour patterns is either to clear first the dearer dues keeping in abeyance their obligations to the soft-creditor-the cooperatives, or to clear the heavier of the two, consequently no surplus is left and the inevitable outcome is default to the cooperative societies and stagnation in the cooperative dues.

There are again defaults which arise out of the uncertainties of rain and of very little acreage having ensured supply of water through irrigation, Indian agriculture has been proverbially, "a gamble on the monsoon." Generally not less than three out of every five years of bad crop yields are either due to floods or scarcity of rains. In such conditions, it is necessary to provide a built-in device for ensuring uninterrupted flow of credit to the agriculturists in the financial system, so that they could waive such loans during crop failure.

Crop damages should be covered by a comprehensive crop insurance policy so that the farmers are assisted to pay back their loan in full. This would help to reduce the loan burden of the farmer and keep the credit flow uninterrupted.

The present procedure for granting extension, conversion, replacement and consolidation facilities needs rationalisation, so that such action can be taken expeditiously; of course, with proper arrangements to ensure that the facility is not abused. The cooperative credit institution should not have favouritism and nepotism prevailing in the granting of a loan or it should not grant a loan to a person, because he is ready to take up a share or if he had applied for a loan. It should ensure that a member really deserves a loan to be utilised for some productive purpose. Moreover, the cooperative society should not think that its work ends in sanctioning a loan. Strictly speaking, it is only there that the work of the society begins. That is, once a loan is granted the society must follow it up, whether the amount lent is utilised, the purpose for which it has been granted, because by experience its misutilisation is a factor, which contributes a considerable extent to non-repayment of cooperative credit.

Timely visits for verification of documents during loan disbursement and the life of the loan enables planning and implementing of corrective actions. Beside it can be assured that the project develops on schedule (according to plan) with utilisation of funds for authorised purposes only. It would ensure the maximum utilisation of credit and facilitate better repayment performance.

If a loan granted for some productive purpose is seen as being misutilised by a member, the society should take instant steps to recollect the amount granted.

In 1992, a regional seminar on agricultural cooperative credit was conducted in Thailand. It would be worth-mentioning here about a passage from the seminar report, "Absence of proper supervision and poor end-use verification of credit were also important problems resulting in delinquency of members." In the absence of proper supervision, members tend to delay repayment. A tendency generally grows among the members to consider that cooperative loans are not repaid." This was compounded, according, to the seminar, by reckless statements made by politicians.

In recent years the loans of the defaulting members in certain countries were written off notwithstanding, the reason to default. This action put the disciplined members who repaid their loans earlier to the announcement of the write-off policy at a disadvantage as the defaulters were rewarded. Some of the problems connected with overdues identified by the seminar were:

1. delay in taking action against defaulting members,
2. delay in disposing arbitration cases and execution of awards,
3. covering of loans by influential sections and their wilful default and choking the line of credit,
4. lack of proper coordination among the various agencies under the multi-agency system, resulting in dual financing, and at times, weakening the cooperatives by weaning away their members.

> "Many societies lacking in administrative and financial viability suffer from inadequate equity, weak structure, poor resources, improper loaning procedures and policies, inadequate supervision and monitoring, absence of a climate of recovery due to shifting governmental policies, multiplicity of agencies in the field with inadequate coordination among them, lack of adequate arrangements for supply of inputs and farm guidance, poor infrastructure facilities. The cumulative effect of all these difficulties is the high incidence of overdues in agricultural credit cooperatives, which are the major problems affecting the healthy growth of the primary agricultural credit societies in most countries of the region."

It was also discussed in the seminar that "Credit counselling may be undertaken to advice as to availability and effective use of credit and income." The atmosphere and counselling etc., of the society should unconsciously develop an ethical or moral tendency within the borrowers to make repayments in accordance with the loan agreements, enabling the societies to recover their loans in time and recycle the funds.

One of such notable suggestions was, "The societies or banks should emphasis that all borrowers maintain saving accounts and the repayment of the loan should be routed through this account and the balance in the saving account should not be less than at least one instalment of the loan borrowed. This can be called linking deposits with loans."

It has been identified that poor loaning policies and procedures followed by the societies is an important area of weakness. It is understood that there is no proper evaluation of credit limit—application to determine the credit requirement on the basis of approved scales of finance for different crops and also the absence of seasonality in disbursement of credit as well as recovery of the loans, absence of production-oriented lending, ultimately disbursement of credit, absence of proper scales of finance leading very often to over-financing had resulted in the accumulation of overdues. The absence of well-conceived credit policies leads to haphazard lending, resulting in misutilisation of loans, which finally results in non-repayment. So the loaning policies and procedures should be proper and well-conceived so as to enable the cooperatives to keep the credit cycle moving without any stoppage.

In fact, it would appear overambitious to say that a stage has come to think in terms of evolving a system of financing agriculture, analogous to the cash credit accommodation. The total business and other operations of the cultivator should be considered and a comprehensive limit fixed for him which he should utilise as per requirements. Every withdrawal should be supported by the agriculturists with an appropriate explanation about the utilisation of the funds.

The members' attitude of withholding repayment deliberately should be weeded out. This tendency needs to be put down by several penal actions against the miscreants.

The review shows that not only the financing agency but the beneficiaries, nature of the government and similar factors are equally responsible for the non-repayment of loans. An attempt has been made to remould not only the implementing authorities but the member beneficiaries to make them reciprocate in terms of loyalty and prompt repayment.

Critical analysis shows that both human and non-human factors are involved in the repayment of cooperative credits.

While only very little could be done to control non-human factors (to mitigate natural calamities) more could be achieved by developing and inculcating ethical considerations in the minds of the members (human factors) towards repayment of cooperative credit.

It is a fact that a major chunk of the farming community is economically weak; but morally strong. Despite their illiteracy, ignorance and superstition, they are not morally ignorant; with no intention to deceive circumstances such as consumption needs, social demands, political commands and the administrative bureaucracy (environmental factors) compel them to become defaulters.

The decision of the borrowers either to repay or not depends however, on the psychology of the individual. When the farmer is well received, well respected, well treated and well guided either to avail loan or to adopt improved technology by the bank staff, his first loyalty goes to the bank only. When he received credit from the "clean hands" in time, in adequate quantity without harassment by all probabilities, he is likely to be a good paymaster.

If the reverse is the case, certainly he turns into a defaulter. The influence of environmental factors does not cause much damage to his integrity. When the aforesaid psychological needs of the farmers are met and the banker becomes a friend, philosopher and guide, he reciprocates through his gratitude in prompt repayment. He persuades others, to keep up the credit discipline.

Hence, the man behind transaction is more important than his valuable assets. Nothing can be achieved in a cooperative form of organisation with a dishonest personality, however creditworthy he may be. Trustworthiness should be upheld and the credit-worthiness should be given only secondary importance in cooperatives in general and credit cooperatives in particular.

Coming back to the reasons for non-repayment, we realise that the programmes of the cooperatives are good, the problem is with the implementation in such a way that it is helpful to the weaker sections of the community so as to ensure beneficiaries do not misuse the benefits, with a moral bond rather than a legal bond, to be loyal and prompt in enabling the credit cycle to keep moving.

So, at the outset, the giving end should be made to be prompt, pure and clear without any malpractices. Then the receiving end should be tried. Loans should be given only for productive purposes with effective supervision-disposed in many installments at many stages of raising the crop or whatever. There should be no bribe or delay in sanctioning a loan. The morality of the borrowers should be given fair weight in granting a loan. In no way should the members be made to feel that the money lent to them is free and not to he repaid.

Sometimes if the need arises, case should be taken to pressurise the members in favour of repayment. Member education programmes, member relation programmes, deposit mobilisation campaigns, seminars should be organised in an educative informative, stimulative, thought-provoking and useful manner, but not just for the sake of ostentations.

It will just not be enough if education programmes are conducted. It should be coupled with the departmental employees going from door to door, at least once in a week, to impart the philosophy of cooperation, in cognising them of their rights, duties and privileges.

In those days, people felt it to be a stigma, had they owed a debt to somebody? It was a social degradation. But today, people feel that the quantum of debt owed is directly proportional to one's prestige. The more the debt, the higher the status. It has become an indicator of status. This tendency should be wiped out.

One of the major issues of repayment of cooperative credit now-a-days is political interference, that has polluted the movement to an intolerable extent. It has shaken the very structure of the movement.

Politicians waive the loans or sometimes the interest gets waived with the tricky intention of turning it into vote bank during electioneering. This develops a tendency in the minds of the borrowers to wait till the advent of the elections. He expects it to be waived at the time, when his party holds the power. This tendency at least in such societies which have attained viability and which are diagnosed as likely to become viable soon, for politicians should not use cooperatives as their playground. As a stepping stone to achieving viability, what needs to be done is to make members evolve certain ethical principles in their minds, thereby rural credit transaction takes place in a proper and peaceful climate.

Today, the borrowers are quite sure that the sky will not fall on their heads, if they do not promptly repay or do so completely. So, it suggests them to think, "Let me wait and see, whether others repay or not", instead of "Let me repay the loan, no matter what others do." It has resulted in an indifferent tendency of "Who repays?" Why should I repay then?"

Cooperatives should make it a rule that in the event of natural calamities, the conversion of one loan into the another may be considered. Because, it is realised by experience that even under the most favourable conditions, a cent per cent recovery cannot be expected.

So, it appears to be an inescapable fact that lack of will and discipline among the cultivators to repay is the principal factor contributing to the prevalence of overdues in cooperatives. The members should be made to realise that the cooperatives are there for the well-being of the members only. If the members do not repay in time or ignore, it means their self-destruction.

So, after having analysed the various issues on repayment of cooperative loans the need of the hour is that a general idea or tendency should be enlivened in the minds of borrowers that money borrowed from cooperatives is not to be forgotten once for all or waived on the eve of election, but to be repaid in time to facilitate the mutual help, existence and growth of the members and the cooperatives as-well.

The traditional values relating to the repayment and

non-repayment need to be viewed and thought afresh, so that people consider this non-repayment a social degradation. Local leadership coupled with personnel working in cooperatives have a vital role to play in making the members, rather prompt in repaying the cooperative credit. The human behaviour and attitudes are an important factor to be reckoned with in agricultural credit operations. Therefore, safety to a loan is not mere security, but the sincerity and morality of the borrower which in turn depends on the character and psychology of the individual.

These socio-psychological considerations are expected to develop a positive feedback ensuring prompt repayment. This may come through education and creation of certain socially useful values which upholds the cooperative movement in India.

If we attempt to give some suggestions to quicken the pace of repayments of loan, we can say things like, providing incentives such as giving priority for further loans in future to those who are prompt in repayment. Non-interference of political parties in organisation and management of cooperatives, discouraging the wiping off loans or conversion of loans only under exceptional circumstances and not as a political expediency, bringing back the democratically elected board of management into action, instituting stringent legal measures against defaulters, blacklisting of defaulters so that they couldn't deceive similar banking/para-banking institutions elsewhere and declaring cooperatives as autonomous institutions are a few suggestions.

Such recommendations can help the cooperatives to have some amount of attitudinal change in the minds of the borrower members and mobilise repayment ethics whereby payment and repayment transactions can take place in a proper and peaceful atmosphere, accelerating the movement a fresh impetus towards prosperity.

Growth of Credit

Vikas Volunteer Vahini (VVV): The flow of institutional credit for rural development has made rapid strides over the last decade or so. While there is a phenomenal increase in the flow of credit to the agricultural sector through institutional sources, parallel growth could be seen in the overdues of such loans. The mounting of overdues restricts the capacity of lending institutions to recycle funds, besides threatening the prospects of continued flow of external credit for agriculture and rural development. This drew the attention of NABARD planners and policy makers and the five year plans laid emphasis on recovery discipline and credit recycling.

Accordingly, there was a need to devise suitable measures (organisational or otherwise) for ensuring a prompt and efficient system of recycling credit. This circumstance led to the inception of the Vikas Volunteer Vahini (VVV) programme by NABARD with a code of ethics for rural borrowers on November 5, 1982. It is embodied in the five principles or "Development Through Credit" policy.

Principles

1. Credit must be used in accordance with the most suitable methods of science and technology.
2. The terms and conditions of credit (or techno-economic parameters) must be fully respected.
3. Work must be done with skill so as to increase productivity and income.
4. A part of the additional income created by credit must be saved.
5. Loan installments must be repaid regularly, in time so as to recycle credit.

An institution called "Friends of Banks Club" established in the villages covered under the programme, consists of borrowers who have fully repaid their dues. In the village, the club serves as the nerve centre for promoting the ethics of repayment, bridging between the borrowers on the one hand and the banks and development agencies on the other.

Structure

Coordinating Bank

Designated Officer

Leader-VVV

Volunteer-VVV

Member

Beneficiaries

Role of Officials

Each service area has been assigned a designated officer. His responsibility is to guide, assist and motivate the leader and the club members to participate effectively in the development through credit by regularly convening the club meetings for various credit requirements with follow-up action whenever necessary.

Function: The club in turn would assist the banker in identifying the potential borrowers and viable activities requiring credit support for recovery, seeking cooperation of the government functionaries such as the department of agriculture, panchayats, trade union office, etc.

Activities: The club, with the support of the designated officer, could arrange for subject-specific talks by specialists on matters relating to new technological innovations in agriculture about the problems and solutions relating to animal husbandry, farm methods and practices, symposia on poultry, dairy farming, etc.

Steps in Planning

In Tamil Nadu, 100 villages spread over 20 blocks in Madurai and Trichy districts are covered under the programme. These clubs have been entrusted to service their respective area bank. Accordingly, cooperative banks, RRBS and seven commercial banks are implementing the VVV programme in these districts. The districts have been selected on the availability of infrastructure, potential for development, branch network, etc. It is expected that this programme would have a ripple effect on the nearby areas as well as on the resistance anticipated from interested quarters, for propaganda against recovery and repayment ethics.

Expectations: It is expected that through the programme, villagers will be shown the success models of good borrowers and exposed to the public disapproval of default by people from amongst themselves. Second, they understand the direct link between credit disbursement and recovery. The message of the success of earlier loans followed by another loan complement leading to economic betterment conveys effectively the benefits of repaying the loans. Third, the people discover that banks are not stressing on recovery alone but concerned as much with developmental schemes for the villages. Fourthy, from traditional bankers, it is envisaged to transform them into development bankers. A healthy communication link is thus established between the rural banker and its borrowers.

Study: With a view to understand the impact of the programme in the psycho-social and economic conditions about the positive changes noticed, if any, in the repayment behaviour of beneficiaries, the present study gives an empirical verification to evaluate the VVV programme in two villages, viz. Vannampatty (Nilakottai block) and Ayakudi (Palani block) in Dindigul, Anna District at a comparative setting. This modest attempt, ultimately, aims at drawing lessons to be diffused in areas, where the programme has not marked up the expected scores.

The Problem: The problem intended to be studied is as follows:

> In India, since the inception of the Planning Commission, many developmental programmes have been designed and implemented to ameliorate the socio-economic conditions of the poor. What still remains uncertain is, have these so-called developmental programmes achieved any concrete and visible developments in the rural life?

One such programme implemented by NABARD (National Bank for Agriculture and Rural Development) is the VVV programme with the cherished objective of ensuring "Development through Credit" in rural areas. From the analysis of the programme by contents, approach and expectation, it is a masterpiece, and an admirable programme. It drew the attention of the researchers to an empirical verification to evaluate the psycho-socio-economic impact of the programme in the areas, under implementation.

"Development through Credit"-Impact of Vikas Volunteer Vahini (VVV) programme.

Objectives

1. To understand the personal background of the members and beneficiaries of the programme.
2. To study the psycho-social and economic impact the programme has effected among the beneficiaries.
3. To assess the extent of awareness generated and repayment ethics—built-up among the members and the beneficiaries.
4. To make a critical appraisal of the role of functionaries of the programme.

5. To evaluate the operational efficiency and development effected through the VVV club in the village.

Hypotheses

1. The recovery performance in wet areas is overwhelmingly appreciable; moderately good in well irrigated area and poor in dry or rain-fed areas, i.e., there is a positive correlation between ecological structure and extent of repayment.
2. The economic status, is directly proportional to the delinquency in repayment.
3. More involvement of functionaries yields to better recovery performance and vice versa.

Conceptualisation: "Development through Credit" means the development to be achieved in the psycho-socio-economic conditions of the beneficiaries, when they follow a code of ethics upon the five principles of development through credit, viz.,

- Utilise the credit scientifically,
- Respect the techno-economic parameters,
- Work to increase productivity and income,
- Save a part of generated, additional income, and
- Recycling of credit by prompt repayment.

"Development through Credit' is the epigraph of an informal organisation of prompt repayers of institutional credit who link bankers and deserving borrowers at the village level, induce borrowers to utilise the credit for socio-economic improvement as guided by the programme tc mobilise them repay the loans promptly, manifesting themselves as a model."

Scope: The subject matter covered by the study pertains to two villages viz., Vannampatty (Nilakottai block) and New

Ayakudi (Palani block) of Anna district in Tamil Nadu. It presents an objective assessment of the programme in these villages. It has been attempted to find out the achievements and weaknesses and suggest the ways and means of overcoming any weakness to improve the operation. It portrays the opinion of the bank managers (designated officers), leaders, members, volunteers and beneficiaries about the programme and its impact.

Sampling

Villages and Banks: The programme is under implementation in 15 villages of 3 blocks in Anna district. Two villages from two blocks have been selected for the study to facilitate comparison.

The bases on which these villages have been selected are: (1) the bank launching the programme and (2) the ecology of the villages.

First, Cooperative Bank was launched in Vannampatty, whereas a commercial bank, namely, Indian Overseas Bank commenced in New Ayakudi.

Second, there is a hypothesis to its operation judge whether any positive correlation exists between ecological character and the extent of repayment. Vannampatty is considered to be a dry region and New Ayakudi a wet region.

These two villages were selected because they fulfil both the bases for selection of villages considered by the respondents.

Respondents: The membership list of the VVV dub of Vannampatty revealed that there are only 11 (eleven) members in the club and nobody else is the beneficiary of the programme. So, it was decided to have a complete enumeration as far as Vannampatty is concerned.

In New Ayakudi, besides members, president and vice-president in the club, there were 171 beneficiaries. In order to have a manageable investigation one-fourth (i.e., 44) of the beneficiaries were introduced to the random sampling. The managers and the designated officers of the concerned banks were interviewed.

Research Tools: For the purpose of data collection from the selected respondents in the villages, suitable interview schedules were designed by incorporating such particulars—demographic and educational.

Debt Burden of Programme Beneficiaries

Source / Village	Money-lenders Relative (1)	Cooperatives (2)	IOB (3)	Moneylenders & Cooperatives	Cooperatives & IOB	Money-lenders & IOB	All the three Sources
Vannampatty	Nil	7	Nil	1	2	1	1
New Ayakudi	1	5	35	Nil	1	11	1

The table indicates the number of respondents who availed credit from various sources for their development. It can be seen that most members, i.e., 7 out of 11 in Vannampatty borrowed credit from the cooperative society, whereas IOB remained the major source of credit for those in New Ayakudi, economic status, level of awareness and participation in the VVV programme, credit availed, standard and quality of life before and after the inception of such club, defaults, if any, attitude of the banker towards the leaders, members, volunteers and beneficiaries.

Similarly, interview guides covered aspects like the awareness, attitudes of the bankers towards the programme and the informal functionaries, the extent of involvement of the bankers' in materialising "development through Credit". These guides were administered by the designated officer or the branch managers of the cooperative banks.

As has been mentioned earlier, the empirical operations were carried out in two villages namely Vannampatty and New Ayakudi in the Athoor and Palani Blocks respectively. The primary data collected from the beneficiaries were analysed and the results of the empirical data evaluated.

The particular of the respondents covered such aspects as the personal, socio-economic status of the respondents, the development observed through credit, repayment position, and the attitude of the banker towards development of beneficiaries. Table indicates the source-wise borrowal of programme beneficiaries. Table portrays the landholding particulars of the respondents. In Vannampatty, of the 11 respondents interviewed, 5 respondents (45.45 per cent) held land to the extent of 2.5 acres to 5.0 acres. And the second majority, i.e., 4 respondents (36.37 per cent) with above 5 acres.

In New Ayakudi, of the 25 respondents who possess land, majority, i.e., 13 (52.00 per cent) respondents owned land extent of below 2.5 acres, and only 5 respondents (i.e., 20.00 per cent) held above 5 acres. The size of land owned by Vannampatty respondents remained bigger. Majority of the New Ayakudi respondents were landless who switched pursuits other than agriculture—small scale business, fruit sales, etc. In New Ayakudi, even those who possess land had comparatively smaller sizes of holdings.

Land Holdings of Respondents

Land in possession	*Vannampatty (No. of respondents)*	*New Ayakudi (No. of respondents)*
Below 2.5	2	13
	(18.18)	(52.00)
2.5-5.0	5	7
	(20.00)	(28.00)
above 5.0	4	5
	(36.37)	(20.00)
Total	11	25*
	(100.00)	(45.45)

(figures in parentheses indicates column percentages).

In New Ayakudi 27 respondents (i.e., 54.55 per cent) are landiess labourers and other occupants.

Table highlights the income levels of the respondents before and after the inception of the VVV club in the villages under study. The income levels of five respondents of Vannampatty before the inception of the club have been Rs. 6,000 and six respondents had incomes above Rs. 6,000. After the inception of the club the income of four respondents remained below Rs. 6,000 and the income of seven respondents was above Rs. 6,000. In New Ayakudi, the income levels of 41 respondents before the inception was below Rs. 6,000 with a change in the income levels of 14 respondents in the category of above Rs. 6,000.

A comparative picture of the income levels of the respondents of Vannampatty with New Ayakudi before and after the inception of the club reveals that in Vannampatty, though the income after the inception increased, it could not improve their standards of life. The position in New Ayakudi showed only a slight improvement in income levels. By and large, the programme, though it has not marked any significant development in the income levels of the respondents, generated stability in the income levels.

Change in Income Level

Income Levels (in Rs.)	*Vannampatty*		*New Ayakudi*	
	Before the inception of the club	*After the inception of the club*	*Before the inception of the club*	*After the inception of the club*
Below-2,000	2 (18.18)	1 (9.09)	14 25.46)	12 (21.82)
2,000-4,000	1 (9.10	2 (18.18)	10 (18.18)	10 (18.18)
4,000-6,000	2 (18.18)	1 (9.09)	17 (3091)	19 (34.55)
6,000-8,000	3 (27.27)	4 (36.36)	5 (9.09)	5 (9.09)
8,000-above	3 (27.27)	3 (27.28)	9 (16.36)	9 (16.36)
	11 (100.00)	11 (100.00)	55 (100.00)	55 (100.00)

(Figures in parentheses indicate column percentages)

As far as the income levels of the respondents were concerned, the respondents of Vannampatty were better-off, whereas a state of relative poverty was noticed among the New Ayakudi respondents. Table indicates the expenditure levels of the respondents before and after the inception of the club in the villages under study.

In Vannampatty, the expenditure levels of six respondents before the inception of the club was below Rs. 6,000 whereas after the inception only five respondents spent below Rs. 6,000. Before the inception, the expenditure levels of five respondents was above Rs. 6,000 whereas, after inception six respondents spent above Rs. 6,000.

In New Ayakudi, the expenditure levels of 40 respondents before the inception of the club was below Rs. 6,000 and that of 15 respondents was above Rs. 6,000. After the inception, the number of respondents whose income below Rs. 6000 was 38 and whose income above Rs. 6,000 was 17.

A comparative picture of the expenditure levels of the respondents of Vannampatty with New Ayakudi before and after the inception of the club revealed that in both villages, the levels have increased to some extent. It could be said that almost a proportionate growth is seen in their expenditure and income, so their standards of living.

Table highlights the savings position of the respondents of the villages under study before and after the inception of the club.

The savings position of the respondents of Vannampatty before the inception of the club indicated that most (i.e., three out of five) operated their accounts between Rs. 1,000 to 2,000 and the remaining two accounts were either unoperative or operative below Rs. 500. Similar conditions prevailed after the inception.

In New Ayakudi before the inception of the club most i.e., 18 respondents deposited below Rs. 500. (In most cases they remain unoperated or operated below Rs. 50). There was not much change in the saving habits of them after the inception of the club.

A comparative analysis of the two villages showed that the clubs in both villages have not taken any systematic and effective measures as far as mobilisation of savings or its habits. All those who held accounts opened their bank accounts before the inception of the club.

Change in Expenditure Levels

Expenditure (In Rs.)	Vannampatty		New Ayakudi	
	Before inception	After inception	Before inception	After inception
Below-2,000	1 (9.09)	0	13 (23.64)	13 (23.64)
2,000-4,000	4 (36.36)	5 (45.46)	18 (32.73)	16 (29.09)
4,000-6,000	1 (9.09)	0	9 (16.36)	9 (16.36)
6,000-8,000	1 (9.09)	2 (18.18)	8 (14.54)	9 (16.36)
8,000-above	4 (36.37)	4 (36.36)	7 (12.73)	8 (14.55)
Total	11 (100.00)	11 (100.00)	55 (100.00)	55 (100.00)

(Figures in parentheses indicate column percentages)

Savings Position of the Respondents

Amount (Rs.)	Vannampatty		New Ayakudi	
	Before inception	After inception	Before inception	After inception
Below-500	2 (40.00)	2 (40.00)	18 (23.69)	19 (73.08)
500-1,000	Nil	Nil	6 (23.08)	5 (19.23)
1,000-1,500	2 (40.00)	1 (20.00)	Nil	Nil
1,500-2,000	1 (20.00)	2 (40.00)	2 (7.69)	2 (7.69)
Total	5 (100.00)	5 (100.00)	26 (100.00)	26 (100.00)

(Figures in parentheses indicate column percentages)

Position of Liability of the Respondents

Village Value (in Rs.)	Vannampatty		New Ayakudi	
	Before inception	After inception	Before inception	After inception
Below-500	Nil	Nil	7 (13.46)	12 (21.82)
500-2,500	Nil	Nil	18 (34.62)	17 (30.92)
2,500-5,000	Nil	Nil	11 (21.15)	9 (16.36)
5,000-7,500	1 (9.09)	1 (9.09)	4 (7.69)	5 (9.09)
7,500-10,000	1 (9.09)	3 (27.27)	3 (5.77)	4 (7.27)
Above-10,000	9 (81.80)	7 (63.64)	9 (17.31)	8 (14.55)
Total	11 (100.00)	11 (100.00)	55 (100.00)	55 (100.00)

Contd...

The savings of Vannampatty respondents were higher than Ayakudi respondents, due to their higher income and asset position.

Magnitude of Repayment

Position	*Agriculture and Allied*
Fully Repaid	1 (9.09)
Repaid ¼ of the loan amount	1 (9.09)
Not repaid	7 (63.64)
Yet to mature	2 (18.18)
Total	11 (100.00)

(Figures in parentheses indicate percentages)

Table reveals the purpose of loan and the magnitude of repayment in Vannampatty village, where members of the club got only for agricultural and agriculture allied purposes.

In Vannampatty, only one repaid it fully. Out of the eleven respondents, who defaulted the loan amount fully (63.64 per cent), one member displayed in the table repaid XA the loan amount have not repaid. He got waived of interest. The two members whose loans, yet to mature were beyond the scope of the present study. The above Table manifests the purpose of loan and magnitude of repayment in New Ayakudi.

In New Ayakudi, 22 (about 43 per cent) of the 52 respondents, who borrowed repaid their loan fully; 18 other respondents (about 34 per cent) repaid part of their lent sum. And 8 respondents (around 15 per cent) fully defaulted the loan amount. A comparative analysis of repayment position in Vannampatty village with New Ayakudi revealed that the recovery performance in New Ayakudi village was many times appreciable, whereas in Vannampatty though the members had considerably strong asset base and income levels but don't have the practice of repaying loans promptly. Table revealed the change in the response of the banker towards the members of the VVV club, before and after the inception of the club.

In Vannampatty, the response of the banker, before the inception of the club was either uninterested or indifferent according to eight and three respondents respectively. The response of the banker after the inception of the club as opined by six respondents is "Uninterested" and five respondents opined that the banker was "indifferent".

In New Ayakudi, the response of the banker before the inception was: According to 26 respondents, the banker was uninterested, another 15 respondents opined him as indifferent and yet another 14 opined him as satisfactory. The response of the banker after the inception was: Majority, i.e., 44 respondents (80 per cent) opined that the banker's attitude was satisfactory and two respondents held that it was "exemplary", five perceived to be different whereas four told him to be uninterested. A comparative analysis of the attitude held by the banker in Vannampatty with New Ayakudi revealed that the banker was either indifferent or uninterested, before and after the inception.

Hence, the Vannampatty banker was unfavourable towards the development of the members, before and after the inception of the club. The New Ayakudi banker too was uninterested and indifferent prior to the inception but changed himself to satisfy them and at times remained exemplary even. Hence, an attitudinal change took place in the approach of the banker with the introduction of this programme. It was favourable and facilitative towards the development of the members and other beneficiaries.

Evaluation: Based upon the analysis of the data in the empirical situation, an attempt brings here out the major findings of the study with possible suggestions to improve the performance of the VVV clubs in the study villages, and elsewhere, where the programme was operative.

Magnitude of Repayment II

SI. No	*Purpose of Loan Repayment Position*	*Agri & Allied*	*Percentage Business*	*Small scale Sales*	*Percentage*	*Fruit*	*Percentage*	*Total*
1	Fully Repaid	10 (45.45)	41.66	7 (31.82)	35.00	5 (22.73)	62.50	22 (43.31)
2	Repaid ¼ of the amount	4 (57.14)	16.67	1 (14.29)	5.00	2 (28.57)	25.00	7 (13.46)
3	Repaid ½	4 (66.66)	16.67	2	10.00 (33.34)	Nil	—	6 (11.54)
4	Repaid ¼	1	4.17 (20.00)	4 (80.00)	20.00	Nil	—	5 (8.62)
5	Not repaid	2 (25.00)	8.33	5 (62.50)	25.00	1 (12 50)	12.50	8 (15.38)
6	Yet to mature	3 (75.00)	12.50	1 (25.00)	5.00	Nil	—	4 (7.69)
	Total	24.00	100.00	20.00	100.00	8.00	100.00	52.00 (100.00)

(Figures in parentheses indicate low percentages)

1. The VVV club members of Vannampatty borrowed from primary cooperative bank as primary source and members of New Ayakudi did it from Indian Overseas Bank.
2. Compared to the New Ayakudi members, the sizes of landholdings possessed by the Vannampatty members were considerably bigger. Majority of the VVV club members and beneficiaries of New Ayakudi were either landless or own a small piece of land. They resorted to pursuits other than agriculture such as, small-scale, business, fruit sales, etc., whereas the Vannampatty members had agriculture as their main occupation.
3. New Ayakudi was categorised as wet area, where repayment was appreciable and Vannampatty was rain-fed area, where the repayment position was at stake. This leads to one of the hypotheses of study, as: "The recovery performance in wet areas was appreciable, and poor in rain-fed areas."
4. As far as the income levels of the respondents, members of Vannampatty were better-off with a relative state of poverty among the New Ayakudi members.

   Comparison of the income levels of the members and beneficiaries of VVV club in the study villages revealed that though the programme could not make any significant improvement in income levels of respondents, it generated some stability in income levels of them and beneficiaries.
5. Though the New Ayakudi members and beneficiaries lived in a relatively poverty state, most of them promptly repaid their loan amounts, justifying the morality developed through the programme. It has fertilized the minds of the New Ayakudi members. This should be attributed especially to the functional effectiveness of the functionaries of New Ayakudi.

Though not all, they have frequently supervised the utilisation of loan and enabled in the recovery of the same. The initiatives of the president and vice-president of New Ayakudi was commendable. This justifies another hypotheses of the study, i.e., the more the involvement of functionaries, the better is the recovery performance and results of the programme.

6. No serious efforts were made by the functionaries of Vannampatty, with a lethargic attitude towards the club by the bankers and, so the club remained dormant in Vannampatty. The disagreement between bankers and members of VVV in view was, that bankers perceived that the club members think, being a member of the VVV club used to command the bank for a sanction of the loan to somebody; the members perceived that bank does not recognise or honour the club members, so they were practically at loggerheads.

7. Neither of the village VVV clubs took systematic and effective step as far as mobilisation of the savings or its the generation habits were concerned. All such members, who had accounts opened their accounts before the inception of the club.

   The savings possessed by the Vannampatty respondents were higher than New Ayakudi respondents, due to higher income and asset position of Vannampatty respondents. In spite of these savings held in the same bank where they borrowed the repayment was not prompt.

   Moreover, the banker was constrained by government orders not to initiate any legal proceedings against the member borrowers to realise the overdues.

8. Comparison of the asset position of the members of VVV club of Vannampatty and New Ayakudi before and after the inception of the club showed that in both

villages, the asset position of the members could not show any significant development.

9. The income, asset possession including the size of land holdings, savings position etc., of the Vannampatty respondents were several times better than that of New Ayakudi members. Hence, the economic status of Vannampatty members remained at par. But as far as repayment, forthcoming from the Vannampatty members it was not appreciable. They defaulted in spite of their capacity to repay. This proved the third hypotheses of study The higher the economic status, the higher would be the delinquency in repayment.

10. The members of Vannampatty had greater amount of liabilities. And most of New Ayakudi members had comparatively smaller amount of liability or debt burden.

    If we make a correlation of the income levels, asset and savings positions against the magnitude of repayment, it could be said that though the members of New Ayakudi, economically poor with low income and savings were appreciable as far as repayment, those members of Vannampatty though had the capacity to repay, either wilfully default or delayed the repayment.

    When the leader and members, expected to set an example as "good borrowers" themselves in the village were delinquent, the very foundation upon which the idea of VVV has been built get an unbearable shock in Vannampatty. And, so the club remained dormant.

11. With a view to bringing the facts to the knowledge of the members, the science and technology in agriculture, the members of New Ayakudi were taken a tour (sponsored by NABARD) around Tamil Nadu.

    They had observed the functioning of cooperative farming, gobar gas plants, poultry centres, sericulture units, sprinkle irrigation etc., yet they were not following any scientific method of cultivation as embodied in the principles of VVV programme. The members felt that loan amount was so meagre that they could not go in for scientific method of cultivation.

12. The out-of-pocket expenditure incurred by the club leader and members were promptly returned, while the programme was launched by NABARD. After it was entrusted to the banks of the respective villages, these sums were not repaid promptly to the members, which contributed to the futility of the programme as days grew by.

In aggregate terms, the programme, by and large, made an impact on the participating members and beneficiaries in the following aspects.

1. In New Ayakudi, the programme had a psycho-social impact in terms of positive repayment behaviour, concern for others, and selflessness amongst members and attitudinal changes were visible on the part of the banker. As far as the economic impact of the programme, it achieved very little. Though hardly there was any visible development in terms of generation of savings, creation of assets, redemption of prior debts, etc., the programme generated some stability in the living standard of the beneficiaries.

   In Vannampatty, the programme don't have any psycho-social impact. The mentality of the members and the attitude of the banker were as they used to be, by and large quite visible. There was some development in income levels, creation of assets, savings position etc. What needs emphasis here is that members of Vannampatty borrowed loans not in their capacity as the members of VVV club, but by personal influence.

2. In New Ayakudi, awareness of members both in terms

of the programme and the banking transactions were rather good. Most of them were aware of the principles and ideology of "Development through Credit." This was mainly because of the perfect coordination between the village leader and members, who acted as catalyst to ensure development amongst the borrowers on the one hand and the banker on the other, whereas in Vannampatty, the members gave up convening monthly meetings some time before. So, they totally forgot so to say, or were unaware of, the aims of the programme.

This study proved the prompt repayment behaviour of the New Ayakudi members, despite their poor economic conditions and non-repayment behaviour of the members of Vannampatty following their higher income asset and savings position. This strengthened the earlier statement on positive correlation between (higher) economic status and the delinquency in repayment.

3. The functionaries (Leaders, Vice-President and Members) of New Ayakudi can be said to be effective and interested in the programme. This is supported by the fact that they convened regular meetings, assisted the banker in recovery, etc. But the functionaries of Vannampatty took hardly any interest in the programme, but did not realise that the programme is for the well-being of the members and they should be cooperative and persuasive with the banker.
4. Finally, in New Ayakudi, though the programme could not make any visible economic impact, it achieved something concrete in terms of psycho-social awareness built-up, development of repayment ethics ensuring the recycling of credit in their midst. Hence, the programme has realised the principles of "Development through Credit" to a considerable magnitude.

Contrastingly, in Vannampatty, although there was visible economic development of the member borrowers, yet strictly speaking, it is not routed through the VVV club. On account of improper coordination, the club remained, by and large, dormant. Hence, from this point of view, the motto of the programme that is "Development through Credit" was not operationalised.

Conclusion: To sum up, a logical conclusion could be drawn from the major inferences of the study. In New Ayakudi the appreciable repayment behaviour, selflessness of the president, vice-president and some members and the mentality of concern for others we tend to conclude by saying that principle "Development through Credit" has been effectively put into practice by the functionaries, for, the club was operationally efficient. Though no visible economic development through credit-in terms of income generation, savings generation, asset creation—took place, the programme facilitated the generation of stability in the standard of living of the members. Hence, in New Ayakudi the impact of the programme brought stability in living by improving the quality of life.

In Vannampatty, due to non-cooperation of the banker and the VVV club members the principle of "Development through Credit", was not put in practice at all. Here, the leaders and members were the beneficiaries of the programme as against the selfless service rendered by the New Ayakudi President, Vice-President and some Members.

In Vannampatty, even the leader and the members defaulted, they failed to manifest themselves as models of good borrowers. The impact of the programme, as such has failed to realise the principles behind this programme.

Suggestions: Based upon the findings of the study, the following suggestions are made to improve the performance of weak and dormant clubs organised through the VVV programme.

1. One of the important considerations in selecting the village for launching VVV programme should be a village with the extremely poor people are in overwhelming numbers.
2. In selecting the functionaries (leaders, members and volunteers) considerations should not only be of the influence capacity, but also the heart to work for a common cause.
3. "Development through Credit" should be for the development of the people of small means and not for the development of those who've already developed.
4. On no account, should the monthly meeting be foregone; for, it would lead to decline in interest and dormancy at a later stage.
5. All government officials concerned should bear in mind to attend the monthly meetings regularly.
6. For the identification, follow-up action and recovery of loan, the banker should utilise the services of local club functionaries.
7. The leaders and members shall make it a moral-bound rule to repay in time and set an example to others.
8. That habit of thrift and savings should be inculcated in the minds of the members of VVV club.
9. The members and bankers should work shoulder to shoulder with their views at loggerheads in contradictory to the principle "Development through Credit."
10. If the case is lending for agricultural purposes, the banker can initiate repayment soon after the harvest. If it is for non-agricultural purpose, the bank should insist on periodical repayment by members.
11. At the time of lending, the bank should insist that the loanee open a recurring deposit, whereby an arrangement is made in such a way that at the time of

maturity of the loan, 50 per cent of it has been deposited recurringly. The loanee needs to repay only the remaining 50 per cent out of the sale proceeds.

This approach is believed to benefit multi-dimensionally. First, it encourages the habit of thrift among borrowers, second, it enables the banker to mobilize more towards deposit and thereby any continuous recycling of credit. Third, the banker's effort in recovery could be minimised. Fourth, the borrower also feels it to be a easier way of redeeming his debts.

12. Loans for continuous income generation activities through application of modern science and technology should be encouraged.
13. Distraint proceedings on overdue loans should be initiated in cooperative banks. Government orders should not be a constraint to this process.
14. Waivery of loans should be strongly discouraged from the government.
15. Leaders who rendered selfless services or known for exemplary work must be accorded due recognition through a discussion with the beneficiaries. It is expected that such type of people finds encouragement to intensify their services to ensure the motto "Development through Credit."
16. In order to encourage the functionaries—the leaders, volunteers, and the sponsoring bank particularly must meet their incidental expenses, when they undertake periodical visits prior to, and after, the release of credit. By doing this, they are encouraged to involve themselves intensively in order to realise the principles behind this programme.
17. The practice of giving awards and prizes to the best dub and its members may be continued as effective incentives to motivate members.

Social Justice through Cooperative Bodies: India is a country composed of villages, primarily engaged in agriculture and allied activities. Due to uneven distribution of land, the landless poor are unable to participate effectively and contribute their mite in agricultural production. As agriculture still grumbles in the monsoon, the worst sufferers are the landless, women, and rural artisans in the event of frequent occurrence of natural calamities like flood, drought, pest attack, crop failure in most parts of our country. The scheduled castes and tribes, on account of socio-economic deprivation and alienation have been greatly affected, as they were overwhelmingly known for landlessness. Moreover, these are the broad segments with whom most socio-economic problems were observed in view of vagaries in monsoon and uncertainty in agriculture.

Since Harijans, by and large, are deprived of land—both men and women are left with no option except to employ themselves locally as agricultural labourers as they don't have any skills other than what is required in agriculture. The rural artisans—carpenter, blacksmith, cobbler, well digger, mason, barber, dhobi who once served as support structures to agriculture under the Jajmani system were affected either due to the elimination of the system or technological transformations in agriculture.

In addition, the system of social stratification has affected these segments further and subjected themselves to the practice of social inequality in the form of casteism, untouchability, exploitation, social segregation and social distance. Moreover, those people belonging to the lower echelons in the social hierarchy lead a life of subordination owing to superordination and socio-economic domination of upper caste and class people. In view of these social practices social segments are pushed against the wall with the prevalence of socio-economic problems such as illiteracy, ignorance, unawareness, unemployment, poverty, indebtedness, exploitation, migration, superstitious beliefs and practices, untouchability and the domination of upper class. The people, who are affected in one way or other, experience socio-economic alienation, deprivation, inequality, humiliation, etc., are termed as the weaker segments for whom programmes of social justice are extremely necessary.

Collaborative Migration

Keeping in view of the socio-economic problems experienced by weaker segments, the cooperative movement strives to alleviate them by providing an opportunity to them by pooling their resources for collective and cooperative social action, to mitigate their problems and promote development in their midst.

The concept of cooperation took shape in India way back in 1904, since the introduction of the Cooperative Credit Societies Act—a measure to eradicate rural indebtedness through institutional credit to weaker segments. Since then, the cooperative movement made considerable progress and penetrated all walks of rural social life, especially the fields of credit transaction, supply of farm inputs, processing, marketing and employment generation. Later organisation of industrial cooperatives specially meant for women and rural artisans accelerated the process of rural industrialisation. As a voluntary organisation, cooperation became an integral part of India's route to democracy, on the development strategy and paved the way for the socio-economic uplift of the weaker segments.

The cooperative movement is based primarily on the "spirit of working together, to eliminate the monopoly of individual." It is based on the principle of open and voluntary membership, democratic participation and control, equality and fair distribution of benefits on the philosophical basis of "All for each and each for all." The cooperative organisation is marked by mutual help and the social welfare of individual members. As modern society, is marked by the weaknesses of individual domination and exploitation, the weaker segments are deprived of their due share and recognition. Although in modern life, exploitation cannot be easily eliminated, yet organisation of the affected segments under the banner of cooperation relieves them from the clutches of domination and liberates them from further exploitation.

Further, the definition of cooperation highlights social justice and the need to organise cooperatives in bringing the weaker segments under its fold for elimination of their socio-economic problems which is more apt and relevant in the Indian milieu. "Cooperation is a form of organisation in which persons voluntarily assist on the basis of equality for the promotion of their economic interests.

Those who come together have a common economic aim which they cannot achieve by individual isolated action, because of the economic position of a large majority of them." The element of individual weakness is overcome by pooling of their resources and making self-help in strengthening the bond of moral solidarity between them.

The organisation of cooperatives in India promoted development in the socio-economic sphere amongst the weaker segments and played the role effectively of a catalyst, to promote social justice in our society, known for the prevalence of social evils and economic hardships.

Cooperative Organisation and Social Justice: Since the introduction of the cooperative movement in India, the weaker segments were given opportunities to enrol themselves in specific cooperatives which, in turn, ensures their economic development.

As cooperation is popularly known as the socio-economic organisation of the affected segments, it effectively serves for the promotion of social justice in a society of our kind be set with certain social evils. The role of the cooperative organisation as a catalyst for promotion of social justice is observed through the following functions of cooperatives.

Making Aware

As the rural poor are greatly affected by illiteracy, they are ignorant of the opportunities for development. Their enrolment in cooperatives due to motivation by the promoter exposed them to the answers of development, their rights, duties, provisions in cooperatives, enlightening them on the benefits of cooperative action. The cooperative education undertaken in their midst further accelerated the process of awareness generation, resulting in their awakening, to development of unity, integrity, coexistence, mutual aid and participation in cooperative business.

Equal Drive

One of the cardinal principles of cooperation is equality and practice of democracy in the cooperative endeavour. The rural poor and affected segments are brought under the fold of cooperation for the promotion of economic betterment, irrespective of their personal background of caste, class and creed. The cooperative action warrants on the part of members, abstaining from personal characteristics, on the basis of equality. This tendency ultimately results in elimination of inequality.

Eradication of Untouchability: One of the outcome of cooperative action, as stated already, is generation of equality amongst members. Since Indian society is known for perpetuation of social inequality due to an identity of an individual in the system of social stratification, social inequality in the form of untouchability is still practiced. As there is no chance for social identity of individual members in the cooperative business transactions, this social evil is gradually eliminated in the minds of members.

Existing Together

As cooperation invariably involves togetherness, it is evident that their collective and cooperative action stimulates coexistence, recognising problems of individuals for its amelioration. This sense of togetherness and recognition of problems leads them to interdependence and peaceful coexistence. In view of such developments, the members tend to forget their social bias towards one another.

Existence of Democracy

One of the principles of cooperation, as has been pointed out, relates to democratic control being exercised by the owners of cooperatives (the members). It provides equal opportunities to all members in the affairs of cooperative management, to exercise their right of control in such a way as to result in the equitable distribution of benefits among them. Hence, equality is being practiced in the administration of cooperatives, by offering one vote to each member—irrespective of their personal background, which is the cardinal principle of democracy.

Decentralisation of Leadership: The organisation of cooperation in villages has not only facilitated the practice of the values of democracy at the micro-level, but ensured the decentralisation of leadership amongst the members regardless of their socio-economic status. To be specific, the people belonging to lower castes, women and rural artisans, once neglected are now offered the opportunity of being office-bearers; either through a contest or nomination to the board of directors, to share power in cooperative management. Further, the organisation of cooperatives exclusively meant for women, scheduled castes and tribes and rural artisans has further accelerated the process of development of leadership qualities amongst these segments.

Socialistic Behaviour

Organisation of people under the fold of cooperation facilitates the practice of socialism at the village level. The principle relating to open and voluntary membership ensures the enrolment of members for the promotion of economic interest, irrespective of their personal identity such as caste, religion, class, occupation, etc. This leads to the elimination of socio-economic prejudices in the minds of people at large.

Development of Women (Status Upgradation): The Indian women, due to the practice of sex bias, inequality and other socio-economic restrictions were subjected to exploitation, domination, harassment, etc.

The organisation of cooperatives, particularly the industrial units have provided opportunities for their permanent employment with continuous income flow. The women are very much conscious, about their potentialities and establish rural industrial enterprises through cooperation towards the total development of entrepreneurship.

Establishment of Industry

Besides women, the rural artisans are now-a-days brought under the fold of cooperative action through the establishment of guilds for rural artisans which act as the forum for their development. Such development have ensured the tapping of fiscal assistance with subsidies from the government for generation of employment. This has helped to a great extent in alleviation of poverty, checking the issue of migration and indebtedness in their midst.

Social Harmony

In view of the collective action under the fold of cooperation, there emerges social solidarity amongst the participating members, towards development of certain socio-psychological characters such as the 'We' feeling, homogeneity of interest, integrity and morality in business transaction for peaceful coexistence and communal harmony which in turn, promote social solidarity in society as a whole.

The organisation of weaker segments such as scheduled

castes and tribes, women and rural artisans, affected by certain socio-economic problems have facilitated the promotion of their socio-economic development. One of the outstanding response of cooperative action of such segments is the promotion of equality in democratic setup. In addition, the organisation of the weaker segments under the fold of cooperatives facilitates the elimination of certain socio-economic evils and divisive forces in society. Developments observed in the business transactions of cooperative bodies seem to ensure ultimately social justice in our society, known for the prevalence of socio-economic evils. To that extent, the cooperatives act as catalysts and saviours of the downtrodden.

Psychological Study

Society is a web of social relationships, said Maclver and Page, the distinguished sociologists. The social relationships are invariably built through social interaction of human beings in societies. Social interaction is the means, and achievement of such social relationship is the end. Being the means, social interaction however plays a significant role in social actions of human beings, as the base of social relationships.

The application of this concept of social relationships in society with specific reference to the cooperative (society) movement reveals the truth of cooperative social interaction on the basis of equality for promotion of socio-economic interests of the interacting individuals. Consequently, the individual members in cooperative societies or organisation in the process seem to develop the cooperative social relationship of friendship, belongingness, 'we' feeling, togetherness, peaceful coexistence, unity, integrity, harmony, leading to the cultivation of a team spirit in their "midst.

A scan on cooperative action of individual members in such societies highlights the following areas of social psychology:

1. Social Interaction
2. Group Formation
3. Basic Psychology
4. Felt-needs-Expression and Realisation
5. Communication
6. Socialisation
7. Formation of Attitudes
8. Leadership Traits: Emergence and Development
9. Personality Development
10. Cooperative Social Order.

Mutual Interaction

Social interaction refers to the reciprocal relationship between two or more individuals, whose behaviour is mutually dependent. It involves a communication process, influencing upon the actions and outlooks of individuals. Interactions take place in an interpersonal situation i.e., a face-to-face relationship. The interactions of a more enduring kind involve inter-dependence, mutual expectancy besides evaluation. As we shall see later, interactions affect the very development of personality and the concept of self influencing the individual's basic psychological process of perception, motivation, learning. Social interaction in respect of a cooperative society yields positive influence on individual members due to similar socio-economic background. The members seem to develop certain values of interdependence and mutual assistance for their collective benefits. In the process, they exert an influence on one another and thereby develop the culture of cooperation towards collective action, which ultimately leads them to betterment of socio-economic conditions.

The social action observed amongst the interacting members in such a society certainly promotes association of weaker segments like small farmers, agricultural labourers, rural artisans, marginal farmers, scheduled castes and tribes and women. Consequently, they understand each other better and appreciate the problems of another with sympathy, empathy and constructive suggestions in the boards of management of cooperatives. Accordingly, the cooperative social action tends to avoid dissociation, disruption, enmity and eliminate prejudice among the interacting individuals.

Segment Creation

The getting together of individuals upon similar socio-economic background facilitates the articulation of interest to promote the interests of members in a group formation of their organisation. In common parlance, we use the term group for the members of an organisation with a definite structure, people who have a sense of belonging to the given group.

The organisation of individuals under the aegis of a cooperative society provides a structure and specified functions on the basis of bye-laws framed for cooperative business transactions to govern their behaviour. In view of the formation of such structure under the specific name of cooperative society and accompanied by specific functions, the interest group promoted gets strengthened for the realisation of its objectives of cooperative action.

Fundamental Psychology

The interest based organisation of individuals under the banner cooperation, as pointed out earlier, precipitated the formation of well-knit group with its own structure and functions supported and regulated by bye-laws. Initially, the operation of the basic psychological processes of perception, motivation and learning sets in. Accordingly, the members perceive the organisation as their own for it helped in promoting their development. They are motivated to imbibe the values of cooperation and involve themselves in cooperative business transactions. In addition, they on account of recognition and appreciation of needs of one another, learn the advantages of self-help for mutual help consequent to the realisation of things in such organisation—the basic psychological process of perception, motivation and learning take its shape in the social situation of members marked by similar interests and characteristics.

Felt Needs—Expression and Realisation: Felt needs are the expressed needs by individuals. Expression of individual needs in the Indian social milieu hardly get realised due to cultural obstacles. If the individuals are organised for a common purpose, then there is a chance for collective expression of their needs without any fear. To that extent, the cooperative organisation of interested members however, need expressed in the fora of management provided the officials concerned put their efforts in the organisation. In this context, the cooperatives play a significant role in the generation of awareness among members, articulation of interests, the expression of needs followed by subsequent realisation.

The Interaction

The individual expression of needs under the aegis of cooperation accords a shape to the aspirations of members for their overall development. In such a process they are free to communicate any ideas and thoughts. Consequently, the identity of their common causes is revealed in an atmosphere of cooperative social action. Cooperative education undertaken periodically amongst them accelerates this process of communication for an awareness on to the promotion of their socio-economic interests with suitable knowledge on the values of cooperative democracy. The inter-communication between leaders in cooperative bodies, i.e., official, management, membership leaders orients them towards cooperative and collective actions, for the benefit of organised members of cooperative society.

Process of Socialisation

Socialisation is the international process by which the behaviour is modified to conform to the expectations held by the members of the group to which he belongs. It also includes the process by which an adult acquires the behaviour appropriate to the expectations associated with a new position in a group, an organisation associated with it or society at large.

Thus the socialisation process involve social leanings, which ultimately result in the internalisation of the values and norms of the society. Internalisation of values results in a stable personality. The values sanctioned by culture through internalisation become part of the personality.

The personality of the individuals is shaped in cooperative society through his involvement and participation in the cooperative business transactions. In the process, he is being socialised through learning the cooperative societies values of equality, democratic participation, self-help for mutual benefit and adherence to norms by following the rules, regulations, bye-laws and other cooperative constitutional requirements. The cooperative socialisation of individual members transmits the culture of cooperation and its traits.

Attitude of Creation

Attitudes are the "mental and neural state of readiness, organised through experience, exerting a directive or dynamic influence upon the individuals response to all objects and situations with which it is related." An attitude is an enduring system that includes a cognitive component, a feeling component and an action tendency. Attitudes involve an emotional component. An attitude involves beliefs as well as evaluations.

A cooperative attitude is formed primarily due to exposure of individuals to cooperative education, objective principles and the philosophy of cooperation. The knowledge they are exposed to and the awareness generated on the benefits of collective and cooperative action lead to conditioning of their mental and neural state, which is organised through the individual member's experience as a participant of cooperative action, which in turn exerts a dynamic influence upon himself. As a result of this, the participants associate more intimately with others and take cognizance of mutual aid feeling that their actions are for the collective benefit. They believe the cooperative institution is a creature of, for and by them, working for the promotion of their socio-economic interests.

Behaving as a Leader

One way of becoming a leader is being appointed by someone outside the group. All the persons in positions of authority in the administrative services of the government, industrial concerns, business concerns, banks, etc., are all 'appointed' leaders. Another way of becoming a leader is by election process. The members of the group elect their leader. This involves a formal procedure and it is the choice of the majority. The appointed leaders, as well as the elected leaders, may adopt either a democratic or the autocratic style of functioning.

The democratic leader is one, whose basic techniques are persuasion, conciliation and tolerance. He is not preoccupied with the problem of disciplining the members of his group. He trusts in the good sense of people and believes that with proper guidance they can be made to work for their goals.

In contrast, the authoritarian leader is characterised by dominance and aggressiveness. He believes in the value of discipline, forcefulness and deference to authority. He likes to display the external symbols of status and power. Since he does not have a high opinion of the intelligence and abilities of the masses, he uses many techniques of propaganda to make them believe, and do what he wants them to believe and do. He depends more on power and punishment than on persuasion.

Cooperative leadership subscribes to the values of democracy and philosophically "all for each and each for all." Therefore, the leadership in cooperative bodies invariably conforms to the democratic form. The leadership in a cooperative movement is classified in terms of (i) membership, (ii) management and (iii) official with definite specialisation of their functions.

Since cooperative bodies are the micro-institutions of democracy, leadership in their transactions is significant for the promotion of socio-economic betterment of members. In addition, the coordination between and amongst leaders of these categories are very much essential for rendering better service to the members.

Therefore, in the selection of such leaders, the members must effectively exercise their choice judiciously to elect the democratic type of leaders to the cooperative bodies. Moreover, the leaders having been elected, must understand the social psychology and the needs of the members, and strive to fulfil the same during their tenure.

Growth of Personality

Personality is the more or less a patterned body of habits, traits, attitudes and ideas of an individual, as these are organised externally into roles and statuses and relate internally to motivation, goals and various aspect of self-hood. Personality, has two aspects: role and status with respect to conduct affecting others and life organisation or self-hood with regard to internal motivation, goals and the ways of viewing one's own behaviour as well as the behaviour of others. Thus it concerns, in brief, the overt action and meaning.

The development of personality in cooperative society takes place in consonance with the ideals of cooperation and other values inherent in it. As the individual is exposed to cooperative views, there takes place the formation of cooperative mind by imbibing the values of cooperative social action for collective benefits. The external manifestation of this is the way in which the duties and responsibilities in the form of the role played as members or office-bearers in a cooperative society are taken up and the status that is derived on account of that. The cooperative values influence the individual in such a way to develop his personality according to the tenets of cooperation, which is founded on the basis of equality, love for democracy, generosity, open mindedness, sacrifice, peaceful coexistence. All such traits of cooperative personality are revealed through the overt actions and meaning derived out of it.

Social Order in Collaboration

The social psychology of cooperative action identified in the cooperative (society) movement involves social interaction among members leading to the formation of groups and associations to practice and promote socio-economic development on the basis of equality, democracy and all for each and each for all. The recognition of individual members in the cooperative as an equal partner in the process of each other's promotion sets in motion the cherished values of cooperation namely unity, integrity, equality, national development through cooperative action.

The practice of all such values of cooperation by the members leads them towards the operation of the basic psychological process of social perception, motivation, learning for the purpose of tapping the benefits through the collective action. This in turn socialises the members in the formation of cooperative attitudes in their minds and develops democratic types of leadership ensuring the personality development on these lines. In view of this, there emerges and gets established a cooperative social order not only in their midst, but in the larger society.

Collaborative Learning

One of the principles of cooperation deals with its education which was included, owing to the pioneering endeavour of Rochdale who, emphasized the need for 'Promotion of Education' in the cooperative sector. The need for such education is not overemphasised in the less-developed countries, where cooperative bodies play a significant role in the promotion of economy and social welfare of the downtrodden. Education, concept-wise, involves the generation of knowledge, creation of awareness, development of intellectual, physical, aesthetic, moral faculties in an individual either through formal or non-formal channels. Hence, education is an effective means of human resource development, facilitating the integrated development of the individual, society and nation at large. As an organisation of weaker segments, the cooperative body undertakes education programmes with a view to imparting education amongst its members. It is expected that through cooperative education, the requisite knowledge and awareness on the principles, philosophy, objectives, and benefits of cooperative action are created amongst the members, who were comparatively marked earlier by illiteracy, ignorance and unawareness.

Collaborative Aspects

Before we proceed, it is essential to highlight the principles and philosophy of cooperation. They are:

1. Open an voluntary membership,
2. Democratic control,
3. Limited interest on share capital,
4. Fair distribution of surplus,
5. Promotion of cooperative education,
6. Cooperation among cooperative bodies,
7. All for each and each for all.

The entire field of cooperative education, as such revolves around these principles and philosophy of cooperation. Cooperative education is specifically concerned with the following objectives concerned in the cooperative bodies and society at large:

1. to impart knowledge about the principles of cooperation,
2. to create awareness on the rights and responsibilities of members,
3. to expose the members widely on the ideologies, methods, aims and practices of cooperation,
4. to create a climate of cooperation amongst the general public.

Importance of Cooperative Education: The importance of cooperative education arises, when we consider the behavioural characteristics of the people in India. Owing to their dependence on monsoon for agricultural reproduction, they are greatly affected by the consistent failure of monsoon putting the rural masses under economic stress. At times, the people are also affected due to certain natural calamities like flood and drought, which render them untold misery and hardships. Those who are subjected to such problems are either frequently unemployed or under-employed without job-contentment, leading to poverty, indebtedness, migration.

It is these segments that the cooperative bodies have to care for their economic development. Moreover, these are the people, who are affected by illiteracy, ignorance, unawareness, untouchability, social segregation, etc. The cooperative bodies as an organisation of these segments strive to alleviate their problems, they are confronted with in a society of, known for proliferation of such problems. The best or only alternative available for these segments in India is the cooperative organisation.

But when we look at the practical side of cooperation, the

due share in participation, management and benefit are not identified with these segments. Hence, the urgent need to generate awareness amongst these segments and to create an awakening of the facilities, benefits, rights etc. for which knowledge of cooperation in terms of its principles, objectives, philosophy are essential. It is expected that the awareness amongst these segments would pave the way for their active and democratic participation in the affairs of the cooperative institution.

Purpose

1. To bring people within the fold of the cooperative movement.
2. To produce entrepreneurial qualities in a population, where business management is unknown.
3. To keep the feeling alive in members that the cooperative society is an organisation that belongs to them.
4. To instil, the requisite knowledge, motives, meritorious skills, and ability in them.
5. To wage war against illiteracy and ignorance among its members.
6. To counteract the bad propaganda against cooperative movement.
7. To create personnel trained in the cooperative movement.

Necessity

1. To teach members about the cooperative principles, methods and aims of such movement.
2. To increase efficiency in the cooperative movement among the employees.
3. To teach the people to have faith and loyalty in the movement.

4. To enlighten the people on their rights, aims, privileges in the organisation.
5. To develop the spirit of (togetherness) cooperation.
6. To develop morality and repayment ethics which make them realise their moral obligation towards one another in such business transactions.
7. To develop leadership within the movement.
8. Cooperation aims at providing work and responsibilities to individuals outside their ordinary life and experience.
9. To check the obstacles in the process of establishment of cooperative bodies.
10. Cooperative bodies as a democratic organisation facilitate the practice of democracy at the micro-level. To practice democracy, they need enlightened membership. The members should understand their right and responsibilities and be vigilant in their transactions.
11. Cooperative education is needed to educate the members and to develop a sense of responsibility in them to decide and prepare them to exercise their rights and responsibilities intelligently, honestly and judiciously.
12. As cooperative bodies promote group action, it is essential that the members and others develop the cooperative spirit and attitude.
13. Cooperative education makes the participating members eliminate their ego, selfish and parochialistic tendencies.

Hence, the indispensable guide to promote cooperative spirit for collective action amongst the participants and others concerned is education in the principles and practice of cooperation.

Profit Holders

Cooperative education intends to cover, by and large, the entire society. To be specific, the following segments are involved in cooperative education.

1. Members of cooperative societies
2. Leaders of cooperative societies
3. Employees of cooperative societies
4. The youth
5. The general public at large

The Members: The members in the cooperative society are considered to be the owners, who need to be educated on the following objectives and needs:

1. to impart knowledge on cooperation, its principles and philosophy,
2. to know their rights and responsibilities,
3. to generate awareness about cooperative actions,
4. to restore the zeal for working together,
5. to keep the ideology of cooperative movement, alive in their mind.

The Leaders: The leaders of cooperative bodies are considered as the representatives of members in a particular cooperative society, who need to be exposed to the ideology of cooperation so that they lead the members and employees on the right path towards the effective service to members and the public. They have to perform the following functions:

1. to impart knowledge of the principles, aims and practices of the cooperative society,
2. to increase their functionality,
3. to know their rights, responsibilities and obligations,
4. to inform them of the cooperative laws,
5. to increase the efficiency of liaisoning.

The Employees: The employees of cooperative society's bodies are the actual managers of the cooperative movement, who are engaged in the provision of services to the owners i.e., the members of the cooperative bodies. Therefore, they are to be enlightened every now and then in the form of inservice training so that they work for the total satisfaction of the members. It is desirable on their part to develop the following:

1. the sense of cooperative endeavour and work culture,
2. to increase their efficiency,
3. to develop the proper service mentality.

The Youth: In order to ensure a continuous flow of committee leadership to the movement, the emerging generation needs to be educated. Since youth possess high potentialities to deliver the goods through their hard work, cooperative education generates cooperative spirit through a base for cooperative action in future. Therefore, the youth being the future cooperators are highly eligible for cooperative and collective action.

The Public: Since the cooperators come from the general public there is a need for their awareness as part of motivation, so that the public is informed about any such action and the benefits in lieu thereof. It ensures creation of cooperators with sufficient knowledge before the establishment of cooperative bodies.

Types of Learning

In order to disseminate such knowledge, various media of communication must be effectively pressed into service in a society, where about 50 per cent of the people are affected by illiteracy. Hence, a multi-media approach could produce the desired results in India, considering the characteristics of people. The following methods of communication ensure effective dissemination of cooperative education for various segments.

1. Radio
2. Television & Video
3. Documentaries and film shows
4. Newspapers
5. Exhibitions
6. Conferences, Seminars, Workshops and Public meetings
7. Cooperative week celebrations in schools, colleges and universities
8. Short orientation and refresher courses and lectures to leaders and employees in cooperatives
9. Publication of books, newsletters, magazines, journals, pamphlets
10. Folksongs, music, dance, drama projecting themes of cooperation
11. Interviews with successful cooperators, beneficiaries, and the officials managing cooperative societies, etc.

Despite the encouragement of government and the dissemination of cooperative knowledge amongst various segments in our society by cooperative bodies, there remains much to be desired and accomplished. In order to bridge the gap and accelerate the process of effective dissemination of such education, the multi-media strategy may be adopted. A grass-root approach to the scheme of such education and training by utilising the centres of adult literacy and social action for school teachers, would however, stimulate and encourage villagers to accept cooperation as a way of life and a movement to ensure their integrated development.

Collaborative Growth

The cooperative movement plays a significant role in the Third World countries, beset with umpteen issues and socio-economic problems. As a democratic organisation, the rural cooperative bodies facilitate organisation of the weaker segments, who are in dire need of external assistance for socio-economic upliftment. The cooperative movement took shape with the cherished objectives of service and assistance to such segments through their organisation to promote collective social action. The dawn of independence in India further accelerated the process of establishment of rural cooperative bodies, for the purpose of integrated rural community development.

In the Constitution of India, there is a division of spheres of administration between centre and state governments. Cooperation is included in the state and the responsibility of implementing the provision under the Directive Principles of State Policy is left to the state governments. In this respect the Directive Principles lay down that the state shall try to secure a social order for promotion of social welfare of the people. The social welfare can be better ensured through the organisation of such institutions at the grass-root level.

Cooperative societies have been established by the state government with a view to transforming the traditional social order in the rural areas amongst weaker segments through their collective social action. To do this, each state government has a department that takes care of and runs the cooperative movement. The cooperative societies existing in India may broadly be classified in terms of primary and secondary units.

The purpose behind the organisation of primary cooperative units is two fold, i.e., provision of credit and non-credit assistance and service to the vulnerable segments. Again, the credit assistance is issued for agricultural and non-agricultural purposes. Similarly, non-credit units may also be classified as agricultural and non-agricultural societies.

The secondary cooperative societies include the cooperative union at the state level, central cooperative bank at the district level and the state cooperative bank, the apex bank at the state level. The following chart illustrates the structure of the cooperative societies organisation.

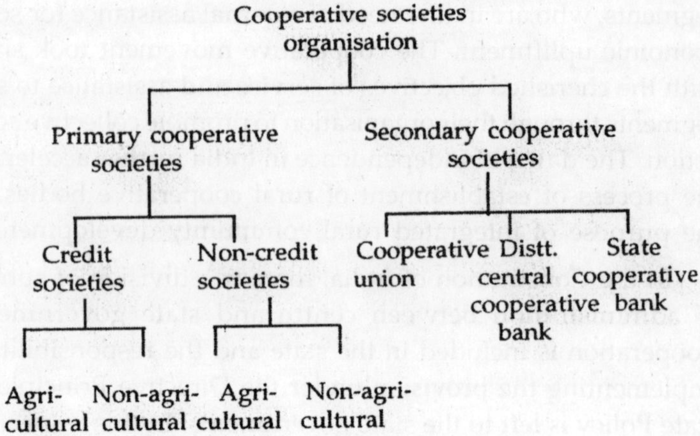

Need for Cooperative Organisation: Being an agricultural country, India lives in villages, where one could gauge the existence of socio-economic problems such as unemployment, poverty, indebtedness, exploitation, illiteracy, ignorance, religiosity, superstitious beliefs and practices, untouchability and the domination of the haves over the have-nots etc. The organisation of cooperative societies amongst people known for and affected by such problems pave the way for their development.

The cooperative movement is based primarily on the 'spirit of working together' and thereby eliminating monopoly of individuals. It is based on the principle of "All for each and each for all." The cooperative organisation is characterised by mutual help and welfare of the individual members. As modern society is affected by the weakness of monopolisation and exploitation, the weaker segments are deprived of their due share and recognition. It is true that in modern life, exploitation cannot be easily eliminated.

The organisation of such affected segments under the banner of cooperation relieves them from the clutches of capitalist domination and liberates them to a great extent from exploitation. Furthermore, the definition of cooperation itself bears testimony to the need for organisation of such weaker segments in India. "Cooperation is a form of organisation in which persons voluntarily assist one another, on the basis of equality for the promotion of economic interest. Those who come together have a common economic aim, which they cannot achieve by individual isolated action, because of the weakness of the economic position of a large majority of them". This is overcome by pooling their resources and making self-help effective through mutual help, by strengthening the bond of moral solidarity between them.

Awakening regarding Collaborative Movement

The concept of cooperation took concrete structure in India after the introduction of the Cooperative Credit Societies Act-1904, a measure designed to eradicate rural indebtedness and provide institutional credit to the weaker segments.

Since then the cooperative movement has made progress and penetrated in all walks of rural social life especially, those fields of rural credit transaction, supply of farm inputs, processing and marketing of farm produce. Later, the organisation of industrial cooperative bodies accelerated the process of rural industrialisation. As a voluntary organisation, cooperation now becomes an integral part of Indian development plans, for socio-economic development of the weaker segments.

Cooperative Organisations and Development: The introduction of cooperative enterprises in our rural society effectively set in motion the socio-economic uplift of the weaker segments particularly since independence. As a catalyst, the cooperative bodies organised the weaker segments in rural areas and acted as the common parlance for ensuring socio-economic development of rural people. The development role of cooperative bodies in rural areas can be summarised as:

1. Organisation of weaker segments in the cooperative institutions facilitated collective social action by an awareness about their deprived condition.
2. The awakening of conscientiousness through cooperative education further accelerated the process of their social awakening.
3. Such awareness and its impact however, minimised problems of illiteracy, ignorance and unawareness in their social life.
4. Being a democratic institution, the cooperative bodies helped to set in the democratic participation of members irrespective of caste, class or creed eliminating some of the problems like casteism, untouchability and physical segregation, etc. This has ultimately ensured the principle of democracy, i.e., equality and one vote for each individual.
5. Through cooperative societies, now, the peasants can come together and bring about agricultural development. Cooperative societies facilitate the purchase of quality seeds, fertilizers, pesticides, modern agricultural implements etc., to solve many of their difficulties.
6. Before the introduction of cooperative bodies, the rural society was subjected to the domination of non-institutional credit, particularly, the moneylenders and traders, who lend money to the needy at exorbitant rates of interest. Cooperative bodies relieved the weaker segments from the clutches of such middlemen, exploiters and parasites in rural credit transactions. Moreover, the peasants now can get loans at nominal rates, without running the risk of losing their landed property.
7. On account of their enrolment in cooperative society, the members can develop the spirit of self-service

through collective actions and other such social qualities as working together, social adjustment, fellow-feeling, open-mindedness, concern for mutual welfare, sympathy and above all unity, integrity, equality, social solidarity, homogeneity and peaceful coexistence.

8. The change in the leadership pattern another important development, since the inception of cooperative societies in rural areas. The formal leadership came into being through such institutions and facilitated the election of meritorious and hard-working individuals. This culminated in the elimination of tradition bound caste-class based hereditary informal leadership, identified in village social life.
9. Through cooperative societies, women development and their emancipation could now be achieved. The rural women, who were deprived of opportunity hitherto for their socio-economic development against certain taboos effectively used these cooperative institutions for their socio-economic development. This has brought about social honour and economic importance for their career prospects.
10. The fora organised in the rural society in the name of cooperation undertook several income generation activities through self-employment in their own environment. The employment generated through them, not only promoted their economic status in the family but improved the overall income of the family and standard of living.
11. Yet another significant outcome of cooperation in rural society is the rural industrialisation. The cooperative movement in India has facilitated the establishment of cottage and village industries by utilising the locally available raw materials. Rural industrialisation seen through cooperation generated local self-employment for men and women.

12. Cooperative societies besides being a voluntary business organisation of the needy are considered now as a moral organisation as well. In the process of transmission of morality to members, they discipline the borrowers or beneficiaries of cooperative action. This has resulted in the inculcation of repayment ethics in the minds of members.
13. Through cooperative societies, the interested people could undertake social work. The cooperative societies are meant for the socio-economic welfare of the affected segments and so the spirit of social service develops in their minds. These qualities are largely responsible for the development of moral faculties in them.
14. The democratic values like equality, opportunity, rule of majority are all put into practice at the micro-level through cooperative organisation in villages. This, in turn, lead to political consciousness among the participants in the cooperative organisation, is essential for the development of the country.

Thus, cooperative organisations act as fora for collective social action of the people of meagre means, primarily for the promotion of their economic development. In the process, owing to their cooperative action, they develop certain socio-psychological characteristics such as sense of equality, unity, integrity, peaceful coexistence, aid, etc. The organisation of weaker segments in cooperative societies has helped in the long run, elimination of certain socio-economic evils. Above all, the cooperative organisation in rural society has led to the minimisation of poverty and the generation of local self-employment. In view of these developments, the rural societies have experienced a transition from tradition to modern social order leading to the integrated development of weaker sections, who were once subjected to deprivation and alienation.

4

CASTE SYSTEM

Changes in traditional caste system of India are associated with various changes in social institutions at the micro as well as at the macro level. Urbanisation, industrialization, education and other such factors have contributed to the changes in the caste system. The welfare measures taken up by the government have also helped in weakening the caste system.

However change and continuity in caste system of Indian society has been of special interest to many Sociologists. We see changes taking place by eroding the traditional set up through modernization. Rules of endogamy has been weakened due to education, mobility etc. However, we witness endogamous marriage as preferable one when we look at the matrimonial alliance. In cities, towns, urban areas, many workers do migrate from villages and they interdine and share with the fellow beings. But these are to be completely avoided when they go back to their respective villages. Brahmans are no more given the same kind of respect they traditionally used to enjoy. Economic and political power become important for social status. Individual mobility rather than Jati mobility has been encouraged. Yet Brahmins enjoy this traditional social position and they are the people who amassed wealth and got modern education too due to which they are capable of holding their higher social position. The structure of caste stability is not without continued tension which keeps the balance of power among castes at a precarious situation that one caste group acts against the other caste group for political ends. Democratisation and the various welfare measures of the lower caste groups have enabled them to challenge the ritual and economically powerful upper caste groups. There is stiff competition in terms of mobility.

But such competition is not always healthy. It takes the form of ugly face which one cannot ignore *e.g.*, formation of different caste associations, loyalty to particular caste groups give rise to communalism.

Even though we witness the weakening of caste in terms of pollution and purity, social interaction, inter caste marriage, occupational mobility. Indian society is not but without caste and it has penetrated into our lives however the changes could be.

Gandhi, Ambedkar and Caste

Gandhian Views on Caste: Gandhi interpreted caste as a degenerated form of varna system for the creation of division of society. According to Gandhi, varna' system is functional so far as its members perform their ascribed functions. Thus, according to Gandhi varna is a method to distribute functions to people according to their traits and capabilities. "All are born to serve God's creation. Brahmins fulfill the function of priestly and religious functions, Kashatriya perform the warfare function, the Vaishyas engage in trade and commerce while the Sudras perform all manual labour."

Gandhiji believed that if a person was assigned a particular role in society, it did not mean that he was absolved of his duties towards others. A Brahmin could not absolve himself from the responsibility of physical labour and a Sudra could not be denied his right to acquire knowledge. According to Gandhiji, this however does not mean that a Brahmin is absolved from bodily labour or the duty of protecting himself and others. The birth makes a Brahmin predominantly a man of knowledge, the fittest by heredity and training to impart it to others. There is nothing again to prevent the Sudra from acquiring all the knowledge he wishes; only he will best serve with his body and need not envy others special qualities for service. But a Brahmin who claims superiority by right of knowledge fails and has no knowledge. And so with the others who pride themselves.

Though Gandhiji upheld the Varna Ashram Dharma, he opposed the degenerated form of caste system. He based his Varna Ashrama Dharma on division of labour and clarified his argument in the following line:

It would be wrong and improper to judge the law of Varna by its caricature in the life of man who profits to belong to a Varna, whilst he openly commits a breach, it is only an operative role. Arrogation of superior status by any of the Varnas over another is a denial of the law. And there is nothing in the law of Varna to warrant people to untouchability. Down with the monster of caste that masquerades in the guise of varna. It is this travesty of Varna that has degraded Hinduism and India.

Gandhiji did not oppose intermarriage, interdining but wanted that these should not be operated as against the wishes of others. With regard to inter-marriage and interdining, Gandhiji has remarked. "Prohibition against inter-marriage and interdining is essential for a rapid evaluation of the soul. But this self-denial is not to test Varna. A Brahmin may remain a Brahmin though he may dine with his Sudra brother, provided he has not let off his duty of service by sharing his knowledge with others. It evolves from what I have said above that restraint in matters of marriage and dining is not based upon notions of superiority. If a Hindu should refuse to dine with any other from a sense of superiority it altogether misrepresents his Hindu religion".

When Gandhiji was taking the lead in Indian National Congress session in 1920, removal of untouchability was incorporated as one among many constructive programme. In the freedom struggle movement against the British yoke, there were many programmes launched against the various ills of society. Removal of untouchability was one of such propaganda. He founded the Harijan Sevak Sangh and underwent 21 day fast as a form of protest against the closing of temples to the untouchables. Further, he pointed out that in the inception, untouchability was a rule of sanitation. An unclean person or the thing may be untouchable, immediately when his or its uncleanness is shed, he or it is no longer untouchable. Therefore persons who are to attend to scavenging, whether a paid bhangi or an unpaid mother are unclean until they have washed themselves clean of their unclean work. If instead of being regarded as untouchable for even the bhangi was treated as brother and was given an opportunity and even made to become clean after performing an unclean service for society he would be acceptable as any other member of that society.

Gandhiji considered the practice of untouchability among the Hindus as a sin against God and man, a poison slowly eating into the very vitals of Hinduism. He believed that it has no sanction whatsoever in the Hindu Shastras taken as whole. Untouchability, he maintained, had degraded both the untouchables and the touchables. He accepted that it was an old institution but argued that if it was an evil, it could not be defended on the ground of its antiquity.

He argued that untouchability and its ugly face has pervaded all corners of our society. Further "the existence of untouchability amongst untouchables", he said, "was an additional reason for the cultured Hindu society to rid itself of the curse." If the untouchables are so because they have to work with flesh, blood, bones and night soil, every nurse and every doctor should become untouchable and so should Christians and Muslims and all so-called high-class Hindus who kill animals for food or sacrifice.

For Gandhiji removal of untouchability was perhaps the biggest religious reform movement in India. He wanted orthodox sections that disapproved of the movement to be given every courtesy and consideration, to win them by love, by self-sacrifice, by perfect self-restraint and "by letting the purity of our lives produce its own silent effect upon their hearts. We must have faith in our truth and love converting the opponents to our way" he said.

He regarded it is as a movement purely and simply of purification of Hinduism and 'that purification can only come through the purest instrument', he proclaimed.

Gandhiji further pointed out that law alone cannot help in removing untouchability and hence he calls for all the Hindus to involve by realising the fact that it is a crime against God and man. Further Gandhiji put forth, "If it was demonstrated to me to my satisfaction that the political or social economic regeneration of Harijans would be enough to retain the Harijans in the Hindu fold, I would still want to open the temples and remove every trace of inequality, because for me it is as it must be for you, a question of repentance and reparation for the wrong we have done for our fellowmen".

But he did not want the untouchables to force their way into the temples. He was even willing to reserve a part of the day for the untouchables to offer worship or even build common wells, schools, temples specially designed for the convenience of untouchables but open to others. He desired that temple entry for the untouchables should be given more importance than even their economic upliftment. Public places such as schools, wells, places of worship should be open to all section of Harijan community.

Untouchability without Religious Base

He argued that no religion could sanction inhuman behaviour and that no scripture that categorized human beings as inferior or superior on the basis of birth, could command our allegiance. Gandhi also did not approve of citing varnadharma to defend untouchability and inequality. He did not see varnadharma as a system of social gradation but as a system which assigns different duties—a healthy division of labour.

Gandhi's main aim was to incorporate the untouchables among other caste groups and always wanted to treat them equally with other caste groups. He had reserves about the existing varna system though he strongly opposed the practice of untouchability.

Ambedkar's Views on Caste: Both Gandhi and Ambedkar fought against the existence of untouchability. However the way untouchability as social ill was looked upon differently by the two and their methodologies of fighting against untouchability was different. For this there were tension between the two which got resolved later on mutual understanding.

Ambedkar strongly believed that untouchability could be abolished only if caste society would be abolished. But caste has pervaded every nook and corner of our society. Ambedkar strongly proposed the suggestion that untouchables can enhance their position only through political assertion for themselves. He strongly endorsed separate political representation for the untouchables in the 1932 Communal Award. Positive discrimination was implemented separately for the untouchables. In an attempt to improve the status of the untouchables he strongly propagated the untouchables to convert to Buddhism which does not recognise the hierarchy of human beings. It is basically an egalitarian religion.

Ambedkar analysed the problem of caste as based on the problem of endogamy which is one of the features of caste in

India. Endogamy implies marriage within the group and discourages marriage between groups.

The various races of India occupying definite territories have more or less fused into one another and do possess cultural unity which is the only criterion of a homogeneous population. Given this homogeneity, caste becomes a problem altogether new in character and wholly absent in the situation constituted by the mere propinquity of endogamous social or tribal groups.

Hindu society was composed of classes such as (1) Brahmin or the priestly class; (2) Kshatriya or the military class; (3) Vaishya or the merchant class and (4) Sudra or the artisan. This was considered as a class system according to Ambedkar. Among Hindus, the priestly class maintains social distance from others through a closed-down policy and became a caste by itself. The other classes underwent differentiation, some into large and some into very minute groups. This sub-division of society is quite natural. The unnatural thing about these sub-divisions is that they have lost the open-door character of the class system and have become self-enclosed units called castes. Ambedkar answered to the point, "some closed the door; others found it closed against them". One is psychological interpretation and the other mechanistic but they are complementary and both are necessary to explain the phenomena of caste-formation in its entirety.

He farther argues that since the Brahmins remains detached from others through endogamy it was wholeheartedly imitated by all the non-Brahmin sub-division or classes who became endogamous castes. The influence of the model's example is efficacious inversely to its distance as well as directly to its superiority. The conditions for imitation, according to this standard of authority are (1) that the source of imitation must enjoy prestige in the group and (2) that there must be numerous and duly relations among members of a group. These conditions were present in India and the lower classes imitated the

Brahmins. Ambedkar concludes four main points in the study of the caste system: (1) that in spite of composite make-up of the Hindu population there is a deep cultural unity; (2) that caste is a parcelling into bits of a larger cultural unit; (3) that there was one caste to start with and (4) the classes have become castes through imitation and ex-communication.

System of Caste and Politics

Many Sociologists and others have highlighted the relationship between caste and politics peculiar to Indian society. Andre Beteille Rajni Kothari, Rudolf and Rudolf have highlighted the role played by caste in Indian politics and *vice-versa.* Rajni Kothari studied the relationship of the two in the following ways. (1) By examining the nature of relationship between caste and politics and (2) By examining the type of changes that have taken place in the political system as a result of the involvement of caste organization. Thus his focus was not so much on what happens to the cast system as a whole but on what happens to the political system because of the vote of castes.

Caste has three important indigenous elements (1) secular which refers to relevance of caste in politics in terms of the relations within and between castes (2) integrative which refers to castes being relevant to politics through differentiation and integration and (3) ideological which is heightened by its value structure. This is where gestures for cultural mobility, such as Sanskritization, westernization and secularization, assume or disguise political overtones in their manifestation.

The analysis of "Dominant Caste and Political process" by Anil Bhatt reveals the crucial role played by castes in politics and awareness of the lower castes of their political gains. He analyses U.P., Gujarat, West Bengal and Andhra Pradesh, middle, low and higher caste member responses towards their part in castes politics. The high caste groups had lower political interest and low castes higher political interests. Political awareness was high among the higher castes, and was low among the lower level castes. As regards identification with political parties, there is practically no relationship between caste status and partisanship. Persons of low status castes are almost as likely to support political parties as those of the high status castes.

Lower castes by organizing themselves in pursuit of collective interests were able to emerge successfully. The involvement of these caste organization in politics has changed their position in hierarchical pattern of Hindu society. Caste solidarity and political power helped them to achieve higher social, economic and political success. This was highlighted by the studies conducted by Rudolf and Rudolf. The same was highlighted by Andre Beteille's study of Tanjore district in Tamil Nadu.

In India it has been a tradition for different caste groups to affiliate themselves to different associations, organisation, political ideology etc. These caste groups have used politics as tools for improving upon themselves since group assertion can be expressed most successfully through political means.

The Mahars of Maharashtra, who occupy lower position in caste hierarchy ultimately used politics for ameliorating their social condition. Ambedkar organized them into a political entity, formed a Scheduled Caste Federation, which was ultimately used as a political means, forwarded the goal of social equality. The traditional place of a Mahar in the village community was as village servant watchman, village guide or messenger to the Government, sweeping roads, carrying death notices etc. Mahars were untouchables because of their lower position in the caste hierarchy ritually and economically. Brahmins had to maintain social distance that the image of the Mahars could not be touched by any Brahmin since the Mahars were considered to be pollutants.

But today the Mahars are capable of asserting themselves about their' rights and aspirations through political means. Ambedkar played the most important role in making the Mahars to politically organised group during just in the event of ending the British rule in India.

Politics played a crucial role in Gujarat on caste level where economically depressed communities of cultivators federated together in 1940s and 1950s into a common organization for achieving political power. Several Rajput intermediary castes, Kolis to Tribal Bhils, and even high castes, formed the Kshatriya Sabha, mobilized mass political support and bargained with their aged old rivals, pallidars. They achieved their goal of upgrading the position of the lower castes and winning elections against Congress through a Patidar-Kshatriya alliance. The process was one of mobilization of group support whereby many castes were accepted into the Kshatriya fold. Politics worked as a cementing force.

Caste has assumed the most significant element in the politics of Bihar, U.P., Andhra Pradesh, Gujarat etc. Lower caste groups in pursuit of collective interest could organise themselves and it has resulted into the improvement of their social standing in the hierarchy. The Yadavs of Bihar is noteworthy. Today the importance given to ritual superiority has also been declined.

By participating in the modern political system, castes is now exposed to divisive influences and a new form of integration. In the present scenario the relationship between politics and caste has taken different shape. Extreme loyalty to one's own caste group has created conflicts and tension between different caste groups.

Many people talk of the role of casteism and communalism in politics. An impression prevails that when things like education, industrialization and urbanization were diminishing the traditional caste loyalties, electoral politics has strengthened them and re-established their legitimacy and that this has given rise to disintegrative tendencies that will disrupt the existing democratic political system. But this is not true. In reality the consequences of caste-politics interactions are just the reverse of what is usually stated. It is not politics that gets caste-ridden; it is the caste that gets politicized as being put forth by Rajni Kothari.

Caste has become one of the most formidable element of group formation within political parties in India. In Bihar politics is mainly based on caste. The patronage and pecuniary resources available to the political leaders enable them to create a coalition of factions on caste basis, whose leaders are bound to political elites in power in a complex network of personal obligational ties. Each of these leaders had a group of followers tied to him in accordance with the same set of caste principles. The personnel of these castes factions may vary but whatever may be their social composition they demand and to a higher degree receive from their members full support.

It is thus the caste cohesion which keeps the leaders in power. Same is the case in Karnataka, U.P, Gujarat, Maharashtra, Rajasthan, M.P. etc. The mobilization of schedule caste members by their caste leaders of Jats by Jat minister, of Reddy by Reddy Chief Minister, of Kurmis by Kurmi Agricultural Minister illustrates the way in which caste is used in politics by a skilful organiser to transform his own caste into a viable political force. Same is the case with different association and institution affiliated to different castes.

Political parties mobilize caste supports in various ways. Andre Beteille has discussed about Tanjore district of Tamil Nadu. He suggested that two kinds of changes seem to be taking place in relation between caste and politics: Power shifts from one dominant caste to another; and the focus of power shifts from one caste itself to another on caste basis.

Andre Beteille maintains loyalties of castes are exploited

in voting. New alliances cutting across castes areas are also formed. Rudolph is of the opinion that caste association has given caste a new vitality and democracy has enabled caste to play an important political role in India. Caste federations are formed not of one caste but many. His further observation pointed out that caste enters the political process (1) by making appeals to caste loyalties in a general way like exhorting Vanniyans to vote for Vanniyars (2) by activising networks of inter personal relation both during elections and at other times for mobilizing support along caste lines and (3) by articulating caste interests in an organized manner. Beteille has also pointed out that the political process has a dual effect on the caste system. To the extent that caste and sub-caste loyalties are consistently exploited, the traditional structure is strengthened and to the extent that it leads to new alliance cutting across caste, it loosens the traditional structure.

Political parties utilize the support of caste for their functioning and seek their support in winning elections. Grass-root political arenas as well as political parties have always remained and continue to remain dominated by elites of castes which compete with each other to form caste coalitions of supporters strong enough to maximize control over local resources and enhance opportunities to became players in political system.

Backward Class Uprising

Backward class movement is one of the important arenas on social change. For decades these group of people were subject to inhuman conditions and after become victim in the hands of the high caste groups. When they became aware of their extreme exploitation it became intolerable for them to accept inhuman treatment from other high caste groups and started challenging the power of the high caste. Such movements definitely helped the lower caste to enhance their social position though not ritually and it enabled them to avail of facilities. In Madras, non-Brahmin caste found themselves in a disadvantageous position because the Brahmin caste on account of their education, were holding higher posts. The non-Brahmin movement laid stress on two aspects: with respect to reservation in admission to college courses and with respect to the recruitment to government jobs. In both, they wanted that the reservation should be according to the population proportion. Both the demands created a good deal of resentment among the Brahmins who now found themselves being discriminated on the ground of their caste. The members of the aggressive groups of Dravida Kazhagam and Dravida Munnetra in Tamil Nadu carried on a virulent campaign against Brahmins.

But in North India when the lower castes claimed higher status, there were violent clashes. The Sudra castes Sanskritized themselves and wanted to put on the sacred thread in order to register themselves in the census as members of the Vaisya or the Kshatriya caste. This led to violent clashes between the Brahmins and Kshatriyas on one hand and the Shudra castes on the other.

Many of their movements took a political turn. The non-Brahmin leaders of the old composite state of Madras formed the South India Liberation Federation in 1916 to advance and protect the interests of the non-Brahmins. The federation later on called itself the Justice Party. It started newspapers in English and other languages to educate and put forward the case of the non-Brahmins. In the same way many weeklies were started in various languages by caste organisations in different parts of India.

Thus the aim of backward classes movement was to limit the Brahmin monopoly in the two fields of education and appointment to government posts. But this was not a mass movement. The opposition of Brahmin dominance did not come from the low and the oppressed castes but from the leaders of the powerful rural dominant castes such as the

Kammars and Reddis of Andhra Pradesh, Tamil Nadu and the Nayars of Kerala.

These backward classes include tribes, Hindus etc. Various steps have been taken up to improve upon the lot of the backwardness such as the positive discrimination, Mandal commission.

The Backward class commission was appointed according to the Article 340 of the Constitution. The Commission was to determine the criteria to be adopted to provide concessions to 'socially and educationally Backward Classes' besides the scheduled castes and scheduled tribes. The Commission was also asked to prepare a list of such classes.

But the commission's report of backward classes on the basis of caste was not the criterion to be taken into consideration. The commission submitted its report in 1955 by listing 2399 castes as backward but it was rejected since caste was taken as the criterion of identifying the backwardness instead income was taken into consideration. The commission also recommended to include certain sections of Sikhs, Christians, Muslims to be included in the backward classes.

Economic backwardness is the result of many social evils. With respect to criteria of backwardness, the Commission recommended for general guidance (1) Low social position in the traditional caste hierarchy (2) Lack of education in the major section of the community (3) Inadequate or no representation in' government service and (4) Inadequate representation in the field of trade, commerce and industry. The list of other backward classes were published by the Education Ministry and by the State Governments. The commission also revised the list of SC and ST on the basis of such available information. The Commission noted that the great majority of the backward classes were ignorant, illiterates and poor. This was due to the traditional exploitation practised by the high social caste groups.

Resulting from the various benefits offered to these backward class groups, many of these groups have improved upon the socio-economic conditions that the economic status has been improved, they have their political representations. But at the same time, one should not ignore its negative implications. That it fails to create capable men of merit in the job market plus there has been conflict between those who avail of these facilities and those who are deprived of these facilities but belong to the same economic position. Further there has been clamour on the part of many who try to get a place in the backward class group so as to avail of these facilities through reservation. Backward Classes who manage to get all the benefits are the most vocal in their professions for the welfare of the backward sections of their caste or group. It is also true that these sections of the caste make full use of the backwardness of their group to consolidate their own political power. Because of this, there is also a clamour for more and more to include in the list of backward class.

M. N. Srinivas explained that the rise of the backward class for education and economic opportunities was fundamentally a movement to achieve mobility on the part of the groups which had lagged behind the Brahmins in westernization. In the process of participating the modern political and other processes assumed significant changes-(1) Freeing the caste from its traditional local and vertical matrix, within the local matrix the emphasis was on the independence of castes or local section of castes. (2) The coming into existence of new opportunities educational, economic and political, brought about an increase in horizontal solidarity.

M.N. Srinivas maintains that reservation policy in an attempt to bring equality has improved the conditions of the backward class. Social movements have not been but without ideological backing for example S.N.D.P. movement in the south, the Mahar movement in Maharashtra, the Telengana Movement in Andhra Pradesh.

Lower castes by organizing themselves in pursuit of collective interests were able to emerge successfully. The involvement of theseom conditions of acute relative deprivation within the framework of the caste system as characterized by the principle of purity pollution. This principle was legitimised by the priests of orthodox Hinduism (Brahmins) and by the kings who wielded secular authority. During British rule, these two sources of legitimacy were undermined to a great extent, and new sources of status were established, based on occupation, income, education and an egalitarian value system. Under such conditions, the leaders of the deprived sections were awakened to alternative sources of identity. Two ways of protest were open to them. One was to reinterpret Hinduism and claimed a new identity within its fold, and the other was to abandon Hinduism and embrace another religion and culture. The Izhavas choose the former, although they did make several attempts to choose the latter, because of the presence of a charismatic leader, Sri Narayana Guru Swamy.

Sri Narayana Guru Swamy established a new identity for the Izhavas of Kerala based on a reinterpretation of orthodox Hinduism. He denied the existence of a plurality of Gods, religions and castes. He argued against the criterion of birth as the basis of differential access to the highest forms of spiritual knowledge, and demonstrated the efficacy of training in gaining this knowledge. He established a set of beliefs, rituals, temples and priests which was parallel to those of the upper castes. The world-view of his reinterpretation of Hinduism was both enlightening and simple, on the basis of which Izhavas were able to claim a new identity with honour, esteem and self-respect. This movement was basically known as Self-respect Movement.

Further Sri Narayana developed Dharma Paripalana movement among the Izhavas (toddy-tappers) of Kerala. Until 1935, the Izhavas belonged to the schedule castes. They were considered to be untouchables by the clean castes. The Izhavas, who formed about twenty-six per cent of Kerala's total population, suffered from many religious, educational and political disabilities. It was he who gave them a new lease of life. Temple entry movement was organised by him. The Mahar movement in Maharashtra completely rejected Hinduism and adopted its sect which stressed on egalitarianism such as Buddhism.

The Mahars were deemed as an important section of the scheduled castes of Maharashtra constituting about ten per cent of the state's population. They served as village watchmen, messengers, and removers of cattle carcasses. These services were hereditary and were paid for in kind. The Mahars were also weavers, petty traders, carpenters and cultivators. Thus, they occupied, educational and political disabilities. In the third decade of the present century, the Mahars organised themselves under the leadership of Dr. Ambedkar. Dr Ambedkar vacillated between adopting one of two themes of identity to fight against the discriminations imposed by the upper castes—whether to stay within the Hindu fold or to abandon Hinduism altogether. He finally resolved the dilemma in 1956 by accepting Buddhism and abandoning Hinduism which also meant giving up caste. A large number of his followers embraced Buddhism which upheld egalitarian values.

Thus these Backward Class movement did not occur in vacuum. Exploitation, social injustice provided the fertile ground for such movement.

These movement have been dominant in establishing new identities among the Backward Classes, characterized by conflict with the dominant groups.

Because of this new identity, it becomes a threat to the dominant groups since this dominant position socially and economically has been challenged by the new emerging class.

Mandal Commission Report: The Mandal Commission, its chairman as B.P. Mandal was constituted to look into two issues of other Backward Class so as to implement various measures pertaining to reservation of education and jobs.

The main recommendations of Mandal Commission are:

* Socially and educationally backward classes should be accorded 27 per cent reservation of seats in educational institutions, in jobs under the control of Central Government, Public sector and Private sector, receiving financial assistance from the Government in one form or another.
* Candidates belonging to OBCs recruited on the basis of merit in an open competition should not be adjusted against their reservation quota of 27 per cent.
* The above reservations should also be made applicable to promotion quota of all levels.
* Reserved quota remaining unfilled should be carried forward for a period of three years and reserved thereafter.
* Relaxation in the upper age limit for direct recruitment should be extended to the candidates of OBCs in the same manner as done in the case of SCs and STs.
* A roster system for each category of posts should be adopted by the concerned authorities in the same manner as presently done in respect of SC and ST candidates.
* The above scheme of reservation in its toto should be made applicable to all recruitment to public sector undertakings both under the central and state government as also to nationalized banks.
* All private sector undertakings which have received financial assistance from the Government in one form or other should also be obliged to recruit personnel on the aforesaid basis.

* All universities and affiliated colleges should also be covered by the above scheme of reservation.

To give proper effect to these recommendations, it is imperative that adequate statutory provisions are made by the Government to amend the existing enactments rules, procedures, etc. to the extent they are not in consequence with the same.

An intensive and time bound programme of adult education should be launched in selected pockets with high concentration of OBC population. Residential school should be set in these areas for backward class students to provide a climate especially conducive to serious studies. All facilities in these schools including boarding and lodging will have to be provided free of cost to attract students from poor and backward homes.

Seats should be reserved for OBC student in all scientific technical and professional institutions run by Central as well as State Government.

Those states which have already reserved more than 27 per cent seats for OBC students will remain unaffected by this recommendation.

Suitable institutional finance and technical assistance is made available to such members of village vocational communities who want to set up sway scale industries of their own. Similar assistance should also be provided to those OBC candidates who have obtained special vocational training. Some State Government like Karnataka and Andhra Pradesh have already set up separate financial corporations, etc. for OBCs. Separate financial institutions for providing financial and technical assistance shall be established for the backward classes.

All the state government should be directed to enact and implement progressive land legislation to effect structural changes. Certain sections of some occupational communities like Fishermen, Khatives, Banafares, etc. suffer from the stigma of untouchability in some parts of the country. They have been listed as OBCs, by the commission, but their inclusions in the list of SC/ST may be considered by the Governments.

Backward Class Development Corporation have been set up both at the Central and State levels to implement various socio-educational and economic measures for their advancement. A separate Ministry/ Department of OBCs at the centre and states should be created to safeguard their interests.

With a view to giving better representation to certain backward sections it is recommended that areas of concentration may be carved out into separate constituencies at the time of delimitations. At present no Central Assistance is available to the State Government for implementing any welfare measure for other Backward Classes. All development programmes especially designed for Other Backward Classes should be financed by Central Government in the same manner and as to the same extent in the case of the Scheduled Tribes and Scheduled Castes. The entire scheme should be reviewed after twenty years. OBCs should be redivided into two categories *i.e.* Intermediate Backward Class and Depressed Backward Class. The former is awarded 12 per cent and latter is awarded 15 per cent in the OBC reservation scheme. In Chairman, Mandal's opinion Article 15 (4) of the Indian Constitution will not permit such a provision.

The Mandal Commission reviewed (a) Various court judgements with reference to reservation schemes (b) The related debates in various state assemblies and parliament (c) The reservation schemes now in force in various states (d) Opinions of State Government and Central Government in the question answer format (e) Ideas and suggestions from General Public and (f) Reports of the previous Backward Class Commissions set up by the Central government. It also gathered opinions from Central and State Government, VI and VII parliament members, voluntary organizations, social workers, intellectuals and the public.

Awareness among Dalits

Dalits and the social groups occupy the lowest position in the local hierarchy of castes. They are the out caste made up of former 'outcaste' groups of 'ex-untouchables' who form the inner core of poverty, adopted the nomenclature of 'Dalits' following the original usage of the term by Mahatma, Jyotiba Phule (1827-1899) backward caste Maratha social reformer to describe the outcastes and untouchables as the oppressed group.

Dalits existed from the time of Rig Vedas. Purusa Hymn mentions the existence of four castes. The Brahmin was his mouth, of both his arms was the Rajanya (Kshatriya) made, his thighs become the Vaisya, from his feet the Sudra was produced." Thus the origin of the existence of Dalits is attributed to religion. On the basis of the hymn we understand four-fold division of society existed. But many scholars believe that this hymn has been composed at a later time and therefore does not represent Rig Vedic period. But at the same time it is also true that Dalit problem took root at the time the hymn was written. In the Upanishad period, the problem seems to have been crystallized and is becoming deeper and clearer. The Chandogya Upanishad not only refers to the first three upper castes but also compares Chandala (outcaste). They are born against the rule of endogamy. It refers to only three upper castes and fourth caste Sudra was not mentioned. Instead it refers to Chandala.

In Manu Smriti references to mixed castes are made—the Chandalas and how and where they were supposed to live. During this time the negative development of the Dalit problem or state had reached its climax. In the recent years when British ruled India, their situation remained status quo and they followed the policy of non-interference, actively upholding the distinctions in Hindu society. During British period a number of small movements came into existence, who showed concern for the Dalits for various reasons. Even before this, during

Muslim period Bhakthi movement helped the cause of the Dalits particularly in spiritual sphere. This happened through Bhakthi Saivas who belong to Backward Class or they themselves were Dalits. These efforts had little impact on improving the condition of Dalits Mahatama Jyotiba Phule, Dr. Ambedkar, Mahatma Gandhi, E.V.R. of Chennai, Sri Narayana Dharma Paripalan of Kerala and reform movements of Karnataka, and Pant movement in Punjab were few leaders who fought for the Dalit Cause.

Among all the social reformers, Jyotiba Phule's contribution for the cause of Dalit is notable. It was in 1873 that he started Satyashodhak Samaj. He strongly condemned the tyranny of caste system. His revolt was against caste in so far as caste denied ordinary human rights at all. In 1851 he started a primary school for untouchables in Poona. He criticised Manusmriti because it was a stumbling block in the way of social change. Mahatama Phule made efforts to unite all the non-Brahmins and the Dalits and to remain united for their own cause.

The depressed classes were used in place of scheduled caste in British India, and also by the members of various reform movements. But till 1932 the latter expression was used more or less for all kinds of depressed people including the 'untouchables' Until then no effort was made to differentiate it, to define on the basis of religion. In 1932 for the first time the term 'The Depressed Classes' was used for people with an untouchable background. At that time the British Government was also trying to help all the other communities such as Muslims, Christians, etc. which according to them, were not covered under Depressed Classes with special benefits, like separate electorates in the aftermath of independent India.

Religious and legal sanctions against discrimination made the scheduled tribe accessible for political and constitutional rights through positive discrimination.

With the numerical majority the political democratic structure created potential vote banks among the scheduled castes. The Reservation of electoral candidates for parliament and Assembly was the last straw with which all leading political parties dilly dallied for creating fusion and fission among the scheduled caste members. Parallel and vertical caste organizations marked cleavage of social and economic and political between them to usurp power.

The legal and democratic rights, with numerical strength made the homogeneous groups make use of the existing situations. The access to power through political emancipation was easy and principle of hierarchy has been rejected and egalitarian and competitive ideologies prevail and caste consciousness among the Harijans has been consolidated all the more.

But developmental awareness of the Dalits depends much on the personality of their leader.

Table highlights the income levels of the respondents before and after the inception of the VVV club in the villages under study. The income levels of five respondents of Vannampatty before the inception of the club have been Rs. 6,000 and six respondents had incomes above Rs. 6,000. After the inception of the club the income of four respondents remained below Rs. 6,000 and the income of seven respondents [illegible] above Rs. 6,000. In New Ayakudi, the income levels of 41 respondents before its inception was below Rs. 6,000 while a change in the income levels of 14 respondents in the category of above Rs. 6,000.

A comparative picture of the income levels of the respondents of Vannampatty with New Ayakudi before and after the inception of the club reveals that in Vannampatty, though the income after the inception increased, it [illegible] not improve their standards of life. The position in New Ayakudi showed only a slight improvement in income levels. By and large, the programme, though it has not marked any significant development in the income levels of the respondents, generated stability in the income levels.

Change in Income Level

Income Levels (in Rs.)	Vannampatty: Before the Inception of the club	Vannampatty: After the inception of the club	New Ayakudi: Before the inception of the club	New Ayakudi: After the inception of the club
Below 2,000	2	1	14	[illegible]
	(18.18)	(9.09)	(25.46)	(21.82)
2,000-4,000	1	2	20	[illegible]
	(9.10	(18.18)	(18.18)	[illegible]
4,000-6,000	2	1	17	[illegible]
	(18.18)	(9.09)	(30.91)	[illegible]
6,000-8,000	3	4	5	[illegible]
	(27.27)	(36.36)	(9.09)	[illegible]
8,000-above	3	3	9	[illegible]
	(27.27)	(27.28)	(16.36)	[illegible]
	11	11	55	[illegible]
	(100.00)	(100.00)	(100.00)	(100.00)

(Figures in parentheses indicate column percentages)

5

The Tribes

Distinctive features of tribal communities and their geographical spread; problems of tribal communities; land alienation, poverty and indebtedness, health and nutrition, education, tribal development efforts after independence; tribal policy-isolation, assimilation and integration; issues of tribal identity.

Tribal Communities Problem

Alienation of Land: The history of land alienation among the tribes began during British colonialism in India when the British interfered in the tribal region only for the purpose of exploiting the tribal natural resources. Coupled with this, in many places, tribal lands have been occupied by money-lenders, zamindars and traders by advancing them loans etc. Opening of mines in the heart of tribal habitat and even a few factories provided wage labour as well as opportunities for factory employment. But establishment of factories and mines did not always bring increased, more secure and paying employment; on the other hand, destitution and displacement. On the legal fiction that the land not settled belonged to the Government, and shifting cultivation land was traditionally occupied and owned by villagers or clans without specific recognition by the Government—mines could be opened on Government land without compensation and rehabilitation, and even without warning. The fate of those who lost settled lands to factories is not less worse but only differently affected. In Rourkela area, 1231 families were dispossessed of their house-site and agricultural land.

The tribes were promised employment in factories which never happened in reality and the tribes because of their acculturation were inclined to participate in various opportunities and avenues opened for them. But training was denied to them. Funds which was to be invested for tribal development were grabbed by authorities and it was never utilised for their welfare, the Madras Agency Tracts Interest and Land Transfer Act, 1919 was meant to protect the aboriginal's land from alienation to non-tribal. But despite these laws, the tribals were made deprived of their land. Thus the national policy was implemented in order to look into the problem of tribal land alienation.

In the beginning it was believed that the forests were under the administrative control of the Rajas' or estates under whose jurisdiction the area came. For all practical purposes, the tribal population inhabiting the jungle area were free to make independent use of the forest resources. After the British came to power, the Forest Policy of the British Government was more inclined towards commercial considerations rather than human. Some forests were declared as reserved ones, where only authorised contractors were allowed to cut the timber, and the forest-dwellers were kept isolated deliberately within their habitat without any effort to ameliorate their economic and educational standards. The expansion of railway in India and in England heavily devastated the forest resources in India. The Government started reserving teak, sal and deodar forests for the manufacture of railway sleepers. The Indian

Forest Act of 1855 was enacted, asserted state monopoly right over the forests. The forest dwellers were however free to use the forest produce, subject to an annual payment of fixed rent. The post-independence forest policy in India essentially derives its root from the policies of 1865 and 1878. No doubt, it was amended several times till the National Forest Policy of 1952.

The Committee on Forests and Tribals in India, with Prof. B.K. Roy Burman as its chairman, observed that the individual tribal, the local tribal community and the national interest should be regarded as the three corners of a triangular forest policy" and hence, there should be ample provisions in the National Forest Policy to implement comprehensive plans for an integrated development of the tribals and the forest on equal footing, so that commercial and humanitarian aspects of the policy go side by side.

Forest land and its resources provide the best means of livelihood for the tribal people and many tribes including the women engage in agriculture, food gathering and hunting, they are heavily dependent on the products of the forest. Therefore when outsiders exploit the tribal's land and its resources, the natural life cycle of tribal ecology and the tribal life is greatly disturbed.

Economic Backwardness and Indebtedness: Majority tribes live under poverty line. The tribes follow many simple occupations based on simple technology. Most of their occupation falls into the primary occupations such as hunting, gathering, agriculture. The technology they use for these purposes belong to the most primitive kind. There is no profit and surplus making in such economy. Hence their per capita income is very meager, much lesser than the Indian average. Most of them live under abject poverty and are in debt in the hands of local money-lenders and Zamindars. In order to repay the debt, they often mortgage or sell their land to the money-lenders. Indebtedness is almost inevitable since heavy interest is to be paid to these money-lenders.

The demands of the supernatural, sometimes too insistent to be neglected, especially in times of family crisis, and those of the creditors quite out of proportion to the principal advanced and the demands of the petty officials, not to speak of those of the close relatives, do not leave much for the household after what was saved from the wild animals, rats and weeds. Even then festivals and occasional celebrations in honour of guests eat heavily into their lean resources.

The local creditors have no hesitation in advancing loans, for not only heavy compound interest, but also pre-emptive rights to purchase the standing crops at rock-bottom prices as their privilege. However pressing the claims of others may be, the creditor knows that the Adivasi will honour his word. And the Adivasi knowing no arithmetic always leaves a comfortable arrear in favour of the creditor.

Thus the vicious circle becomes inescapable. One way to break this vicious circle was to go for alternate employment, another to sell land and repay the outstanding debt as the creditors demanded, and the third way led to virtual serfdom known as debt bondage or bonded labur. This is a system of labour whereby "a person on receiving some advance in money or kind engages himself to be a labourer of his creditor for agricultural and domestic purposes as long as the loan together with the interest remains unpaid".

In 1962, a study by the Assistant Commissioner for Scheduled Tribes and Castes, showed that in Koraput district of Orissa, a few persons with, more than 15 acres of agricultural land had become bonded labourers with a maximum advance of Rs. 2000 taken. Bonded labour had become almost a way of life, so much that even tribal money-lenders engaged bonded labourers from among their fellow-tribals. In a study it was found out that most frequent and important factor in becoming a bonded labourer was the repayment of parental debts. At the time of meeting demands of life crisis and of various life cycle related ceremonies such as death, birth, initiation ceremony, meeting food scarcity, crop failures, payment of loans from another creditor, purchasing land and cattle, etc., are accountable for the tribal people's indebtedness to local money-lenders. When they fail to pay them back, their land is handed over to those money-lenders and in turn they become the bonded labourers of these local exploiters. Thus a tribe is born indebted and dies indebted. It is the most unfortunate and sad scene. The indebtedness of tribals multiplied at an exorbitant rate through the cunning ways of the Sahukars, often resulting in the transfer of tribal lands to the money-lenders. Indebtedness eroded the economic base of the tribal family, even as the very reason for indebtedness was the erosion of land settlement pattern.

The shifting cultivation assured to the tribals was snatched away, and thus they were bound to lose their land and access to land. Consequent erosion of their earning power led them to seek loans from the money lending communities. Illiterate tribals were exploited. A study points out that 61 per cent of the households in tribal areas are debtors and the incidence of debt is very high in the case of landless households. From the total loans only one-fourth of the amount is advanced by the officials and governmental agencies.

The study also points out that 67 per cent of loans are used for consumption purposes. The tribals find it difficult to get out of the debt traps. Their wages are so low that they cannot clear off their debts. The studies on the Minimum Wage Policy also suggest that while laws exist in the statue books, they are not even enforced. The low wages account for their poor standards of living, they cannot afford even their minimum needs like food, health and education.

Problems of Health Care

The normal health of the tribal people cannot be said to be very bad but they become chronic after repeated infections.

They suffer from many diseases but water borne diseases happen to be the worst threatening one due to poor drinking water supply. Water is available for the tribes in plenty but is highly dirty and contaminated one. Consequent upon these, they get infection from various water borne diseases such as diarrhoea, dysentry, cholera, tapeworms, etc.

Tribal people suffer from other diseases due to deficiency in minerals and other good nutrients. These problems differ from region to region for example the tribes in the Himalayan region, suffer from goitre due to lack of iodine. Some of the common diseases among the tribes are tuberculosis. Yaws is a common disease among the Andhra Pradesh tribes. Leprosy is also a common problem among the tribes in India.

Study, on fertility and mortality trends among the tribal population of India have been found to be fragmentary and isolated. Limited studies are available on infant mortality and hardly any study is available on maternal mortality among the tribal population. Basu and Jindal (1990) studied in depth a primitive tribal group, that is, Kutiya Kondhs of Tumdibandha Block of Phulbani district, Orissa. The average age of menarche among Kutiya was found to be 14.5 years. It was observed that the average number of pregnancies per month was 5.09 and 3.89 respectively among completed and incomplete mothers of reproductive life cycles.

Infants mortality was found to be very high, that is, 179.75/1000. The fertility record of Kutiya Kondh mothers in various age groups indicate a total fertility of 5 estimated on an average in the age group of 45-49.

Basu and Kshatriya (1992) studied the fertility and mortality trend among the Dudh Kharia of Sundergarh district, Orissa. They reported that the estimated total fertility, crude birth rate, crude death rate and infant mortality rate are 5.39, 38.5, 11.80 and 102.4 respectively. All these demographic parameters show higher value than the Indian national population level according to 1981 census but these are similar with other Indian tribal populations.

The health and nutrition problems of the vast tribal population of India are as varied as the tribal groups themselves who present a bewildering diversity and variety in their socio-economic, socio-cultural and ecological settings. The nutritional problems of different tribal communities located at various stages of development are full of obscurities and very little scientific information on dietary habits and nutrition status are available due to lack of systematic and comprehensive research investigations. Malnutrition is common and has greatly affected the general physique of the tribals. Malnutrition lowers the ability to resist infection, leads to chronic illness and in the post-wearing period leads to permanent brain impairment.

Maternal malnutrition which is quite common among the tribal women is also a serious health problem.

The nutritional status of pregnant women directly influence their reproductive performance and the birth weight of their children, a factor that is crucial to an infant's chances of survival and to its subsequent growth and development. Nutrition also affects lactation and breast feeding which are key elements in the health of infants and young children and a contributory factor in birth spacing.

Tribal diet are generally grossly deficient in calcium, vitamin A, vitamin C riboflavin and animal protein. Diets of South Indian tribes, in general and of Kerala in particular are grossly deficient even in respect of calories and total protein. A high incidence of malnutrition was observed (Ali, 1980, Basu et al, 1990 Mahapatra and Das, 1989) in some primitive tribal groups in Phulbani, Koraput and Sundergarh districts of Orissa and also among Bhil, Garasin of Rajasthan, Radar, Rabri and Charan of Gujarat and Benda of Orissa (Haque, 1990). Studies of tribal communities in Orissa conducted by Ali (1982) have found that an ecological imbalance caused by rapid deforestation has resulted not only in-depleting food resources, but in prolonged droughts, adding to hunger and starvation of the tribes.

Sexually transmitted diseases are also popular diseases in tribal areas. VDRL is a very sensitive test to diagnose if a person was suffering from syphilis or not. VDRL was found to be positive in 17.12 per cent cases (reactive in dilution of 1:8 or more) of polyandrous Jaunsaris of Chakrata, Dehradun. Out of 17 per cent, 9.92 per cent was found among males and 7.19 per cent among females. Among the Santhals of Mayurbhanj district, Orissa, 8.90 per cent cases (reactive in dilution of 1:8 or more) of VDRL were observed, of which 4.99 per cent were females and 3.91 per cent were males (Basu et. al, 1993).

The prevalence of STD was also reported to be high in the polyandrous Toda tribal group of Nilgiri hills. While conducting morbidity studies among the Kondha tribe of Phulani district, Orissa, Swain et. al,(1990) found syphilis (10 per cent) in Desia Kondhs (reactive in dilution 1:8 or more) whereas it was not diagnosed among primitive Kutia Kondh tribal groups. The presence of STD is also reported among Andamanese, tribal groups of Madhya Pradesh, Rajasthan, Mysore, Laccadive and Minicoy islands.

Because of the extensive felling of trees by vested interest, the distances between the villages and the forest areas have increased, forcing the tribal women to walk longer distances in search of minor forest produce and firewood. In this rapidly changing milieu, tribal are confronted with an extraordinary workload. Given this additional workload, even women in advanced stages of pregnancy are required to work in the agricultural field or walk long distances to collect fuel and minor forest provides. The overstrain on tribal women however is not adequately compensated due to the non-availability of minor forest produce and decrease in foodgrain production.

To malnutrition and additional workload, one has to add

the destruction of traditional herbs through deforestation and the lack of access of the tribals to modern medicine with the increasing ecological imbalance, results in diseases such as TB, stomach disorders and often malaria (Menon, 1987).

Bearing of Child and Maternal Mortality: Child bearing imposes additional health problems on women-physically, psychologically and socially. The complication of health and of childbirth and of illegally induced abortions in areas where environmental and health conditions are adverse, result in large numbers of female deaths. Poor nutritional status and its concomitant problems of poor body weight, and height, poor weight pregnancy, low hemoglobin levels, is one of the primary underlying causes of maternal poverty in India.

Maternal and child health care practices have been found to be largely neglected in various tribal areas. From the inception of pregnancy to its termination, no specific nutritional diet is consumed by women. On the other hand, some pregnant tribal women reduced their food intake because of simple fear of recurrent vomiting and with the belief that the baby may remain small and the delivery may be easier.

The consumption of calcium and vitamins during pregnancy is poor. "The habit of taking alcohol during pregnancy has been found to be usual in tribal women and almost all of them continue regular activities including hard labour during advanced pregnancy. More than 90 per cent of deliveries are conducted at home attended by elderly ladies of the household. No precautions are observed at the time of conducting deliveries which resulted in an increased susceptibility to various infections. Further they are alien to outside nurses and doctors and they have their own way of diagnosis and cure.

From all the aforementioned discussion on health and nutrition and often such related issues the speedy spread of health education among the tribals is very crucial.

Most tribes are illiterate. Therefore, audio-visual methods may be adopted to put across to them the basic principles of health and sanitation. For raising the standard of health and nutritional facilities of the tribals, cooperative endeavour is necessary among the states, the centre, the medical personnels and non-governmental organisations with community participation.

Education on Rules

Educationally the tribal people are at different levels of development but, overall, the formal education has made very little impact on tribal groups.

Before the year 1950, the Indian government had no direct programme for direct tribal education. With the adoption of the constitution and through the provision of reservation policy the government has become responsible for tribal education.

The census figures of 1931 disclosed that only 0.7 per cent of the tribal population were literate, it rose to 32.60 per cent in 1991 against 52.5 per cent for the entire country so the total picture of tribal education is not very encouraging.

Since education is probably the most effective instrument for ensuring equality of opportunity the tribes lag far behind others due to lack of education.

The reasons for this state of affairs are:

Social Reason: Formal education has not been necessary for the members of tribal society to discharge their social obligations. Hence they should be prepared to accept education. Superstitions and myths play an important role in rejecting education among the tribes for example some tribal groups believe that their gods shall be angry if they send their children to schools run by outsiders.

Economic Reason: Most tribes live in abject poverty, it also accounts for their lack of interest in education that it is not easy for them to send their children to schools. According to the present education system any economic benefit a tribal child can bring to his family is after 10 years of schooling, the parents have neither the patience nor the foresight to wait for such a long period.

Absence of Interest in Formal Education: The tribal children cannot follow the same syllabus and curriculum taught at other institutions. They have no taste for this kind of education since their socialisation and exposure has been done in different environment. Instead of teaching them about formal syllabus they should be taught about their local cultures, folklore, music, art and the environment they are dwelling in.

Suitable Teacher: Lack of suitable teacher is one reason why many tribal children fail to go to schools. Most teachers approach tribal people with a sense of superiority and treat them as savage and uncivilized and hence fail to establish proper rapport with the tribal students, so there is a gulf between tribal students and teachers.

Lack of facilities, infrastructure, lack of staff, ecological condition, technical facilities could be other factors accountable for low rate of tribal education.

Aspects of Tribal Identity

A tribe is an endogamous group having a common territory, possessing a common dialect with distinct political, economic and religious organisation occupying particular geographical distribution. However such characterisation of tribes is an oversimplified view specially so in the context of various tribals assimilation and acculrisation.

A number of tribal groups are recognised by the government and they are the scheduled tribes. There are instances where some tribal communities wanted to identify themselves with the dominant group, the Hindus, in a particular period and at a different period, wanted to assert their tribal identity. Approaches to tribal related issues have not been a uniform one. The British adopted the assimilation and segregation method simultaneously. These approaches were followed in the early period of post independence period.

India has 427 "Scheduled" Tribes, each unique in its own right. Constituting about 7 per cent of the country's population, they ostensibly are a major segment of the Indian social fabric. The district self-conceptualisation of tribals in the context of natural, social and historical process is referred to as tribal consciousness, mutual knowledge in distinguishing groups, self from the other. A tribe is regarded as self-sufficient, unstratified, and culturally homogenous, in a universal perspective. When taking into account the dynamics of persistence and change in tribal identities, one notices a significant shift from the earlier view of tribe as a simplistic social formation in the evolutionary scheme to the new approach of teaching tribe as a district to social formation with elements of perpetuity in diverse technological contexts.

The political commitment to uplift the tribals through the positive discrimination policy of the government has geared the tribes to assert their identity.

Voget has also noted a situation, reformative naturism, which he has defined as a relatively conscious attempt on the part of a subordinate group to attain a personal and social integration through selective rejection, modification and synthesis of both traditional and alien cultural components. Various boundary maintaining mechanisms by smailer community has also been noted elsewhere when there is a change of absorption of a minor group within a major or dominant cultural milieu. This process is obviously aimed at maintaining self-identity or group solidarity which usually takes place at a much later stage after the initial contact or exposure with the dominant culture.

Different tribal movements can be said to centre around

the problem of their identity whether tribal community wanted to identity itself with the dominant wider Hindu social system or wanted to maintain group solidarity and identity by preserving its traditional culture. In the latter process there may even by a conscious symbolic revival of typical traditional tribal culture, demand for a separate state, etc. Rise of tribal consciousness, tribal regionalism, frontier tribalism, etc. gained currency after the movements in North East Frontier areas. Tribal regionalism, political in nature, has been said to be a struggle for identity against alienation from basic sources, *viz.*, land, forests, and aspiration for preservation of traditional culture. Of late, the movement in Tripura led by TUJS and Bodoland in Assam, Jharkhand, Gorkhaland movements have transcended that stage of aspiration limited in culture. The newly emerged elites in these regions prefer to have a share in the power structure.

The regional leaders who improvise or manipulate identity symbols to mobilise group sentiment, could rarely assess the likely responses of the political authorities and the dominant social groups. As the movement proceeds and identity assertions tend to transform the concerned ethic to a political conflict group, the leadership and the group have to adopt modern skills and mobilise resources. In the process, they become participants in modernization and get involved in the democratic power game. In both Gorkhaland and Jharkhand, such democratization has been evident.

The Gorkhaland agitation gained momentum on issues such as Indo-Nepal treaty, inclusion of Nepalese language in the eighth schedule of Indian Constitution and other sundry economic factors. The main thrust was on assertion of Indian Nepalese identity through citizenship demand. In the Gorkhaland Accord (1988) enacting the establishment of Gorkha Hill Development Council, both the main issues remained untouched. The identity problem was said to have been solved by putting the word 'Gorkha' in the Council.

According to Bajni Kothan, ethnicity is a response to the excesses of the modern western project of shaping the whole of humanity around three pivots of world capitalism—the state system, world culture based on modern technology, world information order and universalising education system. The nonparty political movement at the grass root levels, and awakening of the ordinary people would form the new process, the establishment of human governance. Together with social movements and citizens' action ethnicity provides security and democracy able to translate into real security and democracy for all, including the most marginalised, even though these could be a far dream for all the tribal population in this country.

Unity in Society

Distinctive features of tribal communities, tribes and castes; acculturation and integration.

Classification of India Tribe: Due to multiplicity of factors and complexity of problems involved, it is not very easy to classify the Indian tribes into different groups. However, the Commissioner for Scheduled Castes and Scheduled Tribes took up the task and investigated the possibility of adopting classification criteria. Keeping this aim in view the state governments were asked to suggest the characteristics which seemed to them most suitable in distinguishing the so-called "aboriginal" groups from the rest of the population.

The Assam government suggested descent from Mongoloid stock, affiliation with Tibeto-Burman linguistic groups and the existence of social organization of the village clan type as the major characteristics. The erstwhile Bombay government considered residence in forest areas as the basic criterion while for the Madhya Pradesh Government tribal origin, speaking tribal languages and residence in forests areas, were important criteria. Similarly, the governments of Madras, Orissa, Andhra,

Mysore, Travancore, etc., suggested various linguistic, geographical, economic and social factors as indicators.

Taking the above mentioned characteristics into consideration the tribes of India may be classified on the basis of their (a) territorial distribution, (b) linguistic affiliation, (c) physical and racial characteristics, (d) occupation or economy, (e) cultural contact and (f) religious beliefs.

Physical Classification

Looking at the physical map of India, and the distribution of tribal population we find that both geography as well as tribal demography permit a regional grouping and a zonal classification. B.S.Guha has classified Indian tribes into three zones:

(i) The north and north-eastern zone

(ii) The central or the middle zone

(iii) The southern zone

The North and the North-eastern Zone: The northern and north-eastern zones consist of the sub-Himalayan region and the mountain valleys of the eastern frontiers of India. The tribal people of Assam, Manipur and Tripura may be included in the eastern part of this geographical zone while in the northern part are included the tribals of eastern Kashmir, eastern Punjab, Himachal Pradesh and northern Uttar Pradesh.

Some of the important tribes living between Assam and Tibet are Aka, Dafla, Miri, Gurung and the Apanani on the west of the Subansiri river. The Mishmi tribes live in the high ranges between the Debong and Lohit rivers. Further east are found the Khamti and the Singpho and beyond them are the different Naga tribes. South of the Naga hills running through the states of Manipur, Tripura and the Chittagong hill tracts live the Kuki, the Lushai, the Khasi and the Garo (now the inhabitants of the newly carved Meghalaya state). In the sub-Himalayan region of Sikkim and the northern parts of

Darjeeling, there are a number of primitive tribes, Lepcha being the best known of them. The Himalayan region of Uttar Pradesh also contains some important tribes like Tharu, Bhoksa, Jounsari (Khasa), Bhotia, Raji, etc.

The entire geographical zone, though quite large in area, does not contain dense population. As a result of geographical similarities most of the tribes of this zone are engaged in either terrace cultivation or *Jhum* (shifting) cultivation and are steeped in poverty and economic backwardness.

Middle Zone

This zone consists of plateaus and mountainous belt between the Indo-Gangetic plain to the north and roughly the Krishna river to the south and this is separated from the north-eastern zone by the gap between the Garo hills and the Rajmahal hills. In this zone we have another massing of tribal peoples in Madhya Pradesh with extensions in Uttar Pradesh, Madhya Bharat, southern Rajasthan, northern Maharashtra, Bihar and Orissa. Northern Rajasthan, southern Maharashtra and Bastar from the peripheral areas of the zone.

The important tribes inhabiting this zone are the Savara, Gadaba and Borido of the Ganjam district; the Juang, Kharia, Khond Bhumji and the Bhiya of the Orissa hills. In the plateau of Chotanagpur live the Munda, the Santhal, the Oraon, the Ho and the Birhor. Further west along the Vindhya ranges live the Katkari, Kol and the Bhil the Gond forms the largest groups and occupy what is known as the 'Gondwan land, On both sides of the Satpuras and around the Maikal hills are found similar tribes like the Koraku, the Agaria, the Pardhan and the Baiga. In the hills of Bastar live some of the most colourful of these tribes like the Muria, the Hill Muriya of the Abhujmar hills and the Bison-horn Maria of the Indravati valley. Most of the tribes of this zone practise shifting cultivation as means of their livelihood but the Oraon, Santhal, Munda and Gond have learnt plough cultivation as a result of their cultural companies with the neighbouring rural populations.

Zone in Southern Area

This zone consists of that part of the southern India which falls south of the river Krishna stretching from Wynad to Cape Camorin. Andhra Pradesh, Karnataka, Coorg, Travancore, Cochin, Tamil Nadu, etc., are included in this zone. Beginning from the northeast of this zone, the Chenchu occupy the area of the Nallaimallais hills across the Krishna and into the erstwhile Hyderabad state. Along the Western Ghats from the Loraga of South Kanara, the Yeruva and the Toda live on the lower slopes of Coorg hills while the Irula, Paniyan and the Kurumba inhabit Wynad area.

The most primitive of Indian aboriginals such as Kadar, Kanikkar, Malvadan, Malakuravan, etc., inhabit the dense forest along the ranges of Cochin and Travancore. They are also included among some of the most economically backward communities of the world. Except Toda, Badaga and Kota who live in Nilgiri hills most of the tribal groups of this zone depend upon hunting and fishing for food gathering.

Although Guha has not included the inhabitants of Andaman Nicobar Islands in any of these zones and has skipped their description, yet these tribal people may be said to constitute a fourth zone. The main tribes living in this zone are the Jarwa. Onge, North Sentinelese, Andamanese and Nicobari. Thus separated from the main body of India's primitive tribes, they are ethnically close to the south Indian tribes.

Classification of Languages

At present people of India may be divided into four speech families *viz.*, the Indo-European (Aryan), the Dravidian, the Austric (Kolor Munda) and the Tibeto-Chinese (Sino-Tibetan). D.N.Majumdar (1955) opines that "so far as the tribal people are concerned the Aryan speech comes into the picture only as a consequence of cultural contract since almost all of our tribal people have pre-Aryan or non-Aryan racial affinities and origins". Most of the scholars, therefore, are of the view that the tribal people of India may be classified chiefly into three speech families: (1) Dravidian, (2) Austric, and (3) Tibeto-Chinese.

The tribal people speaking the languages falling under Dravidian speech family inhabit the middle and southern India. The most developed languages of Dravidian family are Tamil, Telugu, Kannada and Malayalam. Gonds occupy the chief place among the tribal speeches derived from Dravidian family and it is spoken widely by the Gond tribals who are scattered from Madhya Pradesh to Andhra Pradesh. It has no literature but considering the numerical strength of its speakers, it has been assigned a very important place in the realm of tribal languages. Another important language of this group is Koi which is spoken by the Kandh of Orissa, Oraon of Chotanagpur and Malto of Rajmahal hills. The speeches of Toda, Paliya, Chenchu, Irula and Kadar are also included in the Dravidian family.

The Austric family of speeches is also known as Munda speech family. Max Muller was the first scholar who distinguished it from Dravidian speech family and it is he who assigned the term Munda speech family to this group. Speeches of this family are spoken mainly by the tribals of Chotanagpur area but these are also in vogue, to a lesser extent, in some parts of Madhya Pradesh, Orissa, West Bengal, Madras and Terai region of Himalayas stretching from Bihar to Shimla hills. The Santhali speech of Bengal, Bihar and Orissa, Mundari, Ho, Khana, Bhumij and some other speeches of Bihar are also included in this family.

Tibeto-Chinese speeches are spoken most by the tribals of Mongol racial stock. This family is divided into two branches (i) Tibeto-Burman, and (ii) Siamese-Chinese, the tribals of

Assam, Meghalaya and other parts of the north east India speak one or the other speeches of this family.

Classification of Races

D.N.Majumdar (1955) has very rightly described the complexity of the problem of classifying the tribal people of India on the basis of racial affinities when he says that fixing the racial origins or affinities of the tribal communities of India is one of the most complicated tasks that has had to be faced by the Indian anthropologists. There is practically no direct evidence of those ethnic stocks who inhabited different parts of India in prehistoric times. The available knowledge about the racial composition of India in historic times is equally scanty. Therefore, all historical reconstructions regarding the racial history of India have to be based on conjecture.

The first scientific racial classification of India was attempted by Sir Herbert Risely. He published his findings in 1915 in the book *The peoples of India.* He classifies the entire Indian population into seven racial types:

(i) Turko-Iranian
(ii) Indo-Aryan
(iii) Scytho-Dravidian
(iv) Aryo-Dravidian
(v) Mongolo-Dravidian
(vi) Mongoloid
(vii) Dravidian

These seven types may be reduced to three basic types *viz,* the Dravidian, the Mongolian and the Indo-Aryan. Significantly, he gave no separate classificatory scheme for the 'aboriginals' of India.

The latest racial classification of Indian people are those made by 'Hutton, Guha and Majumdar. Guha lists six main races, with nine sub-types:

1. The Negrito
2. The Proto-Australoid
3. The Mongoloid:
   (i) Palaeo-Mongoloids
      (a) Long headed
      (b) Broad headed
4. The Mediterranean:
   (i) Palaeo-Mediterranean
   (ii) Mediterranean
   (iii) Oriental type
5. The Western Brachycephals
   (i) Alpinoid
   (ii) Dinaric
   (iii) Armenoid
6. The Nordic

The ancestry of the present tribal population of India is traced chiefly to the first three types: Negrito, Proto-Australoid and Mongoloid.

The tribals of the hills of Cochin and Travancore such as Kadar, Irula. Paliyan, etc., Angami Naga of Assam and the tribals of Rajmahal hills of western Bihar are included in Negrito racial type which exhibits short stature, black skin colour, black woolly hair, thick lips and broad nose.

The Proto-Australoid racial type exhibits short to medium stature, long and high head, broad and small face and small flattened nose. Most of the middle or central Indian tribals come within this racial type but some south Indian tribes like Chenchu, Bhill, etc. also exhibit the racial characteristics of this type. As far as the Mongoloid racial stock is concerned most of the tribes of north-east India are included in this racial type and exhibit yellowish skin colour, straight and dark hair, flat nose, prominent cheek bones and almond shaped eyes with epicanthic fold. The Naga, Chakma, Lepcha, etc. are some of the important tribes of this racial group. Despite the above mentioned scheme of racial classification, racially the tribes of India cannot be put strictly under any particular type or category, India having been the "melting pot of races" (Majumdaribidi). The generalized types, referred to above, do not account for all the tribes. Thus the Todas of Nilgiri Hills, for just an example, are without a racial label as yet. Serological and linguistic researches are being conducted but these have yet to reveal any new aspect of the racial composition of tribal India.

Classification based on Economy

The Economic classification of Adam Smith and the more recent classifications of Thurnwald and Herskovits have been applied throughout the world in classifying tribes on the basis of their economic life. The scheme presented by Thurnwald is taken as most acceptable in the Indian context and it is as follows:

1. Homogeneous communities of men as hunters and trappers, women as collectors—the Kadar, the Chenchu, the Kharia, and the Korwa are some of the Indian tribes falling into this category.
2. Homogeneous communities of hunters, trappers and agriculturists the Kamar, the Baiga and Birhor are examples of this type from tribal India.
3. Graded society of hunters, trappers, agriculturists and artisans-most of the Indian tribes fall under this category. The Chero and the Aganya among so many others, are famous as artisans.
4. The herdsmen-the Toda and some sections of the great Bhil tribe furnish classic examples in India.
5. Homogeneous hunters and herdsmen-this category is not represented among Indian tribes. The Todas do not hunt, nor do they catch fish or birds.

6. Ethnically stratified cattle breeders and traders—the Bhotiyas of the sub-Himalayan region of Uttar Pradesh breed yaks and are itinerant traders.
7. Socially graded herdsmen with hunting, agricultural and artisan population.

Majumdar opines that such a classification, though useful, does not help much because the purpose herein, in attempting a classification, is mainly to indicate the nature of economic difficulties experienced by the tribal communities.

Taking mainly technological achievements into consideration, a more lucid and clear-cut classification on the basis of the conditions of economic life may be attempted.

1. Tribes hunting in forests.
2. Tribes engaged in hilly cultivation (shifting or slash-and-burn cultivation).
3. Tribes engaged in cultivation on levelled (plain) land.
4. Simple artisan tribes.
5. Pastoral tribes.
6. Tribes living as folk artists.
7. Agricultural and non-agricultural labour oriented tribes.
8. Tribes engaged in service and trade.

Those tribes who live by hunting in forests earn their livelihood through collection of edible roots and fruits, hunting and fishing. This class of tribes is found mostly in southern India. The Chenchu and Chandi of Andhra Pradesh, Kadar, Malapatram and Kurumba from Kerala and Paliyan of Tamil Nadu and Onge, Jarwa, Senegaleses and Nicobarse of Andaman and Nicobar Islands are some of the important tribes living in southern zone. The Raji of Uttar Pradesh, Hill Garo of Meghalaya, Birhor, Korwa and Hill Kharia of Chotanagpur and Juang of Orissa are also some of the notable examples of this class. Although some groups of these tribes are slowly learning cultivation yet their cultural-ethos is still basically of a hunting-gathering type.

A vast chunk of Indian tribes is engaged in shifting cultivation on hilly or mountainous tracts of north-eastern and middle or central India. This mode of cultivation is different from the conventional settled cultivation. Under this system bushes and trees are slashed and burnt. Thereafter seeds are scattered on the ashes and the rest is left to nature.

Almost all the tribes of Assam, Meghalaya, Arunachal Pradesh, Mizoram, Manipur and Tripura produced their crops through this mode of cultivation. Some tribes of Orissa and Gond and Baiga of Madhya Pradesh are also engaged in this mode of cultivation.

Due to intimate contacts with the civilized groups, most of the Indian tribes have taken to settled agriculture on plain land as means of their livelihood. Their technique and mode of cultivation are the same as those of other peasant groups and they also use bullocks, plough and other common implements of agriculture, but most of their land is unirrigated and hence they are often seen to be victims of vagaries of nature. Besides their total dependence on rains, they have to rest content with low and meagre yields because of absence of other agricultural inputs like fertilizers; high yielding varieties of food-grains, pesticides, etc. Among the numerically big tribes, Oraon, Munda, Ho and Santhals are successful cultivators.

Some of the Indian tribes earn their livelihood through cottage industries. They are engaged in basket and mat making, weaving, blacksmith, etc., and supplement the needs of their neighbouring tribal and non-tribal societies. The Gujjar of Kashmir, and Kinnauri of Himachal Pradesh work on wood. Asure of Bihar and Agariya of Madhya Pradesh are proficient in iron smelting, the Kolam of Maharashtra are traditional mat weavers and the Irula of Tamil Nadu make beautiful mats and baskets on bamboo.

Totally pastoral tribes are few in number but Toda of Nilgiri hills, Gaddi and Bakrawal of Himachal Pradesh, Nageshia of Madhya Pradesh, Maldhan of Gujarat and some other tribes of northern and southern India are notable examples of this class of tribes. It is also worth mentioning that not all the pastoral tribes trade in milk. Some of them rear the cattle like sheep and goats for selling them in the market.

Another class of tribes earn their livelihood by performing dances, acrobatics, snake charming, etc., and hence they may be termed as 'folklorist'. The *Nut and Spares* of Uttar Pradesh are good examples of this category. The Mundupptu of Orissa are expert acrobats, the Kota of Tamil Nadu are snake charmers, some groups of Gonds of Madhya Pradesh are tattooers and dancers and some other tribes of eastern India and southern India may also be put in this category.

Among the tribes engaged in agricultural labour are those which are traditionally agriculturists but due to their landlessness they work as agricultural labour on other's land. According to a conservative estimate about one-fifth of the total tribal population is engaged in agriculture as wage earners. Non-agricultural tribal labour force includes those tribes who are working in local factories and mines of Bihar, Orissa and Bengal and tea plantation of Assam and neighbouring areas.

A comparatively small number of tribal people are engaged in government and semi-government jobs as a result of the application of constitutional provisions. Among such tribes are those of Meghalaya, Mizoram and Nagaland on the north eastern fringe of the country and mainly Christian tribals of Chotanagpur.

Classification of Cultural Contacts

Indian tribes can also be classified according to their cultural distance from the rural-urban groups. Majumdar (1976) opines that this comparative approach is the most useful in evolving a plan of rehabilitation because it focuses our attention on those problems of tribal India which are the outcome of haphazard contact with, or the isolation of these tribes from the rural-urban groups. In the fifties Varrier Elwin floated a well demarcated classification. He described four types of aboriginals:

(i) those who are most primitive, live a joint communal life and cultivate with axes;

(ii) those who, though equally attached to their solitude and ancient traditions, are more individualistic, less occupied with axe cultivation, more used to outside life and generally less simple and honest than the first category;

(iii) those, the most numerous, who under external influence are already on the way out by the loss of their tribal culture, religion, and social organization; and

(iv) the tribes like the Bhils and the Naga who are said to be representatives of the old aristocracy of the country, who retain much of their original tribal life and who have won the battle of cultural contact.

Majumdar has aptly termed Elwin's classification as 'crusader's manifesto. He further maintains that though Elwin's classification helps in presenting the contemporary picture of the culture crisis in tribal India but as a basis for a programme of rehabilitation, it is unacceptable. He moves on to present his own scheme of classification. According to him, the tribal cultures fall into three groups:

(i) those who are culturally most distant from the rural-urban groups; that is, more or less out of contact;

(ii) those who are under the influence of the culture of rural-urban groups and have developed discomforts and problems consequently,

(iii) those who, though in contact with rural-urban groups, have not suffered thereof, or have turned the corner and do not suffer any more, though they may have in the past, because they have now got acculturated into rural or urban culture.

Majumdar disagrees with Elwin that every contact with civilized world brings misery to the tribals. He takes the stand that our goal should be to "take ahead all these three types of tribal communities and establish, under planned conditions, healthy and creative contacts between them and the rural-urban groups". The Indian Conference of Social Work (1952) appointed a Tribal Welfare Committee which had suggested the following classification:

(i) Tribal communities,
(ii) Semi-tribal communities,
(iii) Acculturated tribal communities, and
(iv) Totally assimilated tribes.

Classification of Religious Beliefs

The major religious of India have variably influenced various tribal religions and pantheons and only those tribal communities still maintain their native religious beliefs with purity who are leading an almost isolated social existence in dense forests. On the basis of the census data of 1961 and 1971, the tribes may be classified into the following religions:

(i) Hinduism
(ii) Christianity
(iii) Buddhism
(iv) Islam
(v) Jainism
(vi) Other religions

Among the above mentioned religions, the influence of Hindu religion on the tribes is tremendous and almost 90 per cent of tribals follow Hindu religion in one form or the other. Those who have embraced Christianity are also quite considerable in number and about six per cent are under the 'shadow of the cross' but those following Buddhism, Islam or Jainism are negligible in number. One important point which is to be kept in mind in this context is that even those tribes who have embraced any of the above mentioned major religions have not necessarily shed their local tribal beliefs and rituals and many of them are found to be practicising their traditional faith alongwith their newly acquired faith.

When we view this situation in the geographical perspective we see that barring the tribes inhabiting the islands falling under bay of Bengal and Arabian Sea, most of the tribes of South India alongwith the tribes of Western India and Central India are more or less Hindu in faith. Christianity has made tremendous headway among most of the tribals of north-eastern India and more than 90 per cent of the population of Nagaland and Mizoram follow Christianity.

In Central India, some major tribes of Chotanagpur also follow Christianity and notable among these are Oraon, Munda and Ho. The tribes following Islam are mostly scattered in Lakshdweep, Himachal Pradesh, West Bengal, Maharashtra and Jammu and Kashmir. Among such tribes about 98 per cent of the total tribal population of Lakshdweep, Minicoy and Amindivi Islands are followers of Islam. Buddhism among Indian tribes is represented mainly by some tribal groups of Arunachal Pradesh.

Characteristics Tribal Communities: The following characteristics of the tribe are evident from its various definitions:

Common Topography: The tribe inhabits and remains within a definite and common topography. In the absence of a common topography the tribe would also lose its other characteristic features as community sentiments, common language, etc. For this reason a common habitat is essential for a tribe.

Consciousness of Unity: But a group of people living in a particular geographical area cannot be called a tribe as long as its members do not possess a consciousness of mutual unity. This psychological element is an invariable and essential characteristic of the tribe.

One Language: The members of a tribe speak a common language. This also helps to generate and evolve a sense of communal unity among them.

Endogamous Group: The members of a tribe generally marry into their own group but now due to increased contact with other tribes, the consequence of an increase in the means of transportation, the system of marrying within the tribe is also changing.

Blood Relationships Ties: A major cause of the sense of communal unity in the tribe is the tie of blood relationships between its members. The members of the tribe have faith in their having descended from a common, real or mythical, ancestor and hence believe in blood relationships with other members.

Need for Protection: The members of a tribe are very much experienced in the need of protection. Keeping this need in view, a political organisation of the tribe is established and all authority for administration is vested in one person. This leader employs his mental power and skill in protecting the entire tribe. A tribal committee is formed to render assistance in the form of advice to the tribal chief. As a general rule, the tribal chief accedes to the wishes of the committee. The tribe is divided into numerous small groups each of which has its own chief. These chiefs solve the problems of their own groups and act according to the directives of the tribe.

Political Structure

In this way each tribe has its own political organisation which maintains harmony and avoids notes of discord among its members and protects them.

Importance of Religion

Religion is of great importance in the tribe. The tribal political and social organisation is based on religion because social and political laws become inviolable once they are granted religious sanctity and recognition. In the form of ancestor worship, tribal religion has rendered important service in developing the habits of obedience. The authority of a common is an important characteristic of the tribe.

Common Name: The tribe has a common name.

Common Cultures: Resulting from a feeling of unity, common language, common religion, common political organisation, etc., a common culture is found to exist in a tribe.

Clan Organisation: A tribe is constituted of many clans. There exist laws of mutual reciprocity among its members.

Tribe-horde Differentiation

A nomadic horde is a group of a small number of people. When the members of the nomadic horde increase to a very sizable figure it is christened a tribe. A very strong community feeling exists in both horde and tribe which differ from mainly in respect of size. In both, such economic activities as collection of fruit, animal hunting, animal husbandry, fishing etc., are carried on. In both, a similarity of blood relations is to be found. In both, these is a conglomeration of families. The chief of the group is well respected and obeyed in both. In spite of such a great extent of similarity, the horde and the tribe differ from each other in the following respects:

1. In the tribal group the need for protection stands out more prominently, as compared to the horde.
2. The tribe is bigger in size than the nomadic horde.
3. In the tribe, religion is more developed than in the horde because in the former a greater solidarity and strength of political and social laws is to be expected.

4. Being of a large and more cumbersome size the tribe possesses a weaker sense of unity than does the horde.
5. Tribe is divided into many smaller groups but the horde has no such sub-divisions.
6. Agricultural occupation is an accepted mode of life in the tribe whereas in the horde agriculture is not indulged in to any large extent.
7. The tribe inhabits a definite locality. On the other hand, instead of staying at a definite place the horde wanders over a definite geographical area.

Tribal Group and Caste

Marriage within the clan is forbidden both in the tribe as well as in the caste. Both generally condemn marriage outside the group. The modern development in the means of transport and communications has induced contact between members of various tribes and has weakened the laws of endogamy in both.

The two do exhibit considerable similarity, yet they also differ in the following respects:

1. According to Risley, the convention of endogamy is not rigidly enforced in tribe whereas such is the case in a caste. But this view of Risley does not appear to be universally true since the law of endogamy is enforced with extreme rigidity in some tribes.
2. Max Weber writes in *Social Structures* that when an Indian tribe loses its territorial significance it assumes the form of an Indian caste. In this way, the tribe is a local group whereas the caste is a social group.
3. The caste originated, in ancient Hindu society, with a view to division of labour on the basis of profession and occupations. The tribe came about because of the evolution of community feeling in a group inhabiting a definite geographical area.

4. According to D.N. Majumdar the tribe looks upon Hindu ritualism as foreign and extra-religious even though indulging in it and in the worship of Gods and Goddesses whereas in the caste these are necessary parts of relation. The Tribes of Madhya Bharat which are called Hindu and Kshatriya tribes are better acquainted with their own 'Bonga' than with the Hindu Gods.
5. According to Max Weber the status of all people is similar in the caste whereas there is much difference of status and rank in the tribe. This view of Max Weber does not apply to all castes. Differences of rank and status can be found in many castes also.
6. There is greater consciousness of differences in status and rank in the caste than in the tribe.
7. The caste is never a political association whereas the tribes is a political association.
8. The names of clans in castes are adopted from some saint or mystical savant; such as Vashishtha, Vishvamitra, Bharadwaj, Kashyap, etc. In the tribe the clans are based on totem, for example the clans in the Komti tribe of Mysore are named after all kinds of fruits, vegetables, spices, foodgrains, etc. The list presented by Thurston in *Castes and Tribes of Southern India* seems to indicates that hardly any name in the animal and vegetable world remains to be used as the basis for a totem name.
9. In the caste, individuals generally pursue their own definite occupations because functions are divided under the caste system. In the tribe, individuals can indulge their fancies in whatever profession they please because there is no fixed relation between them and the occupations.

Actually, now the tribes are gradually being converted

into castes. Risley has mentioned four processes in this transformation:

1. By changing one's lineage,
2. By accepting the principles of any school of Hindu religion,
3. By joining Hindu religion,
4. By entering into relations with Hindus without changing name.

According to D.N. Majumdar a tribe can enter Hindu society by adopting clan and name of a caste.

As a result of these changes, the differences between tribe and caste are being continually reduced.

Acculturation and Integration: Due to contact with Hindu and Western culture, the tribal culture has constantly changed. This cultural change has been affected by the following processes:

Normal Adoption: In this process of cultural change a tribe simply adopts the culture of another tribe, for example the Worli tribe of Bombay state, formerly used to wear only a cloth. Now they use shirt, turban and dhoti due to the influence of Koli tribe.

Acculturation: Where a culture almost engulfs another culture and changes it the process is known as acculturation. This involves a wider and deeper cultural change. For example, the Indian tribal culture is being constantly influenced by Hindu culture, so much so that some tribes are almost Hindu in culture. An example of this type of cultural change can be found in Gond tribes.

Assimilation: In this process of cultural change, a culture is not only adopted, but also assimilated and therefore becomes an integral part of the adopting culture. This process is seen in the tribes who, leaving their difficult mountain tracks and deep forests, come to plains and stay there. Such tribes in India have been assimilated in Hindu culture in almost all aspects of their social and cultural organization.

According to D.N. Majumdar, the Indian tribes can be classified into two groups on the basis of processes of cultural change. Firstly, the assimilated tribes whose culture has been completely assimilated by some other culture. Secondly, there are adaptive tribes whose culture is gradually adapting to some new culture.

Features and Functions of Clan

Definition of Clan: A clan comes into being by including all the relatives from patrilineal and matrilineal lineages. Thus few lineages combined together will form one clan. The people of the clan have an imagined ancestor who is accepted and respected as the founder of the clan. His name is introduced in the whole clan. It is a collection of unilateral families. A clan has been defined as. *"an exogamous division of a tribe, the members of which are held to be related to one another by some communities, it may be belief in descent from common ancestor or possession of a common territory".*

Each clan has certain peculiar or significant characteristics. A clan is exogamous group and its members do not marry within the tribe. Then the members of the tribe believe that they have common ancestors who can be both real as well as mythical. A clan is unilateral which implies that it is either matrilineal or patrilineal.

Kinds of Clan: Clans can be of different types. It can be matrilineal when all the children of one women are members of the clan. In it a women, her children, her sisters and children of sister are included. Then is patrilineal clan in which a male member, his children, his brothers and sisters and children of brothers are included. Whether it is a patrilineal or a matrilineal clan, its name will be either after some saint or totem or some topography.

Role of Clan: An important function of clan is that its members should mutually assist each other and extend all their cooperation to other members of the family. They should protect each other in time of difficulty. In other words they should have 'We' instead of 'I' feeling. Members of the clan feel that an attack on one of them is attack on them all. The head of the clan ensures that the members of his clan do not indulge in anti-social activities.

Thus he controls the members of the clan. He maintains order in the family and punishes those who try to violate the discipline of the clan. The members of the clan help in arranging marriages outside the clan because marriages within the clan are forbidden. Then the clans settle disputes among various clans by forming committees of heads of clans. In fact such committees perform all such functions which are usually performed by the government. It is then the function of head of the clan that he should distribute agricultural land among its members. What is Clan?

The clan or sib is an important part of the tribal organisation. It is only an extensive form of lineage constituted of blood relations. A clan is constituted by including all the relatives of either the mother's or the father's lineage and all the offsprings of ancestors in such a lineage.

In this way many lineages constitute a clan. The clan emanates from some major biblical or imagined ancestor of the family. Being prominent and respected this ancestor is accepted as its founder. All the lineal descendents of the family are introduced by his name. A clan is never constituted by combining the lineages of both the mother and the father. It is invariably unilateral;. Its descendents are of either matrilineal or patrilineal lineage. According to Majumdar and Madan, "A sib or clan is often a combination of a few lineages and descent who may be ultimately traced to a mythical ancestor, who may be human, human like, animal, plant, or even inanimate". A committee has defined the clan thus "Clan is an exogamous division of a tribe, the members of which are held to be related to one another by some common ties, it may be belief in descent from a common ancestor, possession of a common totem or habitation of a common territory". Thus, in brief, clan is that collection of unilateral families whose members believe themselves to be the common descendants of a real or mythical ancestor.

Traits of Clan

The following characteristics of the clan are evident from its foregone definitions:

Exogamous Group: The clan is an exogamous group since all the members of a clan believe themselves to be descended from an ancestor. Consequently, they do not marry any member of their clan. Marriage is contracted only out of one's own clan.

Common Ancestor: The organisation of the clan is based on the conception of a common ancestor. This ancestor can be real or mythical.

Unilateral: The nature of the clan is unilateral *viz.*, in one clan there is either the collection of all families on the mother's side or of all the families on the father's side.

Kinds of Clan: According to its unilateral nature, clan may be of two types:

Matrilineal Clan: In this all the offsprings of one woman are held to be members of one clan. At the same time the sisters and brothers of the woman are also members of this clan. In this way a matrilineal clan includes the woman, her offspring, her sisters and their children. But it does not include the children of the brothers.

Patrilineal Clan: In this clan are included the man, his children, his brothers and sisters and the children of the brothers but not of the sisters.

(1) Clans have different names based on various different grounds. The main grounds among them are the following:

After the names of saints, for example, Shandilya, Bhardwaj, etc.

(2) After the names of the totem such as Kunjam, Naagsori, etc.

(3) On the basis of substitute names such as Kamaar, Jagat, etc.

(4) On the basis of some topography, for example Mahanadiya, Jaunpuriya, etc.

Important Functions of Clan: The main functions of the clan are as follows:

Mutual Assistance and Protection: The members of a clan possess a 'we feeling' because of their belief in descent from a common ancestor. They are prepared not merely to assist one another but even to lay down their lives for each other. When one member of the clan is injured all the members share his pain. Two sayings are prevalent among them:

(i) "Strike my clan brother and you strike me", and

(ii) "The blood of the clan is my blood".

Members Control: Individuals indulging in anti-social acts are extradited from the clan. In this way, the conduct of clan members is controlled. Extradition from the clan proves more effective and disastrous than even a death sentence for the members.

Legal Work: It is the universal legal function of the clan to punish miscreants and maintain peace and order in this manner.

Exogamy Nature: With the help of the law of exogamy the clan arranges marriage from outside the group. This, on the one hand, avoids conflicts within the clan between men for a woman and on the other hand, serves to increase cordiality and friendship with the members of the other clans.

Governing Function: The clan performs all the Governmental (administrative) functions for its members. The heads of the various clans meet and form a committee for the tribe which serves to mediate in the conflicts between clan members and takes political decisions in war and peace time.

Property Dealing: In the villages where agriculture is carried on, it is the clan which arranges for agricultural land. The head of the clan distributes the land. When a person is deprived of the membership of the clan he is also deprived of this land. Members can only rent the land.

In addition to the above mentioned functions, the clan also caters to the religious preferences of its members. Generally, the head of the clan is also its priest. It is he who consummates the religious undertakings of all the members.

Caste vs. Clan: Clan and caste differ from each other in the following respects:

(1) Clan is a well organised group based on a mythical ancestor. Caste is a real, actual organised group.

(2) Clan is an exogamous and caste an endogenous group. Members of the clan marry outside the clan. Members of the caste cannot marry outside the caste.

(3) In the clan individuals possess the same status. In the caste individuals possess higher and lower social status.

Clan vs. Tribe: The clan and tribe are different and distinct from each other on the following counts.

(1) Clan has no definite topographical area whereas members of a tribe generally live in a definite geographical location.

(2) Clan has no definite language, the tribe has a common language. Clan is an exogamous group. The members of clan do not wed a member of their own clan. The tribe is commonly an endogenous group although with

increasing contact among neighboring tribes consequent upon an increase in the means of transportation the tribe has now lost some of its endogenous character.

Tribal Society Dormitory System: The most important social institution in the tribal social organization is the youth organization. These organizations are found in almost every tribe and their social life is centered around it. They are known by different names in different tribes, for example, among the Nagas of Assam, they are called 'Morung', while the female youth organization is called' Yo', among Angomi Nagas, it is called 'Kinchuki'. In Uttar Pradesh, it is known as Rangbang, while among the Mundas and Ho tribe of Madhya Bharat, it is called Gitiora. The Oraons call it Dhoomkuriya, the Bhuiyan call it Dhangarbassa and the Gonds call it Gotul.

These youth organisations are centered in big buildings known as dormitories. They are buildings of straw and thatch. There are separate houses meant for boys and girls. All the youths of the tribe pass their night in the dormitory. The boys and girls sleep separately. In the village where there is no dormitory for the girls, they sleep in the house of some old woman. Such is the custom in the Munda tribe. In Bastar the boys and girls of the age of 15 and 16 sleep in the dormitories. The Oraon youth has to pass his night in the Dhumkuria situated outside the village. In the Ho tribe the unmarried boys and girls live in separate dormitories. In the Lhota Nagas of Assam the boys can get leave from the Morung only in the case of serious illness of their mothers. Among the Miami tribals of Assam both boys and girls sleep in the same dormitory. While the girls sleep on the ground floor, the boys sleep on the first floor. Similar is the custom in the Muria tribe of Bastar. Their dormitories are situated outside the village. The unmarried boys and girls gather here at night, sing and dance and participate in other social activities and finally pass the night.

CHARACTERISTICS OF DORMITORY

The following are the important characteristics of the youth dormitory:

(1) While at some places there are separate dormitories for boys and girls, in other tribes they live in common dormitory. This is the custom in the Muria tribe. On the other hand, among the Konayak Nagas of Assam, the boys live in the Morung and the girls sleep at Yo.

(2) Normally the dormitories are situated outside the village in the forest, but they may also be near the fields as it is in the case of dormitories of the Nagas. In Oraon tribes the dormitory is situated in the centre of the village.

(3) The life in the dormitory is based on certain traditions and customs which are invariably followed by all the members.

(4) The age of membership of the dormitory differs from tribe to tribe. As a general rule it is four or five years in most of the tribe.

(5) The boys and girls live in the dormitory till they are married when their membership is automatically dissolved.

(6) If a girl becomes a widow she can again enter the dormitory as its member.

(7) In the evening the members of the dormitory gather after taking their meals at their homes. At the dormitory they make a fire, sit around it, tell stories, sing, dance and play and finally sleep.

(8) The members of the dormitory are divided into two classes according to age—seniors and juniors. The head of the dormitory is selected from the senior group. It is his job to take care of all the members of the dormitory and maintain discipline among them. The juniors follow

the commands of the seniors and receive different types of education from them.

(9) It is the duty of every member of the dormitory to keep every thing secret about the dormitory.

(10) The members of the dormitory carry out several functions together *e.g.*, construction of a house on the occasion of marriage or helping the village folk in harvesting the crop etc.

The Gotul of Muria and Gond: Among the dormitories of Indian tribes, the Gotul of the Muria and Gonds of Madhya Bharat is worth mentioning. It is raised on the bamboo poles and the roofs of straw. There is no door or window in it. The members enter through a small hole sufficient to permit entry. All the unmarried boys and girls gather here in the evening, make a fire, sing and dance, tell traditional legends and sleep here. The juniors serve the seniors and receive different types of training from them. Among the members of the Gotul, different boys and girls are given different status and the corresponding roles.

The head of the dormitory is known as Challan or Siledar. Under him there are Dewan, Tehsildar, Subedar and Kotwal, etc. Similar positions are also given to the girls. According to Majumdar, the purpose of the Gotul is to save the village folk from the attack of wild animals. The youths remain awake for most of the night and sleep only in its last lap or in the day. They help their parents on the field or in grazing the cattle in the forest. In the evening they go to Gotul after taking their meals. Among the Muria tribals, the girls massage the bodies of the boys. Verrier Elvin has described the sexual life in the Gotul in details in his book. "The Muria and their Gotul". He has pointed out that the senior girls train the junior boys in matters of sex.

In 'The Gondwana and the Gonds' Shri Inder Jit Singh has denied any type of sexual activity in the Gotul. D.N.Majumdar and Hutton also agree with Singh. In fact Mr. Elvin has himself admitted and wondered that there is hardly any case of conception among the members of the Gotul. According to Majumdar and Hutton, the Gotuls are the centers of social education. In it are shown the dances imitating agriculture, hunting, gathering of honey and economic activities carried out by the village folk. The conceptions of crime and punishment and good and bad actions are taught through different stories.

Group Sleeping Area

Scholars do not agree about the origin of tribal dormitory. According to one view, they are residues of the ancient communal houses when the whole village used to live under one roof and there were no individual homes. According to another view the purpose of the dormitory is to keep boys and girls unaware of the sexual relationship of their parents. According to Majumdar, the purpose of dormitory is to gather the youths of the village at one place to save the village from the attack of wild animals and the village maidens from the attack of males of other tribes.

Besides, the origin of the dormitory may be due to want of houses, the bliss of communal life and the development of tribal culture. Whatever may be origin of dormitory, it is undeniable that it is the center of tribal culture in a tribe. In it are taught the lessons of the traditions, norms, ideals, religious beliefs, methods of earning, livelihood and discipline to the boys and girls of the tribe. According to S.C. Roy, the tribal dormitory carries out the following three functions:

(1) Helping in the gathering of edible things and consolidating economic organization.

(2) Educating boys and girls in social and other duties and imparting them education in the matters of sex.

(3) Following the principle of endogamy and keeping the movement of women limited and controlled.

Dormitory on Decline: At present unfortunately the institution of youth organisation is gradually weakening in the tribes. The two important causes of this development are as follows:

City Contact: Due to contact with urban people the tribals are gradually forgetting then-social ideals and institutions and following urban culture. As the education is now being provided by the schools, the children do not go to dormitory to receive education.

Effect of Christian Missionaries: The spread of Christianity among tribals and the presence of the Christian missionaries among them have adversely affected their youth cultural set up. The institution of youth organisation is gradually weakening, which has led to social disorganization among the tribes.

In fact, it has been rightly pointed out by Elwin, that the condition of the social organization of a tribal group can be rightly estimated from the condition of its youth organizations which are the centres of the maintenance and development of its culture.

Marriages in Tribes

The institution of marriage is another point on which the tribal people throughout the world have been much maligned. Wild and baseless charges were hurled at them, fantastic insinuations were formulated and many pseudo-scholars, claiming to have an intimate knowledge of the tribal world, let their imagination run riot for the benefit of a receptive readership. Some degree of laxity regarding sexual liaison was taken to mean 'promiscuity' or free sex under which, according to such people, the institution of marriage could not exist. Such spicy phrases like 'sexual communism' were coined to describe a nonexistent social situation, 'Interestingly; no ethnographic data collected from any part of the world support this hypothesis. In India too the simplest and the rudest of tribal cultures we know, *e.g.*, the Andamanese, the Kadar, the Paliyan, the Malapanthram, the Chenchu, the Birhor and others do not furnish us any evidence of promiscuity.

Indian tribes like tribes of other parts of the world practise several forms of marriage as a matter of convenience and social acclimatization in their respective cultural-ecological settings.

The Monogamy: Monogamy is a form of marriage in which no man may be married to more than one woman at any one time. A majority of the Indian tribes practise monogamy. Just to refute the allegation that among the most backward and primitive tribes no clear-cut scheme of marriage exists, the example of the Kamar, a very backward tribe of Madhya Pradesh may be cited. This tribe is monogamous.

The Polygamy: Polygamy that is, marriage to more than one person, is fairly widespread all over the world. Among Indian tribes, there are many who are following this type of matrimonial alliance. Polygamy has two aspects: (i) Polygyny, (ii) Polyandry.

While Polygyny is the marriage of one man to several women, polyandry means the marriage of one woman to several men. Both types of marriages are referred to as polygamy in common parlance.

The Polygyny: Polygyny is found among the Naga tribes, the Gond, the Baiga, the Toda, the Lushai and most of the Proto-Australoid tribes of middle India. In most cases such form of marriage comes into existence as a result of disequilibrium in sex ratio. Obviously, in a society where the sex ratio is normal, such type of marriage may force many of the men to remain bachelors. Hence, normally such a practice develops in a society where the number of women is quite larger than of the males. In an otherwise normal situation it is the privilege of the powerful and rich who keep more than one wife as a symbol of prestige and status. Among the Indian tribes like Gond, Baiga and Lushai, this type of marriage is resorted to, to facilitate a better division of labour.

The Polyandry: Polyandry is, comparatively, much restricted in distribution. This type of matrimonial alliance is found in the Himalayan tract stretching from Kashmir to Assam and is popular among the Indo-Aryan and Mongoloid tribes. In its classical form it is prevalent among the Tiyan, the Toda, the Kota, the Khasa (Jounsari) and the Ladakhi Bota. It is also popular among the Tibetans.

Among the Indian tribes, two types of polyandry are in vogue. When several brothers share the same wife, as among the Khasa and the Toda, we have *fraternal polyandry.* Majumdar(1967) opines that in the general type, also found among the Toda of Nilgiri Hills, there need not be any close relationship between the husbands, and the wife goes to spend some time with each husband.

So long as a woman lives with one of her husbands, the others have no claim over her. Nair polyandry was of this type. Polyandry is not everywhere explicable with reference to a preponderance of men over women. In Ladakhi it was actually the women who were more in number. Among the Toda, property considerations and sex-disparity explain this institution. Polyandry is found to lead to fewer children to every woman, more male children, and a high incidence of sterility among women.

The Khasa of Jounsar-bawar have evolved a very practical mode of polyandrous matrimony. Among them, when the eldest brother marries a girl, she automatically becomes the common wife of the rest of the brothers. If a brother is minor, he may, on becoming adult, marry another to match his age. Hence this leads to a situation where a number of brothers have more than one wife which is not the classical mode of polyandry. Observing polygyny-polyandry mixed up,

Majumdar (ibid) coined an interesting phrase, *Polygynandry*, to describe this situation.

Till some time back the Todas of Nilgiri Hills used to observe an interesting ceremony called *how and arrow ceremony* to declare the paternity socially. In this ceremony, all brothers and the common wife assemble amidst the rest of the villagers in the fourth or fifth month of pregnancy of the wife and as a result of consensus one of the brothers presents a seat of bow and arrow to the wife. This is taken as declaration that this particular brother will be accepted as father of the coming child. In this way 'sociological fatherhood' overrides the 'biological fatherhood' in the bewildering mosaic of human affairs.

Beside demographic factors, an economic factor called *bride price* is also responsible for the prevalence of polyandry among Indian tribes. Under the system of *bride price* the husband/husbands are obliged to give an agreed amount of cash/kind to the parents of the bride as price which usually varies according to the physical beauty and utility of the bride. With the passage of time the bride price continued to soar and a stage came when it became almost impossible to arrange the bride price individually. Furthermore, the agricultural holdings in mountains are quite uneconomic and the pursuit of cultivation too hard to be borne by a single individual. Hence, to avoid further fragmentation of holdings and sharing the enormous labour, such a mode of marriage might have come into existence.

Another mode of polygamy, which maybe called 'bigamy', is also in vogue, though on a very restricted scale. Under bigamy a man is allowed to marry two sisters at one time. This type of polygamy has been reported from the Holiya and Medara tribes of Mysore.

Marriage—Preferential and Prohibited: It is observed that, on the one hand, the society prohibits sexual liaison or matrimonial alliances between particular kins or in the same clan or *gotra* but on the other hand, it encourages matrimonial alliances between certain other kins. In such cases there is a prescription, or only a preference, expressed for marriage to a particular kin. The following are some of the popular types of 'preferential' marriages prevalent among the Indian tribes.

(1) *Cousin marriage*
  (a) cross-cousin marriage
  (b) parallel-cousin marriage
(2) *Levirate*
(3) *Sorvrate*

Both types of cousin marriage, *viz.*, cross-cousin marriage and parallel-cousin marriage are quite popular among the Indian tribes. The Gond, Kharia, Khasi and Kadar are some of the important Indian tribes practising cousin marriage. Anthropologically speaking, when the children of a brother and a sister marry, it is a cross-cousin marriage while it is parallel-cousin marriage when the children of two sisters or two brothers get married. A Gond is supposed to marry his or her cross cousin, and if one likes to have this prescription waived in one's case, a compensation has to be paid to the losing party. Cross-cousin marriage, as observed by Majumdar, is often explained to be a device for avoiding payment of a high bride price, and also for maintaining property in the household. The Gonds of Madhya Pradesh call this form of marriage *doodh lautawa* (return of milk). The implication is that the bride price paid by 'A' for his wife would be returned to his family when the daughter of 'A' marries her mother's brother's son. Claude Levi Strauss has said that preferential marriage has, for its main purpose, the strengthening of solidarity within a tribe.

Levirate and sororate are two other types of preferential marriages which are also said to promote 'inter-familial cordiality' by making certain linkages imperative. When a woman marries her husband's brother this is called levirate. It may be split into two types: (a) junior levirate, (b) senior levirate. When the woman marries her husband's younger brother, it is junior levirate while marriage with the elder brother is called senior levirate. When levirate occurs in non-polyandrous societies, it is of paramount importance because in the event of her husband's death, the widow finds a guardian, husband and patron while the children get a man as their father who has been loving them earlier too. Among some tribal groups, a degree of laxity is allowed in the matter of intimate social relations and sexual liaison between a woman and her husband's brothers as a prelude to the coming event. This situation may be termed as 'anticipatory levirate'.

When a man marries his wife's sister/sisters, it is sororate. It may occur after the death of his wife or even in her life. The death of a spouse is compensated by giving a new spouse, generally a younger sister of the deceased. Levirate and sororate emphasise the acceptance of inter-familial obligations and the recognition of marriage as a tie between two families, and not only between two individuals. Ways of Acquiring Mates Nine important ways of acquiring a mate have been found to be popular among the Indian tribes:

1. Marriage by capture
2. Marriage by exchange
3. Marriage by purchase
4. Marriage by elopement
5. Marriage by service
6. Marriage by intrusion
7. Marriage by trial
8. Marriage by mutual consent
9. Marriage by probation

When a man forcibly snatches away a woman from her village and marries her, it is called marriage by 'capture'.

Many tribal societies give social sanction to this type of marriage which symbolises valour and chivalry. Marriage by capture has been most popular among the Naga tribes of north eastern region where Naga tribals of one village used to invade the enemy's village and capture grown up girls. This led to female infanticide. However, with the widening application of the Indian Penal Code and growing social consciousness as a result of culture contracts this practice is fast vanishing into oblivion. Cases of capture have also been reported from the Ho, who call it *Operatipe* and the Gond who call it *Posiothur*.

Tribal Society Family Organisation: Marriage is an important institution among the tribal people as well. A tribal family is required to perform the same functions as any other family is required to perform. But the marriage can be by purchase, capture or exchange.

Role of Family

Like any other family in tribal society the family is also required to perform (a) Biological functions, (b) Economic functions, and (c) Social functions. Biological functions include sex satisfaction and producing of children. In the economic functions are included the responsibilities of feeding and nourishing and providing food, clothing and shelter to the members of the family while social functions include socialisation of the children and preparing them to face hard realities of society and social life.

Types of Family: In tribal society, families are of different forms. These are (a) Primary or Nuclear family; (b) Conjugal family; and (c) Matriarchal family. A primary or nuclear family is one which consists of husband, wife and their children and is most common in tribal society. In tribal societies we also find some families in which, in addition to husband, wife and their children, there are few near blood relations who are included in the family. Such families are called conjugal families. Among the Khasis of Assam and some other tribes, matriarchal family is quite common. In such a family all relationship is traced through mother. In it the husband gives some customary gifts to the wife. Patriarchal family is quite common among the tribes and in it after marriage, a wife lives with her husband and all relationship is traced through the father and not through the mother.

Features of Matriarchal Family: As already said in the tribes of India matriarchal families are also found. It is interesting to study the role of male member in a matriarchal society. Then it is also useful to study the features and characteristics of a matriarchal society. The first significant feature of a matriarchal society is that all succession rights are settled through mother's line and after marriage, the husband begins to live with the wife and not the wife who begins to live with the husband.

Then in such a family near relatives of wife and not of the husband succeed to the property. The whole system works on the philosophy that the beginner of the family is not the husband but the wife. In this family all marriage proposals come from female side. Since all property rights are vested with the women, therefore she does not get any money at the time of marriage. In religious functions women serve and act as priest. Divorce is allowed by mutual consent.

The Polyandry: Among the Tujan, Kurumb, Kot, Toda and few other tribes polyandry prevails in which a female marries several males at one and the same time. Both fraternal and non-fraternal polyandry exists among the tribes. In fraternal or Adelphic polyandry a women marries all the brothers of her husband. In it after marriage, a woman is considered to be the wife of the brothers. If a younger brother, after the marriage of elder brother, marries another woman, his elder brother will have equal right over his wife. Such a system prevails in Khasi Tribe of Dehra Dun district.

Then in the Khasi tribe there is slightly different system. Here a woman is considered wife of all brothers, but the eldest brother has a right to ask the wife not to cohabit with others. He is considered to be the father of the children and also he has right to dissolve the marriage. If a younger brother decides to marry another wife, usually he marries the sister of his elder brother's wife. The eldest brother is considered and treated as head of the family and all property belongs to him. When the question of division of property among the brothers comes, the eldest brother gets the lion's share.

In a non-fraternal polyandry a women has right to select her husband, who may not be brother of her husband. If she has more than one husband she stays in the houses of her different husbands. When she is in the house of one husband, her other husbands have no right over her. The practice prevails among the Nayars of Malabar. In this system after marriage a wife can stay in her own house, and allows her husbands to come to her house or she might visit herself to the house of her any husband at her own will. In this family a husband has no right over the children and property of his wife. Why Polyandry?

In all the societies, more particularly among the more advanced societies, it is monogamy which prevails. Now a question arises as to why tribal society is still following Polyandry. One of the important reasons is poverty. Usually it is difficult for one person to provide food and other facilities to the wife. So both men and women like that responsibilities should be shared so that male have less burden and female sufficient for themselves to maintain. Then another reason is scarcity of women. Among Todas the number of male members is much more than those of female members and as such one male cannot have one female. But usually polyandry is decreasing because it is felt that the system is not very healthy. It injures the health of women resulting in many venereal diseases. The women soon become barren and population problem becomes serious. The system has also resulted in increase in divorces. Though it is on the decline, yet the system still continues.

Blood Relations

Man has the gift of a highly developed brain which enables him to engage in organized behaviors to exploit and harness nature. The groupings thus come into existence may have for their immediate cause and binding force several principles of integration: the simplest and most obvious of these is the principle of kinship, that is, relationship between different members of family based on marriage and on descent. "This relationship is of a three fold nature: that between husband and wife, that between parents and children; and that between children of the same parents" (Majumdar, 1967). Family Tribal Indian exhibits a colourful diversity of families because of varied rules and customs among different tribes. Two types of families may be distinguished on the basis of the number of family members: (i) simple or nuclear family, (ii) extended and joint family.

The first type represents the basic grouping of the mates and their children. Such families have very limited number of members. Many Indian tribes like the Birhor, Pariya, Korwa, etc., maintain this type of family. If this nucleus is extended by the addition of other closely related kins, then it is called an extended family. If this is still further extended by the principle of kinship, then we get a family like the Hindu joint family. The Nairs of Kerala are taken as a classical example of this type of family and the Nair's *Thanwad* is an important institution in itself.

A variety of families may also be distinguished on the basis of the number of marriage partners. Although most of the tribes have monogamous families, *i.e.*, families consisting of a husband, a wife and children but polygamous families are also not very uncommon. Such families come into existence on the basis of two forms of polygany *viz.*, Polygyny and polyandry.

A polygynous family consists of a husband, two or more wives and their children. This is a condition of marital arrangement common all over the tribal India. Then there are polyandrous families in which the husbands are more than one, as for instance among the Todas of Nilgiri Hills of Tamil Nadu and the Khasas (Jounsaris) of Jounsar-bawar in U.P. where several brothers many one wife without any exclusive right of cohabitation for any one spouse. The shortage of women was formerly due to the custom of female infanticide which tilled the sex ratio heavily towards the abundance of males. This does not imply, however, that sexual relations are promiscuous. Actually, strict rules are observed by the parties concerned; and when a child is born, its paternity is established by means of a social ceremony instead of biological considerations.

Several other forms of family are also found among the tribes on India or the basis of authority of father and mother. Who is more important in the family, father or mother? This determines the patriarchal and matriarchal nature of the family. This situation further leads to two more sets of situations: patrilineal/ matrilineal and patrilocal/matrilocal. Most of the Indian tribes acknowledge the authority of father in family affairs and hence they have patriarchal families where descent is also traced from father, *i.e.*, patrilineal and the wife leaves her parents' home and comes to reside with her husband, *i.e.*, patrilocal. However the Khasis of Meghalaya and the Nairs of Kerala are the classic examples of the rare matrilined matriachal and matrilocal family.

The Khasis live in the Khasi and Jaintia Hills of Meghalaya. They are famous all over the world as the best example of a society which is nearest to being matriarchy. They trace their descant from mythical female ancestresses. Their family consists of mother, her unmarried children, male and female, her husband, her married daughters and their husbands. The Khasis are matrilocal at the time of marriage, but later on, when a husband shows evidence of his ability to support himself, his wife and children, he may set up an independent household of his own.

According to traditional law, men have no individual right to ownership, whether they are husbands or sons. Property is inherited from women to women. Majumdar aptly remarks that whereas the Khasi family grows round a nucleus of blood-related females who are surrounded by a fringe of males-unmarried brothers and sons, fathers and husbands and whereas property, authority, religion, residence are all in the hands of women, menfolk also are respected and even exercise some authority. The all powerful Khasi woman addresses her husband as her lord. The above description is the traditional situation and the Khasis are also changing with times.

Kinship: People in all parts of the world and in all the societies, irrespective of their technological level, are bound together in groups by variouskinds of bonds. The most universal and the most basic of these bonds is that which is based on reproduction, an inherent human drive, and is called kinship. But social recognition is seen to override biological fact in the affairs of kinship, especially among the primitive societies all over the world.

The tribes of India are divided into lineages. While most of the tribes are divided into patrilineal lineages, Khasi and Garo of Meghalaya have matrilineal lineages.

Like other people of India, the tribal population too recognizes both types of kinship *viz.*, consanguineous kinship and affinal kinship. While consanguineous kinship includes all the kins related through blood or biological ties, affinal kins consist of those recognised through marriage. But an interesting and significant fact, as mentioned earlier, is that the consanguineous kinship among them does not recognise only biological ties. The case of Todas of Nilgiri Hills following fraternal polyandry may be cited as an instance. Paternity is established among them through a social ceremony known as bow and arrow ceremony in which the particular brother who presents the common wife a bow and an arrow before a congregation, is recognised as the father of the child and until another brother makes the ceremonial presentation all children born to her of several brothers are regarded as the children of that brother who last performed the ceremony.

The most profound impact of kinship ties on the social life may be felt through *kinship usages* found in every society. Kinship usages among the tribes of India present very interesting and significant spectacle. Such types of behavioural pattern, verbal and non-verbal, explain many complex intricacies of kinship system.

It has been found among many tribes that many sets of kins avoid each other. The avoidance between daughter-in-laws and parents-in-law is quite common. Likewise, though less universally and also less rigorously, a son-in-law's relations with his parents-in-laws found to be cramped by certain restrictions. Among the tribes of Andaman and Nicobar Islands, the elder brother does not talk with his younger brother's wife. Radcliffe-Brown has given one of the most plausible of contemporary explanations. He points out that avoidance is a social fact and must, therefore, have a social explanation. He says that whenever people come in contact with each other, the possibilities of cooperation as well as conflict are always equally present.

But there are certain kinds of kinship where hostility is regarded as against social norms. The best way to prevent such hostility from becoming manifest is to put restrictions on the growth of intimacy; and hence the kinship usages of avoidance. Freud's psychoanalytical explanation is based on sexual attraction and the need to prevent sexual intimacy between various kinds of relatives.

Another kinship usage which is just reverse of the avoidance relationship is an extreme degree of familiarity expressed through joking relationships. Such joking may amount to exchange of abuse, obscene and vulgar references to sex, ridicule and so on. Apart from joking relationship between sister-in-law and brother-in-law and between a wife and her husband's brothers, such relationships have also been reported between grandparents and grandchildren among the orgaons and the Baigas. The Ho tribe of Chotanagpur also indulge in a variety of joking relationships. Majumdar opines that joking relationships may be indicative of equality and mutual reciprocity. They may also be indicative of a potential sexual relationship. Thus is explained the joking relationship between a man and his wife's younger sister. In each case the two may be potential mates. A joking relationship, when not mutual, assumes the role of social control. It becomes indicative of correction though ridicule.

Avunculate the amitate, as known in anthropological parlance, are two other kinship usages prevalent among the Indian tribes. Among the Khasis, Garos, Nairs, and a couple of other societies the maternal uncle enjoys a preeminent place in the life and affection of his nephews and nieces as a matter of convention. He has special obligations towards them which exceed those of their father and transmits his property to his nephew. The kinship usage is called *avunculate.* Obviously, this is a common usage among matrilineal societies. A special role, similar to that outlined in case of the maternal uncle, for one's father' sister is designated as *amitate.* This is explicable in patrilineal tribes.

Among the Khasi, Toda, Ho, Oraon, and a host of other tribes, a queer practice has been reported, called covuade, on the basis of a similar practice known among the Trobriand Islanders by the same name in their local dialect. The practice consists in "making a husband lead the life of an invalid alongwith his wife whenever she gives birth to a child. He refrains from active life, goes on sick diet and observes certains taboos" (Majumdar, 1967). Thus, the Khasi husband, like his wife cannot cross a stream or wash clothes until the spirits connected with child-birth are propitiated.

Sometimes, among some other tribes, this practice is extended to the extent of putting up the poor husband in an adjacent hut to his wife's where she intends to deliver the child, is made to cry and scream in agony like his wife and made to ape the actions of his wife. Malinowski believed *covuade* to be a cementing bond of married life and a social mechanism designed to secure paternal affection.

Other anthropologists have sought to give a psycho-analytical explanation. They have attributed this usage to the husband's desire to lighten the wife's discomforts, in the absence or lack of proper modern medical care, by a process of participation through identification. Some scholars have attributed this practice to the matriarchal and matrilineal mode of social organisation but the prevalence of this practice till recent past, among some patriarchal and patrilineal societies like the Ho, Oraon, etc., negates this assertion.

Economy and Technology in Tribal Areas: The primitive societies have passed through several stages of economic development everywhere in the world. Thus one finds the stages of food gathering, hunting and fishing, farming, etc., among the Indian tribes. The tribes living in the forests and hills usually earn their livelihood by means of food gathering, hunting and fishing. Such is the life of Kadar of Kerala, Birhor and Kharia of Bihar and other tribes.

The tribes living in dense forests, full of wild beasts, live on hunting. Such are the tribes of Naga, Kuki, Bhil, Santhal and Gond. The hunters leave the females to carry out household activities in the morning and return in the evening after hunting. In some tribes there is a usual custom of hunting collectively. The Nagas use spears and arrows and bows. The

Bhils are very much specialized in shooting by arrow. The tribes living near rivers and seas usually earn their livelihood by catching fish.

The hilly tribes rear the cattle, an example, of which are the *Gujjars* and the tribes of Chamba. The Todas of Nilgiri rear buffaloes. Some tribes also carry out cultivation, but they are generally shifting from one place to another.

Among the cultivating tribes are the Santhals and Gonds. Cottage industries, such as weaving cloth, preparing ropes and skins and utensils of different metals are prevalent in many tribes. The Kharia people are very much specialised in cottage industries.

Kinds of Economy: The Indian tribes can be divided into the following classes on the basis of their economic organization:

(1) Hunting and food gathering tribes include Kadar, Chenchu, Kharia and Korawa etc.

(2) Cattle rearing tribes such as the Todas and Bhils.

(3) Cultivating tribes such as Kamar, Vega and Birhor.

(4) Industrial tribes such as Kharia and Nagas.

Features of Economic Organisation: The tribal economic organization is mainly concerned with producing such things as are necessary for their daily needs and consuming them. These activities are very much determined by the geographical environment of the tribe. Usually the tribals have to struggle very hard to meet their economic needs. The following are the important characteristics of Indian tribal economic organizations.

Production without Technological Aids: As the tribals are illiterate and cut off from the civilized world, they generally carry out production without adequate technological aids with the result that there is much loss of material with very little production. The tribals are, therefore, generally very poor in spite of working very hard.

Mixed Activity

The tribals live in a natural environment where there is no distinction of economic, religious and magical activities. There is, therefore, a tendency to mix all these. In the economic activities also religious and magical activities are utilized to attain economic ends. Many superstitions in this respect are prevalent among the tribals, for example, among Nagas there is a custom of human sacrifice and sprinkling of human blood over land in order to increase its fertility.

Consumption Based Production: In the absence of sufficient technological aids and scientific knowledge regarding agricultural and other production, the tribals generally produce only to consume. Hardly anything is left for exchange or hoarding. In the materials of consumption, food and clothing are generally given first preference, then there is the place for the home.

No Money Dealing: The tribal people do not use currency in deciding the prices of commodities and in exchange. There are no banks of economic exchanges in their societies. They hardly carry out any exchange of economic goods with outside groups.

No Regular Markets: There are no regular markets found in tribal societies and, therefore, there is no competition, monopoly, business or trade in their economic organization.

No Profiteering: There is absence of profiteering in tribal economic organization due to two important causes. First, the absence of currency to fix the price of commodities and secondly the connection of unity sentiments with economic activities.

Community Basis: Thus the chief aim of economic activities in a tribal society is to fulfil the community duties. The organization of most of the economic activities is cooperative and communal.

No Specialists

There are no specialists in different branches of economic organization in tribal societies, with the result that there is no division of labour and specialization.

Issue of Property

Some conception of personal property is found in almost every tribal society. A person is allowed a right over the things produced by his family. There is, however, group ownership over the ponds, the land and the forests etc.

Backward Economy: The above mentioned characteristics of tribal economic organization account for their economic backwardness. They do not know the new changes and inventions in different fields of production. Their methods and implements of cultivation, hunting and fishing are very primitive. They do not know anything about trade and commerce. The cottage industries are carried on by means of unrefined and primitive tools and methods. Hence the economic status of Indian tribes is very much backward.

Traits of Religion in Tribes

Tribal religion is the most primitive form of religion found in human society. The following are the important characteristics of the Indian tribal religion:

The Mana: Defining faith in Mana found in tribal society Codrington has pointed out that Mana is, "A force altogether distinct from physical power, which acts in all kinds of ways for good and evil, and which is of the greatest advantage to possess or control". Thus Mana is a supernatural power which is useful to man in the control of many natural phenomenon beyond his power.

According to Majumdar and Madan, "Entire religious life of the primitive is born out of their belief in certain understandable, impersonal, non-material and unidividualized supernatural power which takes abode in all the objects, animate and inanimate, that exist in the world". According to Maxmuller, Mana is an attempt to define certain natural phenomenon in terms of an impersonal power.

The high mountain, the river, the thunder and all other natural phenomena, according to the tribal people, acts with the power of Mana. This power acts both for good and for bad. It is connected with the soul, ghost of the departed man and the living being. The Ho and Munda tribes of Chota Nagpur call it Bonga.

The Bonga: According to these tribes, Bonga is a mysterious and impersonal power at the back of rains, tempests, cold, floods, epidemics and the wild animals. Everywhere activity is due to the power of Bonga. Thus, Bonga is a form of Mana.

The Animism: Another important characteristic of Indian tribal religion is animism. According to Risley, Tribal religion is animism. The tribal people believe in the presence of supernatural power at the back of high mountains, flooded rivers, big trees and epidemics. They try to please these powers by means of different types of propitiations and worship. Sometimes, they are worshipped even without being given any name. An important type of animism is ancestral worship which is found among the Santhals and Orans. The Santhals worship deities of family and village deities. Among the Korawa tribe, there is a goddesses of crop, one of animals and a deity presiding rains. The tribal people try to please these gods and goddesses by offering the sacrifices of different types of animals and birds before them. The principle of animism is based on the following two beliefs.

(1) There are powerful souls besides powerful gods. The souls are connected with men, and feel pleasure and pain through them. They influence the events in this world and also control them.

(2) The soul of man survives even after his death. The word 'animism' was used for the first time by E.B. Taylor in anthropological literature. Animism, according to Taylor is, "the ground-work of the philosophy of religion from that of savage upto that of civilized man".

Animalism: According to animalism there is some impersonal power behind every material object besides the living beings. Thus, in the tribal religions is found faith in the presence of supernatural power in bones and feathers etc. The impersonal power is worshipped to maintain peace and prosperity in the group. It is difficult to distinguish between animalism and animism. The following distinctions, however, have been pointed out between the two. While according to animism there is some mysterious, unknown, impersonal power at the back of all living beings and things, according to animism there is animal spirit found in all movable and immovable things.

An example of animalism is found in the tribe of Bihar. They consider the bones, beads, stones and feathers to have living and magical powers. The stones are considered to be the children of mother earth and worshipped. The tribal people worship only those powers which can do some harm to them, but sometimes, such powers are also worshipped which can not do any harm, for example, the Sing Bonga of the Munda tribe. Though it is difficult to say as to which types of nature worship is found in a particular tribe in India, generally one finds animism as well as animatism in most of the tribes. From the comparative point of view, however, animalism is more widespread than animism.

Naturalism: A universal characteristic of tribal religion is naturalism or nature worship. The Garo tribe of Assam worships sun and moon. The Munda people worship Sun god. Besides, other tribes worship rivers, mountains, stars, trees and other natural objects.

Soul not Mortal

Among many tribes there is a custom of observing funeral rites two times. This is because of their faith in the immortality of soul. Sometimes the second rite is considered to be more important than the first. The tribals believe that the soul is not destroyed on the death of the body and requires food etc., for a sufficiently long time. Among the Nagas and the tribals of the Nicobar island, the skull of the dead man is placed on a wooden statue believing that the soul of the dead man will pass from the skull to the statue. Now the statue is served like a living human being and efforts are made to fulfil all its needs. Sometimes the statue is made of brass. Such is the custom among the Garo tribe of Assam. In South India in Kerala the statute of a dead person is worshipped at least once a year. The tribals believe that the soul matter can increase the fertility of land and produce life. In the Naga tribe there is a custom of worshipping soul of the ancestors at the time of sowing and in the need of rains.

Rebirth Belief

Most of the Indian tribes believe that after death the soul of a man survives the body and enters into the body of some animal, bird, or other living being. Among the Bhils efforts are done to find out as to which body will be entered into by a particular soul. Similar beliefs are found among Nagas of Assam, Ahirs of Bengal, Kamar and Gond tribes.

The Magic

The most important characteristic of tribal religion is faith in magic. According to M.F. Keesing, "In its technical sense, magic is a term which summarises a variety of methods by which man purports to influence a automatically the course of events by that touch of the supernatural. A magical act is a rite carried out to twist Nature in a specific way to satisfy human desire". Different type of magical acts are prevalent in different tribes. The tribals believe in magicians and witches. If a woman is declared a witch by the magicians of the village, she is given all types of tortures. A strange type of magical act is found among the Bhils to contradict the effect of epidemic. In the event of the spread of epidemic some people hang some pitchers and baskets in bamboo pole and run on the main street coming, 'Toraka, Toraka',. Hearing them other people of the village help them in carrying this load out of the village. The load is carried to the nearest river or jungle and throwing it the people believe that the epidemic has been thrown out of the village in the river or the forest.

Tribal Taboos

The custom of totem is an important characteristic of tribal religion. Different Indian tribes believe in different types of totems. The totem is considered to be the originator of a particular tribe. Its killing and eating is a taboo for the people of the particular tribe. It is worshipped and respected everywhere. Marriages cannot be contracted among the males and females of the said totem, because they are thought to be having blood relationship. In fact tribal religion is the most primitive form of human religion. Thus it exhibits that unrefined purity characteristic of the primitive form. It is the beginning of religious revolution. Hence in it one finds magic, religion and ritualism all in one. In it there is no distinction of utility and religious sanctity. Mostly, the latter depend on the former. The tribal religion is not merely a particular part of the tribal life, but enters in life everywhere. The religious and social activities of the tribal people are closely interconnected.

New Trends in Tribal Culture

Due to contact with Hindu and Western culture, the tribal culture has constantly changed. This cultural change has been affected by the following processes:

Simple Adoption: In this process of cultural change, a tribe simply adopts the culture of another tribe, for example, the Worli tribes of Bombay state, formerly used to wear only a cloth. Now they use shirt, turban and dhoti due to the influence of Worli tribe.

Acculturation: Where a culture almost engulfs another culture and changes it, the process is known as acculturation. This involves a wider and deeper cultural change. For example, the Indian tribal culture is being constantly influenced by Hindu culture, so much so that some tribes are almost Hindu in culture. An example of this type of cultural change can be found in Gond tribe.

Assimilation: In this process of cultural change, a culture is not only adopted, but also assimilated and therefore becomes an integral part of the adopting culture. This process is seen in the tribe who, leaving their difficult mountain tracks and deep forests, come to plains and stay there. Such tribes in India have been assimilated in Hindu society *e.g.*, the Santhals of Bengal have cultural organization.

According to D.N. Majumdar the Indian tribes can be classified into two groups on the basis of processes of cultural change. First, there are assimilated tribes whose cultures have been completely assimilated by some other culture. Secondly, there are adaptative tribes whose culture is gradually adapting according to some new culture.

Effect of Western Culture on Tribes: The impart of cultural contact with Hindus and Christians has resulted both in evil as well as favourable consequences. This culture contact has removed many superstitions and evil customs from the tribes. The Christian missionaries have opened hospitals and schools for the benefit of tribal people. These have decreased the influence of disease and illiteracy. The Christian missionaries are also running several orphanages in tribal areas. They are giving monetary help to the needy tribals and helping in the improvement of the levels of health and education. These favourable influences, however, are nothing before the evil consequences of the cultural contact. The following are the most important evil consequences in this connection:-

Disintegration of Collaborative Life

Due to the influence of western culture many of the tribals have begun to hate their traditions and customs and are gradually disappearing with the result that the collective life is degenerating.

Social Disorganization: This has led to disorganization of family and social institutions. The tribals who have converted into Christian religion, try to imitate European culture and hate their tribal brothers. This has led to social disorganization everywhere.

Exploitation of Economy: The civilized traders, contractors and religious missionaries have also economically exploited the tribal people. Misusing their ignorance they have caught them in the net of indebtedness and robbed their money and land.

Ethical Disintegration

The civilized people have spread gross immortality in tribal society. The poor women have been made to prostitute themselves. The evil of drinking and using all sorts of intoxicants has increased in the tribals. Prostitution has led to increase of venereal diseases. The tribes living near the city are very much morally degenerated.

Gradual Disappearance

The above-mentioned evil consequences of tribal contact with other cultures have led to gradual disappearance of some tribes, as it is in the case of Andmani, Korawa, Toda and Chenchu tribes.

Tribal Difficulty: The Indian tribes at present suffer from mainly two types of problems. Firstly, those which are also found in other people of the country and secondly those which are peculiar to tribal people. In this latter type of tribal problems the following are the most important:

Cultural Difficulty: Due to contact with other cultures, the tribal culture is undergoing a revolutionary change. Due tc the influence of Christian missionaries, the' problem of bilingualism has developed which has led to indifference towards tribal language. The tribal people are imitating Western culture in different aspects of their social life and leaving their own culture. An important influence of cultural contact is seen in the form of disappearance of youth dormitories, imitation of the western dress and modes of living has led to the degeneration of tribal life and tribal arts, such as dance, music and different types of crafts.

Religious Difficulty: Due to the conversion of many tribal people to Hindu and Christian religion, the tribal groups have been divided into several sects on the basis of religion. This has shattered their collective life and conflicts and dissensions are increasing. The tribal people are gradually forgetting their tribal religion. This has led to social disorganisation.

Social Difficulty: Due to the influence of Hindu community the tribals are facing the problem of increasing bride price. This has encouraged elopement of girls and their forcible lifting by males. Another social problem created by the tribal contact with the civilized society has increased the number of pre-marital and extra-marital sexual relationships in tribal society and the number of dissolution of marriages. This has also increased the incidence of prostitution and venereal diseases.

Economic Difficulty: The contact with the civilized world has disintegrated the entire economic system of the tribal people. They have forgotten their ancient crafts. Most of them are working as labourers in plantations, agricultural farms, factories and other jobs. The employers every where misuse the ignorance of the tribal people, take maximum work from them and give them minimum money in return.

Welfare Recommendations

The Indian Constitution has made important provisions for the welfare of tribal people. Posts have been reserved for them in public services, in States and Centre. Seats have been reserved for their representatives in the Legislatures of different States and in the Indian Parliament. Special provisions have been made regarding their administration. District and regional councils have been established to carry out their welfare. The government have given special attention to their educational and economic development. This has not appreciably improved the condition of tribal people. The following suggestions can be made in connection with tribal welfare.

Economic Impovement: Efforts should be made to encourage tribal people to permanently establish for cultivation, because the shifting cultivation practised by them results in much wastage. The co-operative forests utilization societies can help the tribal people in utilizing the forests in which they live. The Government should arrange for technical help and education to improve the condition of tribal crafts and provision should be made for the marketing of the goods produced by them. Laws should be strictly imposed in tribal areas to solve the problem of indebtedness and to restrict exploitation. Co-operative credit societies can be organised to provide money for small scale industries. Labour laws should be strictly enforced in tribal areas.

Educational Improvement: At the base of the fallen state of tribal society is their widespread illiteracy. Educational expansion, therefore, should be given primary consideration. The tribal education should be given through their own language and in their own cultural background. Colleges should be established to safeguard the tribal fine arts. Provision should be made for technical and commercial education in the tribes. Along with education the tribal music, dance, plays and recreation should be encouraged. Religious dogmatism and superstitions should be removed through scientific education.

Health Facility Improvement: Efforts should be made to improve the level of health of the tribal people. This will require provision of medicines, pure water, nutritive food, clean and properly ventilated houses and general healthy atmosphere.

Social Improvement: Whatever may be the opposition from certain vested interests, efforts to carry out social reforms in tribals must be realized. The evil customs of bride price, magic and ritualism, child marriage, prostitution etc., should be removed. These social reforms can be carried out only after economic reforms, have been implemented.

Political Improvement: It is a pity that the Govt. officials posted in tribal areas misuse the ignorance of tribal people and exploit them for different purposes. They scorn the tribal culture and are completely indifferent to their welfare. The Government should appoint such officials as are conversant with the tribal culture and intend to improve the condition of tribal people.

Attempts for Welfare

In free India the State and Central Government have made incessant efforts in the direction of tribal welfare. At the central level a commissioner attached with Home Ministry take care of tribal welfare. Under him there are several Regional Assistant Commissioners whose number has now increased to 16. In the States there are special Directorates of Tribal Welfare. In Assam five District and Regional Councils have been established for tribal welfare. Tribal Research Institutes for the study of tribal culture and language are working in Bihar, Madhya Pradesh, Orissa and other States.

Educational Effort: Efforts are being made to expand educational facilities in tribal areas. Thousands of scholarships have been granted by Central and State Government. Provisions have been made for special seats for tribal people in medical, engineering and technical colleges. Posts have been reserved for them in public services. Primary and Secondary Schools have been established in tribal areas where there is provision for free education.

Political Effort: In the political field the tribes send their representatives to State and Central Legislatures some of whom have risen to the rank of Deputy Ministers and Ministers. Many tribal youths qualify in All India Services and their number is gradually increasing.

Economic Effort: For the economic regeneration of the tribes, the Government has enforced rules regarding land ownership and utilization of land. Crores of rupees have been spent for the development of cottage industries. The Community Projects have been established every where. Grain shops have been opened which provide for improved type of seeds.

Laws in connection with debt have been enforced. Special multi purpose tribal blocks have been created. Shifting cultivation is restricted and tribal families have been permanently established on suitable land. Efforts have been made to provide housing facilities in some tribal areas. Hospitals have been opened which provide free medicines, check epidemics and cure all types of diseases.

Research institutes have been opened for the study of tribal culture and language. New roads have been made and old roads improved in the tribal areas. Personnel working for tribal welfare are given special training for this purpose. Institutes for their training have been established in Madhya Pradesh, West Bengal, Assam, Rajasthan, Bombay and other States.

The above brief outline of the State and Central Government efforts in the direction of tribal welfare show the extent of work that has been done in different Five Years Plans. This has definitely led to some improvement in some directions.

The solution of tribal problems, however, requires a multi-sided planning. To quote D.N.Majumdar, an authority on Indian tribal problems, "There is no one solution to tribal problems, there is no common platform to demand it. There are levels of cultural development and there are different patterns of life that the tribes own. In any scheme of rehabilitation of tribal life, the attitudes and configurations of culture must be known to work out plans, and what is true of one culture area may not be so for a second.

6

Class System

Agrarian and industrial class structure, emergence of middle class; emergence of classes among tribes; elite formation in India.

Group Organisation

The class structure in India has been interpreted by employing different theoretical orientations by the Indian Sociologists. Sociologists like A.R. Desai has utilised Marxian theory while analysing the Indian class structure in agrarian relation. However, attributes such as income, occupation, non agricultural modes of earning are used to the studies on caste, class is, however, not substantial. The reason is partly historical and more importantly, it is because of the continued overlapping between the caste and class status situations or interactions in Indian social stratification. Often, it is difficult to draw a sharp line where caste principle of stratification ceases and the class principle begins. Caste and class are two principles of stratification which have persisted in the Indian social systems in a dialectical relationship.

The Sociology of Indian class stratification should not only take into account the present day processes among the various class strata but also analyse them in the historical contexts of change. Studies which throw light on the class structure and its processes in the traditional Indian society reveal that class structure was related to the modes of production and ownership.

Kings, feudal chiefs, traders, artisans, peasants, labourers and the social relationships of these groups assume significance for understanding the Indian class structure.

The king occupied the highest position with so many loyalties and vassals and his subjects owed allegiance to him and in turn the king was responsible for the welfare of his people. The merchants, the business class were the most mobile. Here wealth and economic factors played important roles in determining one's class position and in that context one's social position based on caste became weakened. The establishment of various economic and political institution by the British enhanced the mobility of these groups of people that they could mobilise economic surpluses from village to towns and cities.

The process of social transformation of classes in India began as far back as 600 B.C. when "there was fusion of Aryan and pre-Aryan peoples and cultures". The period from 600 B.C. to the first millennium A.D. saw the rise of an active material cultural tradition which coincided with the development of banking, emergence of guild organisations and also the religion of Buddhism and the rise of agricultural class. These developments strengthened the growth of artisan and class trading communities as urban traders, town traders and money-lenders. Among different caste groups there was Jajmani system being practised in rural India. It was not just the economic relationship between the patrons and the clients but also social relationships. It was based on mutual interdependence between the two that the lower castes could fulfil the secular function of the upper caste while the upper castes perform ritual function for the lower castes.

There was a decline in this system when British policy on economic system was introduced.

The British economic and political policies in India thus led to the destruction of many older bases of class formation and it also created foundations for the emergence of a feudal agrarian class structure. In cities, new industrial and mercantile middle class emerged and new bureaucratic administrative class as well. The Sociology of the Indian class stratification, nevertheless bears a deep imprint of these historical antecedents in two respects: first, the middle classes that subsequently emerged maintained the structural continuity in terms of recruitment and social background with the previous class structure and secondly, the British contact set a process of new cultural adaptation among the new middle classes.

This class formation was important for the British economic policy. But this could not alter the social base of Indian society.

Agricultural and Industrial Groups

The British in order to facilitate their economic management to suit their own system introduced changes in the agrarian system in North India and South as well.

The Zamindari, the Ryotwari and the Mahalwari system were introduced by the British for revenue assessment on the land. All three systems generated more or less a similar agrarian class structure in the villages. The zamindari system had the zamindars, tenants and agricultural labourers as the main agrarian classes. The ryotwari system consisted of two types of peasants; the ryot landlord and the ryot-peasants. The agrarian class structure everywhere in India had a feudal character; the zamindars collected taxes and were non-cultivating owners of land, the tenants were the real cultivators often without security of land tenure and the agricultural labourers in most parts of the country, had the status of bondsmen and labourers. With the support of the British this highly exploitative system continued to persist all over due to which many peasant movements occurred in the Indian soil.

The challenge to the feudal *class structure emerged with the rise of* the nationalist movement. Not only was radical agrarian ideology accepted but the national leadership actively undertook the cause of the exploited peasantry and led Kisan movements in various parts of the country such as Punjab, Andhra Pradesh, Bihar. Following independence, the land reforms were introduced in most states and it was the beginning for transforming the agrarian class structure and the changes that occurred after this transformation were sociologically significant.

Western authors and Indian sociologists have studied that Indian agrarian social structure by adopting different theoretical orientations. A.R. Desai, Daniel Thorner have used the Marxian approach while studying Agrarian relation in Kumbapaeti village in Tamil Nadu while others such as Dumont used the attributional approach. Daniel Thorner argues that even though there has been land reform measures the peasants continue to suffer the most and the land owning groups such as the Maliks continue to enjoy their dominant positions. This relationship to land corresponds to social relationship as well. The lower castes work as landless labourers for the land owning caste groups who belong to the upper caste. He further maintains these class groups are interdependent on each other underlying different sociological aspects.

A.R. Desai has used the dialectical approach to the understanding of agrarian class relations in rural India.

Ramakrishna Mukherjee has formulated three rural class categories out of the nine occupational categories. He names these as 'land holders and supervisory farmers, 'self-sufficient peasantry' and the group of 'share croppers, agricultural labourer, service holders and others'. These classes roughly correspond with the categories of 'sub infeudatory landlords', 'self-sufficient peasantry' and the 'agricultural labourers'.

The land reform measures in India did not bring about uniform results in land distribution all over India. In some places it moved in a desirable direction while on other places it did not bring about any significant changes.

P.C. Joshi highlighted the trends in the agrarian class structure and the relationships of these agrarian classes in the following ways:

* The decline in feudalistic and customary tenancy.
* Increasing importance commercial tenancy based on the rich and middle state of the peasantry. Decline of feudal landlords and the rise of commercially oriented landlords.
* The socio-economic consequences of these commercial peasants. That, it increased the efficiency and productivity of agriculture but conflicts between the poor peasantry and agricultural labourers has been on the rise.

In present India, there has been changes and mobility too. That traditionally land owning classes sell off land and pursue other economic activities for example the Brahmins were the first among others who sell off their land and get better education and join the bureaucratic job. Brahmins dominate in most bureaucratic jobs.

Because of various opportunities such as industrialisation, urbanisation many abandon agricultural jobs and move to urban places in search of other economic activities. Such mobility also weaken rural agrarian class structure. Using mobility model for analysing the changing class position in villages, Beiteille argues that the traditional class, caste and power factors, these have been dispersed among different groups. That it becomes usual for a member from the upper caste to have a lower class status today. The change from 'cumulative' to 'dispersed' inequalities represents an important element in the changing social stratification. Beteille also uses the term 'harmonic' and 'disharmonic' as two through which the system of social stratification in India and in the West could be compared. In the harmonic system, *e.g.* the traditional caste stratification in India, there was a close fit between the ideology of inequality with the reality of inequalities. In the disharmonic system (of the West) the two diverge, although according to Beteille the pre industrial West also had a system (system of stratification closer to that of traditional India.

Changes in one domain affects the changes in other areas too and such changes is all encompassing even though the rate and degree of such changes differ from region to region.

As industrialisation proceeds, not only does the ratio of working forces engaged in agriculture compared to those engaged in industrial activities go down but the process of social mobility is also accelerated. The number of workers engaged in factories also increase over those engaged in agriculture. Michael Young rightly says the soil grows castes; the machine makes classes'. India is still a peasant society. The class awareness among the Indian industrial workers, if measured through union membership of participation is not quite strong. The trade unions are generally weak in financial resources, although most of them are supported by political parties. Many sociological studies that have been made about the industrial workers in India show that the caste stratification does influence the nature of the industrial working class; it affects its class character. Industrial workers maintain close relationship with their caste and kin-groups, villages and regions and observe caste rules, almost all caste groups are represented in the working population. The recruitment to the industrial class is more on the basis of particularistic ties, achievement, merit and efficiency. India is also known for its soft policy implementation.

In order to understand the class structure in industrial society, it is necessary to know who controls what like the mode of production and different class groups working on the mode of production and the relationship of these classes within the production system.

No single industrial elite controls the economic power but that control is divided among various elites who have stiff competition among themselves despite their corporation. There is a strong symbolic relationship between politicians and economic elites. This is especially true in societies with brokerage-type political parties. Politicians constantly need money to finance expensive election campaigns while economic elites seek legislative favours such as lower taxes, larger governmental subsidies and less restrictive regulation, which only the politicians can provide. This is where politics also interfere in business matters of various industrial units.

Because of the technology they share, all industrial societies have a similar division of labour. If elites want to attract capable people to the more demanding and responsible professional and managerial roles, they have to provide material incentives. When such incentives were withdrawn for ideological reasons and income differences between occupational strata were minimised, the flow of qualified individuals into these positions declined and serious problems developed. Thus despite ideological differences, patterns of stratification in all industrial societies are alike in some basic ways. This has been observed by many sociologists who have contributed in social stratification of industrial societies such as capitalists as well as Soviet Russia.

Income, status group based on income, standard of life, social cliques become important criterion for determining one's class status in industrial society. One's occupation also becomes important in industrial society. For the vast majority of the members of any industrial society, the chief determinant of their access to income and wealth is their position in the occupational system of stratification. In industrial societies, managerial and professional occupations are the most highly rewarded, followed by manual workers in skilled occupations. These are followed by lower white-collar employees engaged in clerical or sales work, while unskilled manual workers are at the bottom of the occupational hierarchy.

Skilled blue collar workers enjoy higher incomes than lower white collar workers. Another change that has occurred in the occupational system of stratification in industrial societies has been the substantial growth in the relative number of high and middle status occupations. There has also been relative growth in the two intermediate occupational classes—skilled manual workers and lower white collar workers, especially the latter. These developments have brought about an important change in the class structure; the majority of people in most industrial societies, are members of the middle class. This is yet another consequence of the technological innovations that have so transformed the conditions of life for members of these societies since the beginnings of industrialisation.

Industrial developments demand more and more capable people, with high managerial skills. Here technical and efficient manpower is highly required. Various institutions provide training to produce such manpower.

Getting into such educational institutions become a fierce competition among the members. Here also we see the reflection of social inequality. That, mostly it is the people who belong to better income and occupational groups that can have access to better and efficient institutions and in turn they prove themselves superior to others who have come from relatively backward institutions in terms of quality. Coupled with these there is also the evidence of selection of people on particularistic ties rather than pure merit or achievement. Because of such persistence, education has been linked with production of external capitals. One most outstanding visible class relation in industrial society is the inequality that exist between the sexes, men and women. Women all over the world are looked upon as minority and one class because of their similar characteristics they share universally. If industrial society encourages efficiency, openess, and talented people and reward on the basis of one's achievement, than in many ways industrial society has not done justice to women folk. That even many educated women's entry in the job market is less. Women's income is substantially lower than that of men. There are a variety of reasons for this, but the most important appears to be the persistence of the division of labour between the sexes. The occupations filled primarily by women usually have lower wages or salaries. There has been improvement but changes occur very slowly. Harassment of women in work places on the basis of gender has become quite evident in many work places and hence the inequality on the basis of gender becomes all the more engendered.

But inequality based on industrial relations is considerably much less than inequality based on agrarian relations as already highlighted in the preceding discussions.

Disintegration of Middle Class and Elite Groups

Elites do not constitute in one particular branch of our social system but exist on different spheres such as the business elite, industrial elites and so on. Mosca and Pareto while studying power elite in America maintain the fact that elites in whatever sphere they are form the most powerful group of people sharing the same status group, standard of living and similar life styles and hence the elites form a group of their own forming a closed group. They maintain that they are the most powerful people in decision making, and influential in policy marking and implementation. They are considered to be superior than the masses in terms of knowledge, experiences and these are all reflected in their life styles. This is almost true in our society too. Traditional elite group and elite formation in traditional India was different than in present India. That, the traditional elites was different in traditional India and correspondingly their elite roles were also different.

The category 'traditional' or charismatic' is used for elites in the old Indian society. The elite role in many studies is related with the caste structure and the theory of varna, especially the charismatic role of the Brahmans, is emphasized. This hypothesis is taken as confirmed by demonstrating the wide extent to which the Brahmans continued to hold predominant elite roles during the British period of the Indian political and cultural movements and after Independence. That, even today, the Brahmins are identified as elites.

The educated middle classes who imbibed western culture in their life style including those of nationalism and liberalism and of religious and cultural reforms emerged as new elite. Introduction of English education and the new educational opportunities for the educated in the modern segment of society created a new phase in Indian elite. These elites played important roles in the formation of policies and propagandas before the British government.

With the emergence of these elites there also took place a functional differentiation among the various types of elites. The political, business and cultural elites did exist in the traditional social structure, but their ideology and function in society was more tradition reinforcing than oriented to structural changes or cultural innovations. The nationalist ideology which the new elites imbibed from the west along with the ideology of economic, social and technological modernisation implied a radical departure from the past traditional elites The new elite continued a new middle class belonging to different professional groups. They were Raja Ram Mohan Roy, Swami Vivekananda, Ishwar Chandra Vidhaya Sagar, M.M. Malaviya, Tilak, Lala Lajpat Rai, Sardar Patel, Gopalachari, Gandhi, Nehru etc. These elites despite of different ideologies were unified for a common goal. *i.e.* India's freedom from the British yoke. This helped in developing the creation of one political unit. Thus new political elites in India emerged through the process of the establishment of Indian nationhood and consolidation of its political freedom. A plurality of structural background characterised the nature of these elites right from the beginning, although elites of the nineteenth and twentieth centuries were functionally diffused. In the process of this political movement, they emerged as the champions of socio-cultural movement. These political elites before independence came from the upper rung of social stratification, irrespective of the variations in their ideologies and ethnic-religious background. The Indian National Congress in a way represents the plurality of most types of ideological traditions of the Indian political elites. The Congress was composed of the new elites of the urban educated middle class such as lawyers, journalists, doctors and teachers. Other political parties like communist party also consisted of elites coming from the upper castes. Reconciliation has been one main feature of these elites.

The business elites come from the traditional merchant castes and many among them have maintained their occupational continuity over a long historical period. They had simultaneous links with the villages despite their dealings in the metropolis and towns. Mobility of these elites from the lower trading occupation to that of business elite or even entrepreneur has been quite popular.

The British was not successful in using the business elites for their political means and they sided with the political elites.

Thus the business elites succeeded in establishing a working relationship with the political elites and evolved a method of response and reconciliation to the industrial policies being followed after Independence.

This also softened the attitude of political elites towards the business elites in India. They were allowed to play an important role in the industrial economy of free India. This development contributed to the growth of the economic power of the business class and elite entrepreneurs in course of the years.

Planned economy has encouraged the process of concentration by facilitating and aiding the growth of big business in India. The concentration of economic power into a few business class also resulted from the licensing policies that the government pursued to augment the industrial sector. The bureaucratic elite and the professional elite constitute another form of elite in our society.

The bureaucratic elites are specially governed by this best attribute of the professional elites. The professional elites like doctors, engineers and lawyers deal in their work more through the normative standard of skill and knowledge. The bureaucratic elites lay more emphasis on conformity to the formally established procedures and rules. The significant role professional elites play reflects the degree to which the country is undergoing social structural differentiation, or changes from tradition to modernity in the fields of occupation, industry and economy; and professional elite assume relevance for the analysis of social stratification also as indicators of social mobility in the class system.

Irrespective of the types of professional elites chosen, it is revealed that the recruitment is heavily biased in favour of the upper castes, the male population and high income group. The upper-middle and middle classes dominate over most of the opportunities and positions in the professional sectors of our society.

The Indian bureaucracy may seem to have passed through three major stages in terms of its dominant orientations. First, at the inception and during the early phases of the company's rule, the 'ethos of trade' was dominant in the civil service. Second was the period of the company crown rule when the civil service as guided by the ethos of professional career of the psychology of masters and guardians'. The third stage following Independence is when the ethos of Indian bureaucracy became professional and developmental. It tends now also to be imbibed with nationalistic values and aspirations.

In various fields Indian intellectuals have produced quality work and have contributed to welfare programmes of the community. This researched work also have been utilised in certain departments of government specially in the field of health and hygiene, women's issues, education etc. Yet, many of these elites remain to be from the upper caste or the more relatively advanced of people socially and financially.

Disintegration of Class into Tribe

Many studies on tribes have shown that they have more or less egalitarian form of society.

Thus social inequality is generally rather limited in most tribal societies of the modern era. Although extremes of wealth and political power are absent, substantial differences in prestige are not uncommon. Political and religious leaders usually enjoy high status, but this depends far more on personal achievements than on mere occupancy of an office. Other bases of status include military prowess, skill in oratory, age, kinship ties and in some cases wealth in the form of wives, pigs and ornaments. Each society has its own peculiar combination of these criteria.

The more advanced the technology and economy of one of these groups, the greater social inequality within it tends to be. Societies that practise irrigation, own domesticated animals, or practice metallurgy for ornamental and ceremonial purposes are usually less egalitarian than groups without these characteristics. However, tribes who reside on fringe regions, near the lowest caste groups of Hindu society tend to convert themselves into scheduled caste and imitate the life style of these caste groups. Such a phenomenon have been in tradition from the early times till date. The tribes, because of positive discrimination and other facilities offered by the government are able to move up in the hierarchy not ritually.

This shows that the two seemingly opposite principles-secular class conflict and religious-cultural-can be seen as transformations. The secular ideology can be recorded into the religious-cultural one and *vice-versa*. At a higher level of abstraction, the opposition is overcome through transformation. The secular and the religious principles can be made to achieve the same end, namely that one establishing a new identity for self-determination and for attacking the monopolies of first-class citizens over religious, economic, educational and political goods and services.

7

ROLE OF FAMILY

Family represents both an institution as well as an association. It is the oldest amongst the other institutions and associations. Also family still forms the backbone of our social structure. Due to these reasons, amongst all associations and institutions of mankind the family is rendered to be the most stable and enduring. As a primary group, the family is the first and most universal of all forms of associations. It is the core of all social organisation, remaining in some even in the most complex system. It is family, which passes on the traditions of a society, and it is family in its comrade and playmate aspects that the first movements of social impulses are felt.

MEANING OF FAMILY

Family has been defined into various ways.

(a) *Burgess and Locke:* "A family is a group of persons united by the ties of marriage, blood or adoption, constituting a single house-hold, inter-acting and inter-communicating, with each other in their respective social role of husband and wife, mother and father, son and daughter, brother and sister, creating and maintaining a common culture.

(b) *MacIver and Page:* "The family is a group defined by sex relationship sufficiently precise and enduring to provide for the procreation and upbringing of children.

(c) *Ogburn and Nimkoff:* "Family is more or less a durable association of husband and wife without children or of a man or woman alone."

Features of Family

The above quoted definitions of family may appear to be quite comprehensive but without more examination a full valuation of family will not be possible. As a social unit family reveals the following important characteristics:

(1) Family is primarily based on mating relationship.

(2) Since family represents an enduring relationship, reckoning of descent either through father or mother is also a characteristic of family.

(3) Child bearing and rearing is a consequence of mating relationship and this involves economic factors, the earning and spending within the family. Hence both child bearing and economic factors also contribute in the constitution of family.

(4) The relationship of the members of a family are socially sanctioned and are traditional in nature.

(5) Living together of various members of a family is also one of its characteristics.

Family has all the characteristics of the other associations of man but besides these and those stated above, family is further distinguished by the following features.

(1) *Universality:* Family is the most universal amongst the innumerable associations of man. It is found in all societies, primitive as well as modern, of pre-historic

times and those existing in our own era. It even surpasses the boundaries of human species and extends amongst the other members of animal kingdom.

(2) *Emotionality:* The profound impulses of mating for procreation and motherly devotions form the main foundation of the emotional life of human beings. These impulses accompanied by secondary impulses concerning economical security, security from the dread of solitude, colour the family life in emotional hues.

(3) *Formative Influence:* Infancy is the most susceptible period in the life of a human being and because a man is born in a family and for greater part of his childhood and adolescence remains strictly within its limits, he is moulded in accordance with the environment in his family.

(4) *Limited Size:* Family due to its inherent nature does not favour a large size. Biological consideration themselves demand the smaller size of family.

(5) *Nuclear Position in the Social Structure:* Though some of the functions of the family have been encroached upon and taken away by other organisations of society, yet family still remains the centre of many activities of man, individual as well as social. Besides the family is looted in human temperament.

(6) *Responsibility of Members:* In other organisations the responsibilities of the members are precise and limited. In family, responsibilities are not limited to one member; first because they appear to the family as a whole and secondly members of a family tend to react with feeling of give and take hence responsibility of one becomes the responsibility of the other.

(7) *Social Regulations:* In a family, its members voluntarily learn to conform to the patterns of conduct setup by that family. Man knows what cooperation and mutual

regard is. Besides, by sustaining the institution of marriage family directly regulates the sex-urge of individuals without which the whole society would disorganize within a short time.

(8) *Its Permanent and Temporary Nature:* The quality of both enduring as well as changing nature of the family is one of its most characteristic features. As has already been stated, family behaves both as an institution as well as an association. As an institution family is of most permanent nature and on the other hand as an association family presents a kaleidoscope of ever-changing patterns.

Role of Family

(1) *Biological Function:* In all societies primitive or modern, simple or complex, human sex-urge requires established and socially recognised channels of satisfaction. The relationship between husband and wife and the act of mating it involves, represents the most important biological function of family. Procreation of the race is generally a consequence of the satisfaction of sex-urge, at least it is so from the viewpoint of the persons involved.

(2) *Psychological Function:* Cry is the only language of a child. But the environment and conditions within a family guarantee that the language of that cry be understood. Long before a child can communicate his feelings and thoughts to other members of the family via media of language a child finds his relative relationship with each member of the family, although his assessments are upon purely psychological reactions are native.

(3) *Social Function:* One of the most important, in fact second in importance to the biological function of the family,

is social functions. Family, in primitive and simpler societies formed the basic unit of social organisation. In a way society was more an aggregation of family organisation than an independent system. The position, however, is not the same in the case of relatively advanced societies. Her family do not exactly represent the basic organisational unit of the society, but its role in the determination of the texture and stability of social organisation has not at all diminished. It would be more correct to say that with the growing influence, larger and more impersonal organisations in the affairs of man, the need and the importance of the family, as the most human and personal association mankind, has considerably increased.

(4) *Socialisation:* Socialisation of human personality is another important function of family. "The child's first human relationships are with the immediate members of his family. He learns first of all from those immediately in charge of him, his mother or nurse or his father or in some societies those who function in their stead. There he experiences love, authority, direction, protection, setting of examples and ideals. Every moment of his conscious life, adult conduct is acting upon his consciousness according to the capacity he possesses to appreciate its meaning. It provides active stimuli to his nervous system. He reacts to this conduct by actions a first purely instinctive but increasingly conscious and perhaps purposive. Habits form according to the treatment they had given him and according to the reaction determined by his inherited capacity. As he grows older limitation of parental actions and exposure to their suggestions lead him to form habits which affect his social life more profoundly than he will recognize until many years after, if at all."

(5) *Formation of Personality Traits:* There are many aspect of human personality which are regarded to be the product of family organisation. No influence is initially as great, however, as the family on the individual. The family is primary in shaping the basic personality traits of individuals.

FAMILY ORGANISATION

The basic structure of the family is provided by the individual nuclear family, the incest taboos, the form of marriage and the rules of residence. Individual nuclear family is of course of significant importance. As Lowie writes: "It does not matter whether marital relations are permanent or temporary; whether there is polygamy or sexual licence; whether conditions are complicated by the addition of members not included in our family circle; the one fact stands out beyond all others that everywhere husband, wife and immature children constitute a unit apart from the remainder of the community." It is nuclear, as it is combined with others to form more complex families. In combining with other families, the component nuclear families always retain their separate identity.

The basic structure of the family depends on the incest taboos. It follows that the nuclear family is linked to two generations. Murdock thus points out that, "In consequence...every normal adult in every human society belongs to at least two nuclear families-a family of orientation in which he was born and reared, and which includes his father, mother, brothers and sisters, and a family of procreation which he establishes by his marriage and which includes his husband or wife, his sons and his daughters". The two families are similar in structure, but for the fact that in one a particular person has the position of son or daughter and in the other that of husband or wife. A third generation can only result from the formation of new families between the existing nuclear families.

Kinds of Family Organisation

Family structure is not the same everywhere. It differs from society to society. Kingsley Davis has listed some major variables that influence the family structure. There are among others the marital relations (number of spouses, authority, strength of bond, choice of spouse, residence etc.), the parent-child relation, and sibling relations. There exists a broad distinction between family systems in which the nuclear family is relatively independent, and systems in which it is incorporated into a larger group, the polygamous or the extended family.

> "The independent nuclear family is characteristic of modern industrial societies. Its predominance seems to be due to the growth of individualism, reflected in property, law, and general social ideals of individual happiness, self-fulfilment, and geographical and social mobility. It has also been affected by the increasing state provision for individual misfortune; the individual is no longer so dependent upon his family in times of distress. This marked predominance of the relatively autonomous nuclear family is a secret phenomenon, and it has appeared most fully in the most advanced industrial societies, particularly USA. The solidarity of this type of family depends largely upon sexual attraction and companionship between husband and wife and companionship between parents and children. This does not seem to be such a firm basis as the wider complex of rights and obligations (economic, sexual and so on) which exist in the extended family. The loss of economic functions is more important than most sociologists have recognised. Divorce is frequent in the USA, and has been increasing in most Western countries. The solidarity of the independent nuclear family is

greater where it includes young children, but as the children grow up the bonds tend to weaken again, first through the influence of peer groups, and later as a result of social mobility and geographical mobility". (Bottomore).

The composite or the incorporated family is of ancient origin and long tradition. In Western industrial society, it has long ceased to exist. It continued to exist in Yugoslavia "until the beginning of the present century". In our country the joint family has existed since the earliest times as indicated above. It was a corporate body. Their concern's, agriculture or commerce was common. The property was held in common. It was quite usual for families to comprise three or four generations, to live under the same shelter, and to eat from common kitchen. Besides property and work, joint worship and ritual was an important force, that kept the joint family united. In China too, a system similar to our family system existed. The ideal family in China was the patrilocal extended family. In each generation the men brought their wives to their father's house; and the strongest social tie in China, at least in theory, was between father and son. The oldest man was the head of the joint house hold. He was succeeded by his eldest son.

Kinds of Family

Broadly speaking, we can divide the various forms of family into two main categories, the patriarchal and the matriarchal. All types of family organisations, primitive as well as modern, fall within one category or the other, or represent a combination of the both.

The Matriarchal Family: Matriarchal family is that type in which the control of the family is centred around some woman member. From family control it is not meant that the woman holds a position of authority in the family. There have been ruling queens in ancient times and in our own times there are women who hold an authoritative position in the field of finance and governance, but the families of which such women are the members cannot be categorised as maternal or matriarchal type of families. Matriarchal families are those families where name, status and material inheritance are transmitted through the female line.

The main features of this type of family are:

(a) Descent is traced through mother.

(b) In most case, the family resides at the home of mother. Husband has only a secondary position in the home and often that is regarded as below the position enjoyed by brothers of his wife.

(c) Due to above, authority in maternal family frequently belongs to some male representative of wife's kin.

(d) According to MacIver and Page, "The maternal system tends to wield the kin-group (or "consanguine family") together but to lessen the cohesiveness of the 'conjugal' family itself. It is usually associated with the principle of exogamy, the tribe being separated into separate intermarrying groups."

The Patriarchal Family: Patriarchal form of family has been the most prevalent type in both ancient as well as modern civilisations. In fact, leaving aside the more industrially advanced countries, where many deviations have occurred in the family structure, patriarchal system forms the basis of families of the majority of present-day societies. The main reason behind the prevalence of this type of family is the pattern of economic relation in which the male of the species plays the dominant role. The economic status of male has remained as such from the early days of human civilisation to our own times. Even in those countries where woman has been given equal rights in the economic sphere, her position has not been shown any marked improvement chiefly due to the reason that old traditions still prevail with almost undiminished strength.

Factors that Favour the Patriarchal System: The mode of production in advanced societies, the specialisation it requires and the relationship it gives birth to, all these tends to strengthen the patriarchal system. That is to say, the-patriarchal type of family is more in conformity with economic patterns of production and distribution and the consequent modification in the social structure than the maternal type of family. This was one of the main reasons of the prevalence of patriarchal type of family over the maternal type. According to MacIver and Page, "The growth of property, the development of agriculture, the concentration of authority, and the specialisation of functions, which characterize the more modern societies, were more in harmony with the patriarchal principle. In many cases, they, doubt, led to its victory over the maternal system. Moreover, the patriarchal principle permitted the family to serve as a compact unit of society, for here there is no division of functions between the father relative by marriage, as the maternal system involved. Under the latter, a society is usually divided into exogamous group, but under the patriarchal system it becomes a system of family units consolidated into larger kin-group."

Modern Family: The new economic forms which the industrial civilisation brought in its wake, and the new cultural trends which began to mould the ideas and ideals of mankind, did not find themselves in harmony with the pure patriarchal system of families, in a like manner in which these happenings could not conform to the old feudal system of society. New forces were more strongly assisted by the vastly accumulated economic factors; they shattered the old order of things-the feudal system of society along with that of the patriarchal structure of family began to crumble.

Patriarchal form of family was best suited to a feudalistic system of society. All other organisations of feudal society tended to strengthen this type of family. The dynastic order of Government, the control of orthodox religion on the family discipline and the subordinate place given to woman by the society, all these were not only in consistency with the patriarchal attitude. But directly supported it.

Many Factors Responsible for Growth of Modern Family: With the breaking of order of dynastic order of Government and the establishment of democracies, with the decreasing hold of religion on the affairs of man and with the enlightened ideas in eighteenth century which insisted on the equality and freedom of all men and women, the old foundation of patriarchal family weakened and crumbled. Accompanied of those came a general diminution in the functional role of the family. This decrease in the functional role of the family, was all sided. Religious, social and economical function of family were taken away by other more efficient organisations of the society. Adding to the aforesaid factors with the establishment of romantic love as the basis of marriage in almost all the developed countries. The factor alone was responsible for freeing the family from old burdensome social obligations and responsibilities and in placing the family on new basis where only the bare biological and emotional factors interplayed.

Functional Aims of Modern Family: As a functional unit modern family aims at the fulfilment of only three major tasks. Firstly, it provides means and ways for stable satisfaction of sex-urge. Secondly, it helps men and women in the production and rearing up children. Thirdly, it provides a home. It will be seen that these functions are not only inter-related but also constitute the functional core of the family throughout ages and of all types and varieties. The crystallisation of the distinction between the first two functions of family mentioned above, *i.e.*, between sexual and reproductive, is more a product of modern scientific achievement in the field of birth control than a product of purely sociological ones. Now, the wife is in a better position to play these roles which in times of patriarchal family system were reserved for concubine or prostitute, because sexual satisfaction minus is productive implications indicate to the new status of modern eve.

With the changed social circumstances, old institutions, associations etc. either modify themselves or perish. Family has not perished chiefly because it was the only socially sanctioned institution, for the satisfaction of one of the basic hunger of man-the hunger for sexual satisfaction, which imply the reproduction and procreation of race. With the separation of sexual satisfaction from its consequence the reproduction, by birth control means, man is striking at the very foundations of family.

Perhaps it is a writing on the wall which proclaimed the coming downfall of the family. There are indications to confirm this, as evident in the experiments that are being undertaken in some of the countries where the state is gradually but steadily breaking the family lives and individual personality and bringing men and women in the world of communes; of group living and thinking. Such are the directions towards which modern family is proceeding and perhaps, some day that direction may lead it to its bloom.

Religious Aspect of Family

In ancient India, life of domesticity was regarded as the basis for the fulfilment of duty. The name 'patni' implies that woman accompanies the man in performance of his religious duties. According to the Hindu shastras no man can complete religious activities without a wife. Even today it is in the family that the individual is educated regarding religious customs and functions.

The important work of imparting elementary religious education to the members of society was everywhere the responsibility of the family. But now the relation of religion to the family has weakened and has been much reduced since now-a-days the interest in religion is declining, and in addition to this religion is looked upon as a private affair in which the family need not interfere.

Family from the Economic View-point: Family is the centre of economic activities. It is the family which utilises the production of society. Sometimes the entire family jointly pursues an occupation. Agriculture, especially, is an occupation which is pursued jointly by the entire family and in it the men do the work of plantation, irrigation and sowing, the women that of cutting the crop while the children take over light work such as grazing the herds of animals. Inheritance also stems from the family. The family protects property, makes arrangements for an adequate income and endeavours to fulfil the needs of the members. It is the family which provides the supports for the old, disabled, unemployed and helpless.

In the ancient Roman family, the head had all the authority of the absolute ruler vested in him. In the Roman law it was prescribed that the father could put his sons into jail, sell them and execute them. In this way, in ancient times the right of administration was the possession of the Pater Familia. Now-a-days the family no longer possesses such unbridled authority to punish the individuals. Only the state has authority to sentence a person to imprisonment or death. Nevertheless the family does much to assist the state in running the government machinery. It exercises control over the conduct of the individuals and prevents them from indulging in antisocial activity. The government consequently finds it easier to maintain order. The family inculcates in the child the habit of discipline from the very beginning.

The family presents to the child an environment which enables him to become a successful citizen in the future. In the absence of training of this kind the child grows up to become obstinate and criminal. In this way, although the importance of the family from the view-points of religion, economy and the government has waned, it still is an important social institution. In all these spheres it assists other agencies.

Separation in Family

The modern family is gradually becoming increasingly disorganised. Some signs of this phenomenon can be seen in the following changes in the family:

Lack of Family Unity: Now-a-days the agreement in objectives, ambitions, thoughts and ideals in the family is at an end or tending in that direction. Men, women, boys and girls each have their own ideals, their own plans, individual programmes and individual thoughts, in which they brook no interference whatever. In this way, even while living together, eating and moving together no one is concerned with another. The house becomes almost a hotel where the family members gather only to take food and rest. Where both the husband and wife are employed, a similar distance is seen to exist between them.

Decrease in Family Control: In modern times the control of the family over its members is continually decreasing. No one wants to be lectured by anybody else. The younger generation finds a bitterness in the wisdom of its predecessors. They do not want to be controlled by them in any sphere. They want to be separated from the family immediately after they start earning or after they are married. In this way, the disorganisation of the family is obvious.

Strife: The strife within the family is presently on the increase because of the absence of family control as well as the absence of a sense of unity among the members. Joint families are rapidly becoming disorganised. Violence, litigation, etc., are common enough occurrences. Faith in one another is decreasing. There are many separate families within one house. The disorganisation of the family is only too evident from this.

Laxity in Marital Bonds: The tie of marriage is the basis of family. Weakening of marriage ties results in a weakening of family ties. Now-a-days marriage is no longer a religious ritual but merely a social contract which can easily be cancelled or annulled on ground of boredom or some kind of misunderstanding. Consequently, there is a constant increase in the number of divorces. A major cause of the weakening of marriage ties is the failure of men to adapt to new circumstances created by the education of women. Previously women were completely dependent upon their husbands. Now, being educated, they also earn as much as their husbands or at least possess the capacity to do so. They want to be equal to the men in every aspect of life. They now demand the same fidelity which their men demand of them. When the men do not want to have women on an equal footing with themselves the result is a struggle due to which the family tends to become disorganised.

Conflict between Parents and Children: Now-a-days an important element indicative of family disorganisation is the conflict between parents and children. The control of the old people over young men and women is constantly decreasing. They do not want to be ordered by their parents in their behaviour, marriage, society etc. Consequently, the misunderstanding between the two parties increases and the family becomes further disorganised.

Lack of Protection: As a result of conflict between husband and wife and parents and children, psychological security is being continually diminished due to which mutual trust is decreasing and the family organisation is being shattered.

It is obvious from the above mentioned causes that the family is being rapidly disorganised in the modern age. The families are becoming smaller. The number of divorces is increasing. Mutual intimacy and belief are being reduced and their place has been taken by selfishness and frivolity.

Familial Change

In the modern period, the institution of family is undergoing rapid change and modification. The main changes, in this connection, are the following:

Reduction in the Economic Functions of Life: In the modern age, many of the economic functions which were previously being performed by the family, are now being performed by the schools, factories, government aid and other associations.

Reduction in other Activities of Family: Many of the other functions of the family have now been taken over by other agencies. The work of looking after and bringing up children is now being performed in creches, children parks, kindergarten schools and by baby sitters. Hospitals undertake the work of delivering children and of treatment. Restaurants make up food for thousands of families.

Increase in Family Recreation: Modern families have been transformed into centres of recreation with the invention of radio and television, and the advent of indoor games.

Laxity in Marital and Sex Relationships: The rigidity traditionally associated with marital a sexual relationships no longer characterises the modern family.

Changes in Relationship of Man and Woman: Now that the women have gained equal rights with men, their mutual relationship has undergone much change. Mawrer has correctly written of the modern woman, "She is no longer the drudge and slave of older days."

Increase in Importance of Children: In the modern family the importance of children has increased. They are now physically maltreated or punished only rarely but are instead taught lovingly. The modern families tend to become filiocentric families.

Decrease in Importance of Blood Relationships: In the modern family there has been a continuous decrease in the importance of blood relationships. The family is now constituted of a husband, a wife and their children.

Disorganisation of Joint Family: The modern family is no longer joint. The joint family is rapidly being disorganised.

Smaller Family: Due to the prolific use of contraceptives and the tendency to regard children as an obstacle in the progress and enjoyment of life, the birth rate is continuously falling and the modern families are becoming smaller.

Family Disorganisation: The process of disorganisation is quite apparent in the modern family. The number of divorces is on the increase. The control which the family exercises over the individual is being lessened.

Instability: The modern family is no longer a permanent association. It is precarious and can be rendered void at any time. Marriage has been reduced to a mere social contract which it is not difficult to break in the event of even the slightest function. According to MacIver the modern family, in comparison with the ancient and medieval families is very weak and unstable.

New Problems Confronting the Family: In this way the modern family is beset with many new problems the major among which now follows:

1. *Problem of Adjustment of the Husband-Wife Relationship:* In the modern family the most difficult problem is that of the mutual adjustment of husband and wife. The educated and enlightened woman of today wants to be the equal of her husband in every sphere of life. But the husbands have not yet adjusted to this situation. Hence a conflict between the two is inevitable. Laxity in sexual relations and the instability of marital relations also tend to create conflict between the husband and wife and to spoil their relationship.
2. *Problem of Sexual Adjustment:* The modern family is also faced with the problem of sexual adjustment, it being the outcome of changes in sex values. D.H. Lawrence, among the Western authors, has presented a graphic

and revealing sketch of this problem in his novels. Psychoanalytic literature has also adversely affected the ancient ideals of sex relationship. Today much importance is attached to the gratification of sexual desires. Some people have gone so far as to declare variety in sex relationships not only desirable but necessary. This tends to encourage premarital and extra-marital sex relationships. All that factors have the effect of creating sexual disharmony between husband and wife and as a result numerous families are disorganised.

3. *Marriages based on Romantic Love:* The third major problem that confronts the family is that of marriages being based on romantic love. After marriages of this nature when the dreams of the husband and wife do not materialise in the family they are seriously frustrated. They start blaming each other and either live in a state of perpetual strife or break the ties of marriage. Elliot and Merill, in their book *Social Disorganisation,* have described divorces as the inevitable consequence of romantic marriages.

4. *Problem of Broken Marriage:* A major problem faced by the modern family is an increase in the number of broken marriages. Marriages have been reduced to a mere social contract. Materialism, individualism, rationalism are the causes of paucity of such feelings as benevolence, love etc. Greater stress is laid on sexual pleasure. The women are far less dependent upon men. The laws of divorce are also not very stringent. All these causes have the cumulative effect of increasing the number of divorces.

5. *Problem of Working Women:* Now-a-days there are more women who are employed outside the precincts of the home. They consequently do not get-sufficient time to look after their children. Returning exhausted from their work they do not have the energy

left to attend to their husband or their children. This hinders the development of children and increases conflict and misunderstanding between husband and wife.

6. *Laxity in Family Control:* A major problem has been created for the modern family by the decrease in the control exercised by the family over its members. This has undermined the administration of the family. Boy-girl, husband-wife, brother-sister each wants to pursue his own course and does not relish any interference, be it advice or be it rebuke.
7. *Family Conflict and Strife:* Changes in the values of life and a reduction of the family control in the modern family have led to increased conflict between husband and wife as well as between parents and children. This conflict is usually not apparent but it does disturb the peace of the family, destroy the faith in one another and remove the sense of psychological security.
8. *Lower Birth Rate:* The birth rate is falling constantly due to late marriages, frequent use of contraceptives, and a tendency to consider children a burden. This tends to accentuate the instability of the family since the absence of children reduces the sense of responsibility in the husband and wife, besides preventing intimate family relations.

Causes of the Instability of Modern Family: The modern family is instable. An increase in the number of desertions, separations and divorces, etc. are a proof of this.

The main causes of this instability are the following:

Less Social Protection in Family Crisis: Previously, a family crisis of the nature of a maladjustment between husband and wife was overcome by the constraining influence of the elders, kinsmen and social mores and traditions and the family was saved from disintegration, but with the existing loss of respect for the power of these modes of social control the husband and wife are deprived of any guide or mediator and in a fit of temper or even vengeance they destroy the delicately and lovingly nurtured sapling which is the family, no matter how much remorse they may experience when they have cooled down. Previously, being financially dependent upon the husband the wife silently bore much injustice and did not dare think in terms of a separation.

Now, the women who are capable of earning their livelihood marry only for love and when that is not forthcoming there is almost nothing to deter them from dissolving their marriage. At some places extreme laxity of divorce laws has led to very great instability and impermanence of the family.

Replacement of Domination by Cooperation: According to MacIver and Page, the basis of husband-wife relationship in the family is no longer domination but cooperation. Previously, everywhere, be it the East or the West, the wife was dominated by the husband and hence the family stability survived. But with the removal of this dominance, in the modern time, the stability of the family can be maintained only by benevolence, sympathy and cooperation. Generally, it is not easy to create these qualities. Hence, the instability of the modern family.

Effect of Modern Civilisation on Family Disorganisation: Many factors of modern civilisation have a major hand in the disorganisation of the family. The main causes are the following:

Industrialism: In the modern Industrial system women and children work in factories along with the man. This reduces the unity of the family and increases disorganisation.

Ideals of Romantic Love: Modern marriages are based on the ideals of the romantic love. When the dreams of the two partners do not materialise in the family, conflict increases and is gradually transformed into enmity.

Hedonism: Modern civilisation is hedonistic. In this, people pay more attention to their rights than to their duties. This increases selfishness and the occasions for conflict.

Individualism: Modern civilisation is also individualistic. No one wants to consider the interests of the family. Everyone is engaged in the consideration of solely his own interest. No one is prepared to sacrifice his smallest interest to benefit another. As a result of this, conflict in the family increases.

Lack of Control in Sexual Relationships: Another consequence of modern civilisation is a change in the values concerning sex. This tends to diminish control in sex relationships, to reduce fidelity in marital relations and also to increase chances for family disorganisation.

Existence of Family

This has led some people to doubt whether the family will escape the present crisis in the highly industrialised and mechanised societies of the West. Will the family survive to continue in the form of a primary association? What will be the future of the family? Actually, there can never be any doubts concerning the continued existence of the family since its basis is the fundamental needs of human beings. It would be no exaggeration to say that the family assuredly exist in whatever varied or transformed form as long as the human society exists.

The desire for procreation is a natural desire in men. Outside the family there can neither be any legal offspring nor any proper arrangement for its upbringing. Some of the other kind of marriage system and a family are needed to afford a permanent means for the gratification of the sexual impulses of men and women. The family satisfies not merely the physiological needs of the male and female but also their psychological needs, the desire to love and to be loved, the sense of psychological security, etc.

The family exercises the control of society upon the individual. The family creates an environment in which the child can be brought up to develop fully his personality and to become an ideal citizen. MacIver has written that many studies have revealed that among people aged more than thirty, the death rate among the unmarried men and women is twice that of the married women and men. Among people who die as a result of tuberculosis, accidents, suicides, alcoholic indulgences and sexual diseases, the proportion of unmarried is greater than that of the married.

In the words of Truxall and Merrill, "Mutual affection guards against many of the mental and physical tribulations of a complicated society." This is clearly indicative of the benefits which accrue to men from the institution of family. Actually, the family is a primary and fundamental unit of society. It is the foundation of all social life. It socialises the individual and assists him in the choice and selection of a life partner. It determines inheritance and procures property. It is difficult to describe all the direct and indirect benefits of the family. It is an inseparable part of human nature. It is the foundation of the social structure. Hence, in the words of Burgess and Locke,... "It seems safe to predict that the family will survive, both because of its long history of adaptability to changing conditions and because of the importance of its functions of affection-giving and receiving in personal satisfaction and in personality development."

Change in Society

For centuries past men lived, and in several countries continued to live fully or partly in agrarian social order, developed institution-economic, social and political in agreement to it. These to the concerned looked inalienable from the social order, and the very props and pillars of it. Industry and technology in the west, shook these foundations, and gave in such direction to society that the past was forgotten.

What remained of it is fleeing like the autumn leaves. It is dying. Changes transforming are in the process in the developing societies as well. The impact of expanding technology on social institution in inevitable. The transition, whatever its character, has never been without pain. It never had been smooth ever before. The Western industrial society as it is known, in Sociology, has passed through a long course of change. It is today on a pedestal not to be recognised by their dead, if they were to walk out of their graves. The one single factor that brought about the social change in the technological revolution. It has affected as we shall see in the following discussion, family and society in the west in manifold manner.

Absence of Social Service: In agricultural society, family was production and consumption unit. Members of the family worked jointly, remained economically interdependent, and the authority of the family remained supreme. The family well being was the primary concern, and individual was a link in the family and kinship chain. One belonged to the bigger group, and it provided the full chances of socialisation. For the young it was a movement from apprenticeship to master status. Agricultural society in Europe, and no less elsewhere had no structure for welfare or social security; the family maintained the aged, nursed the sick, buried the dead, and provided for the mentally or physically crippled.

The kinship system also had to ensure support for widows and orphans and also had to provide a place for the occasionally unmarried woman. Given this, one can understand the growth of a moral outlook that made kinship a most binding and obligatory relationship, regardless of what personal feelings the members may have had for one another. There is obviously now a change in the family system, as indicated elsewhere. In the West most of the functions that were once performed by family, are now performed by the state. Our social structure in general continues to be agriculture-extended family based.

The nuclear family is not yet the dominant reality. Even where it is significant, the family ties have not so weakened as to make family that nuclear, as it is in West. A western type nuclear family system, in view of the peculiarity of our culture, may not take shape here. Besides our polity has yet to take strides even to provide for the primary civic facilities. Directive principles of state policy have much to guide in the direction. After that is realised, then alone, can state take over some of the family services.

Decline of Religion: Rationalist industrial culture, in the west threw religion overboard. The relations between the individual and the divine, family and the church got slackened day after day. Attendance in churches became thinner and thinner. Religion as a matter of practice in general ceased to exist. The rich regal church organisation, now, took upon itself more than ever before to propagate it and that too beyond Europe. Unlike the Catholicism of the past, Puritanism of the seventeenth-eighteenth century and the Methodist church of nineteenth century it had now no significant role to play. The institutional character of family prayer, and of such other supporting practices and beliefs are no more in use. It is much less a social force.

Cultural Disharmony: In modem industrial western complex social system, the role of culture, in the traditional sense of 'sweetness and light' is limited. The institutions like family, church and the corporate character of society, have changed so much as to present complete cultural disharmony. The division of labour, class structure, the rise of nuclear family and dominance of rationalism are contributory to the cultural disharmony. The way of life that culture gave to the collectivity and the standard of social ethics that it had setup is now subject of historical interest. The industrial culture in West, however, has developed, its own norms and values; pressures and compulsion; privileges and privations. Industrial culture, in U.S.A. U.S.S.R. Western Europe and Eastern Europe, is not, however, of the uniform pattern. At some points, it is contradictory, and at others as it has always been very much influenced by the local conditions.

The Dominance of Law: The modern society is dominated by State. Its omnipotence is felt through law at any conceivable points. In modern society while the function of family have been squeezing with every advance of time and technology, the role of state has been ever on increase. One's life at every stage is influenced by law, sometimes it is coercive and sometimes it is cooperative. It exercises full coercive authority in some fields such as matrimony and succession to property, and in some others it cooperates. In providing services from birth to death the western states, have taken pain out of birth misery out of life, and relieved the living of after death liabilities. In the interest of the community and for the welfare of individual, state plays significant and ever-increasing role. The omnipotence of the state is a fact and a reality in modern society-democratic or communist. It is now only in the underdeveloped society, that state plays a limited and a bashful role. Efforts on its part to widen its activity, is decried in the name of state intervention, by the small but powerful pressure group, from their high house tops. The leadership on its part dilates and is dilatory, threatens and persuades, and for reasons known and unknown balances piecemeal reforms and persuasions.

Change in Age and Sex Roles: The traditional consideration for the elderly-the grand parents and all those in that order in modern western society have diminished. At individual level it is not a compelling consideration.

The nuclear family, that is the family in modern industrial society, does not include the aged ones. It is one of the consequences of the increasing social mobility and the neo-local family system that characterises the Western society. The old people, are now the elder citizens, to use the American terms, and not the respected heads of their families. They live by their earned income, the retirement benefits and state security.

In nuclear family, there is the distinct change between the parent-children relation. The traditional patriarchal authority is neither exercised nor felt. The children are not without their say. The democratic ideology that dominates the society supports it. It sometimes also attributed to vanished economic character of the family and, to the absence of the grand parental influence from it.

Sex roles to be appropriate for each sex are culturally defined and structurally institutionalised, in every society. They are determined by ideology, custom and laws. They are basic, "in more ways than in simply determining whether a woman should work or not. They also play a large part in shaping what form of employment a woman should enter and how far she may go in that field of employment." "Thus while sex-roles may be basic roles, it would appear that they are more basic for women than for men. One consequence of this is that the dilemma of multiple roles may appear in a much sharper form for women than for men; to put it another way, there is greater congruence between a man's role and his occupational role than between that of a woman and her occupational role, if she has one".

The impact of change on the sex role is more than apparent. In the process of socialisation the children-the boy and the girl begins with their sex-role training. It begins with parents attitude, the form and the colour of dress they get to wear, the types of toys they play with. More especially, girls learns it by taking the mother as the model, as the two are intimate and close. Boys suffer on this count as the father remains out for longer hours.

The influence of change on the sex roles is clear from the freedom young men and women have in choosing their spouses, the economic independence of the women, the nuclear character of the family, the equality the woman exercises with her husband in decision making and the control they have over property.

Origin of Family

As the jati is fundamental to village society, so is kinship fundamental to the jati. All of a person's kin by descent and marriage, both actual and potential, are within his jati; none are outside it. The boundaries of his jati are continually re-validated through marriage; his closest interactions are typically with his kinsmen. A man's responsibilities to his kin are important considerations in the social enterprises he undertakes. So we must understand how villagers act as kinsmen in order to understand how this social system works.

Kinship begins with the family. In one sense the whole society begins with the family because a society is a living entity that must continually be replenished. The system of a whole society cannot be stopped and started again like a mechanical device. If replenishment is halted, the society ceases to exist. This imperative of replenishment for every society is met by its smallest social component, the family.

Everyone is born, not of a collectivity or into a full-fledged social system, but of parents into a family. In societies of all types, the family is the fundamental multipurpose organisation for many of the principal life functions of the individual and of society. Moreover, as Eric Wolf has written, the family is the bearer of virtue and of public reputation; a man's reputation is linked with that of his family and with his own relations to his family. Although the standards used for social ranking vary widely, Wolf notes, the rankings in each society define whom one can trust and whom one may marry. "Invariably, they refer back to ways in which people handle their domestic affairs" (1966, p. 8). Domestic patterns establish the nature of the relations between the sexes and among the generations. They teach the fundamental lessons of who "we" are and who "they" are; how we may link with others; whom we may marry and whom we must not marry. Such patterns instill motivation in the young so that, in time, they will bring up their own young to seek similar life goals and follow similar cultural patterns.

These common functions of families across the world are carried out through a great variety of family forms, that is, of particular definitions and alignments of family roles. Yet each form of family structure is grounded in the biological constants—in the relation of parent and child, of husband and wife, of sibling and sibling. Another constant feature is a recurrent cycle of family development, in which a family is formed through marriage and mating, expands with the arrival of children, disperses as the children marry and eventually separate to establish new households, and sooner or later is totally replaced after the parents die (cf. Fortes 1958, pp. 4-5; Collver 1963, pp. 86-87).

Among village families in India these general features bear a characteristic Indian stamp, partly because of the widely shared ideal model for family relations and partly because of the common perspective of hierarchy. There are, to be sure, many differences in family organisation according to jati, regional, and economic variations. Yet underlying the variety there is also a notable degree of similarity in family relations.

Fanltless Model and Real Form: The common ideal is that of filial and fraternal solidarity, which prescribes that brothers should remain together in the parental household after they marry, sharing equally in one purse and in common property, helping each other according to need and each giving according to his best abilities. Brothers' should not only cleave to one another, but, even more important, they should remain with their parents and be steadfast to them. This ideal has strongest sway while the father is alive and influential, and fades after both parents are dead and the brothers' children marry (cf. Gore 1965, pp. 211-213). It has more influence among those who are higher and wealthier than among the low and landless. It applies to the men of a family but is a central concern for women also. In most jatis, high and low alike, daughters customarily leave their natal family on marriage. A bride goes to live where her husband lives (which is with his father) and does not share in her own father's and brothers' property. Women, especially as mothers, uphold the ideal at least as vigorously as men do, but they themselves are not implicated in it in the same way.

Indian village society is patrilineal and virilocal except for a few matrilineal groups, notably the Nayars of Kerala who are discussed below. The patrilineal principle defines those men who are expected to cooperate most closely in a family and lineage group. The family ideal governs the relations between close male kin. It is a motif that holds constant interest; villagers hear it told over and again in tales from the *Mahabharata* and other classical sources. It is celebrated in popular song and is a common background of village gossip.

This ideal of filial-fraternal solidarity has been reinforced by being built into the chief textbook of Hindu law, the *Mitakshara* of the twelfth century. Under this code each male is entitled to an equal share of the family property from the moment of his birth; hence all brothers are coparceners, each entitled to the same share his father and brothers have. Joint ownership is assumed by law, and the assumption usually implies, though it does not require, joint residence and joint social and economic activities (cf. Desai 1955, p. no; Mandelbaum 1948). Women, whether in the status of daughter, wife, or widow, are entitled to maintenance by their male kin, but under the ancient law they had no other vested rights in the family property.

No voluntary act is required to establish a close life partnership among brothers that binds them together in a firm legal entity. But the act of legal separation of family property does require voluntary action. When brothers or brothers' sons separate their households and property, as eventually they feel forced to do, they must petition to some formal authority in order to divide the joint property. This family law for Hindus was enforced during the British regime. Though post-independence legislation has changed the inheritance laws, there is still a strong inclination among villagers, men and women alike, to follow the ancient mode of property rights and inheritance.

There were regional variations in legal tradition, notably the *Dayabhaga* code of Bengal, but essentially all the regional codes and local customs postulate that it is desirable for married sons to live, work, and share property with their parents and to remain together after their parents have died.

This kind of family cannot go on indefinitely; there are both physical and social limitations to its continuance. If sons and sons' sons keep adding their wives and children, there is a physical limit to the number that can be fed and housed in one household. Brothers' sons are not under the same obligation to stay together as are true brothers. The fission of the larger family is an inevitable step in the cycle of domestic development.

Taking that step results in the hiving off of smaller family groups, usually nuclear families, each consisting of a married couple and their children. When the sons grow up and a new bride is brought in, the family becomes what is known as a joint family, one that includes two or more married couples. The distinction between nuclear and joint families is one that is made by outside observers and census officers rather than by the villagers themselves.

Family members do not consider that they have merged disparate nuclear families when there are two married couples in a family rather than just one; they regard this change as a natural and much desired growth of the original family. Nor do they use different terms for a single-couple and a multicouple family; there is usually only a single basic term for both. Each son is expected to bring his wife into his natal household. All eat from the same kitchen, live in the same house or compound, and share income. The males pool all property, support each other closely in the village and advance each other's cause in the world—and even into the afterworld.

The inducements to maintain close filial-fraternal relations are considerable. To begin with, most newly wed couples are barely into adulthood and have neither the material nor psychological resources to start a household of their own. Later in their married life, when they have more resources, they may still stay on in the household because the disadvantages of separating are greater than the annoyances of living together.

Brothers are expected to help each other whether they live together or not. I knew two brothers in a village who became bitter enemies, yet when one grew so deranged mentally that no one would care for him, his estranged brother took him into his own house and nursed him until he was well enough to earn his living again. Then the mutual enmity was promptly resumed. Though brothers who live separately may still feel mutual obligations, living together in a joint household makes these obligations more automatic and compulsive.

In the joint family there is immediate aid to tide a member over illness; there is the increased efficiency of pooled labour and the economies of a single kitchen and household; and there is greater strength to ward off encroachments from others. Domestic rites and celebrations can be staged more elegantly by a large family, and the resulting prestige enhances all within the family. Each person is seen by others in the village in the light of his family's reputation. When he comes to a major life transition such as marriage, the reputation of the family weighs heavily in the decisions that are made. He is much advantaged if his family is large, harmonious, and joint, thus demonstrating that its members are reliable, worthy people.

Despite these advantages, centrifugal forces inevitably build up so that every family sooner or later breaches the ideal. Among the very poor the breach typically comes not long after the new bride is brought into the family. Early separation also occurs among families at the other end of the economic scale, those with men in the modern professions. Those families who own and cultivate their land are likely to keep up the ideal pattern longer.

The ideal is acknowledged by almost all villagers and this tends to prolong fraternal cohesion. Cohesion and cooperation are not completely severed when a family splits into smaller households. Though the partition may have taken place in bitterness, family ties are often repaired and some degree of mutual support resumed.

Bibliography

Agrawal, S.N. : *Social Change in India*, APH, Bombay, 1960.

Aurora, G.S. : *Tribe, Caste, Class Encounters*, Administrative Staff College of India, Hyderabad, 1972.

Bailey, F.G. : *Caste and Economic Frontier*, Oxford, New York, 1884.

Barnes : *Social Thought from Lore to Science*, Dover Publications, New York, 1961.

Bell, D. : *The Coming of Post-industrial Society*, Heinneman Educational Books Ltd., London, 1974.

Bhatt, Anil : *Caste, Class and Politics: An Empirical Profile of Social Stratification* in *Modern India*, Manohar Book Service, New Delhi, 1975.

Bipin Chandra : *The Rise and Growth of Economic Nationalism in India*, Publication Division, Delhi, 1977.

Brass, P. : *Factional Politics in an Indian State: The Congress Party in Uttar Pradesh*, University of California Press, Berkeley, 1965.

Brass, Paul R. : *Language, Religion and Politics in India*, Vikas Publishing House, New Delhi, 1975.

Choudhury, R. : *The Evolution of Indian Industries*, Oxford, Calcutta, 1939.

Das, M.N. : *Studies in the Economic and Social Development of Modern India*, MacMillan, Calcutta, 1959.

Datta, R.C. : *The Economic History of India*, Sterling, New Delhi, 1990.

Durkheim, E. : *The Division o f Labour in Society*, MacMillan, London, 1933.

Farquher J.N. : *Modern Religious Movement in India*, OUP, New Delhi, 1914.

Gadgil, D.R. : *The Industrial Evolution of India*, OUP, New Delhi, 1942.

Giffiths, P. : *The British Impact on India*, MacMillan, London, 1952.

Giri, V.V. : *Labour Problems in Indian Industries*, APH, Bombay, 1958.

Habib, Irfan : *The Agrarian System of Mughal India*, Popular Prakashan, Bombay, 1963.

Imtiaz, A. : *Caste and Stratification among Muslim in India*, Monohar Book Service, Delhi, 2001.

Ishwaran, K. : *Social Movement*, Allied Publishers, New Delhi, 1966.

Kathleen : *Class Developments in India*, McGill University Press, Montreal, 1975.

Kothari, Rajni : *Caste in Indian Politics*, Orient Longman, New Delhi, 1970.

Kuppuswamy, B. : *Social Change in Modern India*, Manohar, New Delhi, 1985.

Majumdar, D.N. : *An Introduction to Social Change*, APH, Bombay, 1960.

———— : *Races and Culture of India*, APH, Bombay, 1968.

Merton, R.K. : *Social Theory and Social Structure*, Free Press, New York, 1968.

Mumford, L. : *Conditions of Man*, Martin Secker and Warburg, London, 1944.

Narain, V.A. : *Social History of Modern India*, Manohar, New Delhi, 1972.

Natrajan : *Century of Social Reform in India*, Popular Prakashan, Bombay, 1962.

Nurulla and Naik : *History of Education in India*, MacMillan, London, 1951.

O' Malley, L.S.S. : *Modern India and the West*, OUP, London, 1941.

Perkinson, C.N. : *The Evolution of Political Thought*, MacMillan, London, 1958.

Prasad, N. : *The Myth of Caste System*, Khuda Bakhsh Library, Patna, 1957.

—————— : *Social Reforms: An Analysis of Indian Society*, Y.K. Publishers, Agra, 1990.

Rao, M.S.A. : *Urbanisation and Social Change*, Orient Longman, New Delhi, 1970.

Rawlinson, H.G. : *The Land and People of India*, MacMillan, London, 1961.

Sharma, I.R. : *The Making of Modern India*, Orient Longman, New Delhi, 1951.

—————— : *Social Stratification and Change in India*, Manohar Publication, Delhi, 1989.

Srinivas, M.N. : *Social Change in Modern India*, Orient Longman, Delhi, 1972.

Tumin, M.M. : *Social Stratification : the Forms and Function of Inequality*, Delhi, 1987.

Verba, S. : *Caste, Race and Politics: A Comparative Study of India and the United States*, Sage Publications, Berkeley Hills, 1971.

Whyte, William H. : *The Organization Man*, Simon and Schuster Inc., New York, 1956.

Winch, P. : *The Idea* of *a Social Science*, Oxford, London, 1968.

Zeitlin, I.M. : *Social Change in India*, Appleton-Century Crofts, New York, 1973.

Index

J

K

L

M

N

O

□□□